# Qualitative Research in Education

# Explorations in Ethnography Series

Series Editors: Stephen J. Ball (King's College, London) and Ivor Goodson (University of Western Ontario).

In the past fifteen years qualitative research has had a thorough-going and controversial impact on the field of educational research, both generally and specifically. That is to say, qualitative approaches have colonised, or have been colonised by, almost all theoretical varieties of educational research. Such variation and varigation is evidenced and documented in this volume. But this kind of enthusiastic development and take up has its dangers and problems. The potential of qualitative methods can be blunted or distorted by the cavalier abandonment of first principles or disregard for techniques or rigour. In this collection of papers a careful and systematic review is provided of the current possibilities and necessities of good qualitative research. It is an important contribution to the mature phase development of qualitative methods in educational research.

**Stephen J. Ball**
*King's College London*
Series Editor

Explorations in Ethnography Series

# Qualitative Research in Education: Focus and Methods

*Edited by*
Robert R. Sherman
Rodman B. Webb

The Falmer Press

(A Member of the Taylor & Francis Group)
London · New York · Philadelphia

UK          The Falmer Press, Falmer House, Barcombe, Lewes
            East Sussex, BN8 5DL

USA         The Falmer Press, Taylor & Francis Inc., 242 Cherry Street,
            Philadelphia, PA 19106-1906

First published 1988 **Reprinted 1990**

**British Library Cataloguing in Publication Data**

Qualitative research in education: focus
  and methods.
  1. Education. Research. Qualitative methods
  I. Sherman, Robert R.      II. Webb, Rodman B.
  370'.7'8

  ISBN 1–85000–380–7
  ISBN 1–85000–381–5 Pbk

**Library of Congress Cataloging-in-Publication Data**

Sherman, Robert R., 1930–
  Qualitative research in education.

  Bibliography: p.
  Includes index.
  1. Education—Research. 2. Education—Research—
Methodology.     I. Webb, Rodman B., 1941–
II. Title.
LB1028.S455   1988        370'.7'8        88–3922
ISBN 1–85000–380–7
ISBN 1–85000–381–5 (pbk.)

Jacket design by Caroline Archer

Typeset in 10/12 Bembo by
Input Typesetting Ltd, London

***Printed in Great Britain by Taylor & Francis (Printers) Ltd,
Basingstoke***

*For Lindsey and Laurie — and Joy*

*To see a world in a grain of sand;*
*and heaven in a flower.*

Blake, 'Auguries of Innocence'

# Contents

# Foreword and Acknowledgments

With two exceptions — 'Inside Lives: The Quality of Biography' and 'Putting Life into Educational Research' — the papers that appear in this collection are reprinted from the *Journal of Thought*, Volume 19, Number 2 (Summer, 1984), pp. 24–29 ('Qualitative Research: A Theme Issue'); and Volume 21, Number 3 (Fall, 1986), entire issue ('Qualitative Research: A Special Topic Edition'). They are reprinted with the permission of the authors and the Editor of *Journal of Thought*. We express our appreciation to Dr Chipman G. Stuart, the Editor, for the opportunity first to publish our views and then for permission to republish them. Dr Stuart has shown that editing a journal is more than a service; it is a distinct contribution to research.

Our thanks also to Dr Samuel D. Andrews, our colleague in Foundations of Education at the University of Florida, who helped in preparing the first issue of *Journal of Thought*. We wish to thank Falmer Press Limited, Mr Malcolm W. Clarkson, Managing Director; and Dr Ivor G. Goodson, member of the Board of Directors, for arranging to have the papers republished. Because they have gone out of print in their previous form, their republication makes them available for continued use by students and others interested in qualitative research. We also appreciate the authors' willingness to have their ideas exposed to a wider audience.

Our aim with this collection is to clarify and explain some of the different approaches and methods by which 'qualitative' research in education is being conducted and to develop a sense of what is meant by the term 'qualitative'. It is *not* our view that qualitative research is an alternative, or an antagonist, to quantitative research. We want any research to be rigorous and productive. The contributors explain how that can be accomplished with various kinds of qualitative methods. Our aim also is to provoke discussion and further elaboration of the issues and methods that are represented, so we have taken seriously the matter of citing documentation and giving references for further reading.

A word about the title of the collection. We think it is important to stress the idea of a unity among the methods. There appears to be a general or generic idea of qualitative research that is in the background of all the contributions. But to avoid reductionism or debate over 'unified science', we emphasize unity of 'focus'. The several methods appear to have a similar focus. 'Focus' should be enough to give the sense of what is meant by 'the qualitative' and how qualitative methods are related.

The quest for understanding is never finished. Other qualitative methods may be formulated, particularly combinations of methods, and their use in educational research will need to be demonstrated. What we offer here is a beginning. We trust that our students and colleagues will go well beyond what we have imagined.

**Robert R. Sherman**
**Rodman B. Webb**
*Gainesville, Florida, USA*

*Part I*
# Frame of Reference

*Chapter 1*

# Qualitative Research in Education: A Focus

*Robert R. Sherman and Rodman B. Webb*
*Foundations of Education*
*University of Florida*
*Gainesville, FL 32611*

Qualitative research in education has come into vogue. As the song used to say, 'everybody's doing it'. Yet onlookers, especially students, may not see clearly what is being done and why. We need a systematic discussion of the nature, presuppositions, origins, functions, and limitations of qualitative research; the commonality — if any — among its several methods; and its relation to quantitative research.

## Aim and Method

The aim of the present essays is to explain the nature and use of qualitative research methods in education. We have asked scholars who work in areas and use methods commonly thought to be 'qualitative' to describe the methods and results specific to their interests and styles of inquiry. We present essays in the areas of philosophy of education, history, biography, ethnography, life history, grounded theory, phenomenography, curriculum criticism, the uses of literature in qualitative research, and critical theory. We have asked the essayists to address the following concerns:

1   What is the meaning of 'qualitative'? In what respects and manner is your method and/or area of inquiry qualitative?
2   Are there qualitative 'schools' within the area? That is, sort out the qualitative activities within the area and define the qualitative similarities and differences within the area.
3   Elaborate the qualitative method and show its use through examples. While the aim is not to present a cookbook method, the introduction to qualitative methodology within the area should be explicit enough to enable students to become familiar with it and to build on it.

4    Though the essays are not intended to be a review of the literature about qualitative research and methods, but rather an introduction to what those methods are and how they apply in educational settings, the essays should provide citations to work that has been done so that students may build on them.

5    Suggest a reading list (which may double as a reference list). It should contain citations to qualitative methodology, pertinent to the area being covered, and specific examples where that method is employed.

The essays in this collection follow these guidelines rather well. J. Giarelli and J. J. Chambliss explain, from the perspective of philosophy of education, the evolution of the concern with qualitativeness and the role of philosophy of education in qualitative inquiry. C. H. Edson argues that qualitative inquiry is a form of 'moral discourse', an attempt to 'understand ourselves in relation to the larger world'. That larger world includes both the past and the present, and historical study is a way to reveal the relation. Further, making history personal, J. Campbell argues that the 'new qualitative force' is grounded in biography, getting support from the phenomenologist A. Schutz, who believed that the 'biographic situation' is the basic unit of human understanding. Edson, especially, elaborates some of the methods for doing historical work.

The discussion then turns to ethnography. N. Shimahara traces the connection of ethnography to anthropology and explains the assumptions, strategies, and methodological orientation of anthroethnography. At first it may appear that P. Woods' 'Educational Ethnography in Britain' duplicates Shimahara's discussion, but that would be short-sighted. Woods' essay is unique in its comparative perspective and in its focus on the findings of ethnographic studies as a way to demonstrate ethnographic, and qualitative, concerns and methods. I. Goodson's and R. Walker's 'Putting Life into Educational Research' is a return to history, this time to broaden the interpretive scope of ethnographies, which Goodson and Walker believe too often have a 'timeless' appearance. Classroom events need to be interpreted within the perspective of the teacher's life span, not just of the moment when they occur.

S. Hutchinson describes 'grounded theory', which is concerned with theory generation, rather than verification, through discovery of what the world appears to be to participants and, through an analysis of those perceptions, of the basic social processes and structures that organize the world. This aim is similar to F. Marton's 'phenomenography', which is a way of 'mapping' the qualitatively different ways in which people perceive, conceptualize, and understand — in a word, 'experience' — the world around them. Such observations are analyzed into categories, derived from the experiences themselves, from which one can assess the appropriateness of educational strategies.

D. Ross explains how the techniques of social anthropology and aesthetic criticism are combined in 'curriculum criticism' to describe, interpret, and evaluate curricula. Relying even more on aesthetics and philosophy, M. Greene discusses the uses of literature as an expression of qualitative inquiry. Imaginative literature may be the *par excellence* representation of qualitative concern. J. Dewey (1922) once said that the novelist and dramatist are more illuminating and more interesting commentators on conduct than is the formalizing psychologist:

> The artist makes perceptible individual responses and thus displays a new phase of human nature evoked in new situations. In putting the case visibly and dramatically he reveals vital actualities. The scientific systematizer treats each act as merely another sample of some old principle, or as a mechanical combination of elements drawn from a ready-made inventory. (pp. 155–156)

This is M. Greene's concern. For her, qualitative research is an effort to comprehend not only the modes of cultural arrangements but the ways in which those arrangements are experienced by individuals, in order to provoke intelligibility and involve one personally and intersubjectively in conscious pursuits of meaning. For qualitative researchers, life is not a dress rehearsal; it is the real thing.

Finally in this collection, while education may be less monolithic today than in the past in that different critiques are more tolerated, educational research, according to H. Giroux, still seems to aim simply at understanding what each tradition is doing rather than debate the political and moral implications of the research and its methods. Giroux asks what role educational researchers, as intellectuals, should play in extending free discourse and democracy in public and private life. In other words, though the forms of inquiry may have multiplied (quantitative *and* qualitative, as well as variations within each form), they all continue to avoid the political issue, which enables whatever dominant ideology (and methodology) to continue its hold. The role of 'critical theory' is to uncover, or 'dis-cover', those tendencies and to propose other ways of seeing and behaving.

The essays are presented in a 'rough and ready' order. We believe that philosophic questions have to be raised first in any inquiry. Giarelli and Chambliss note that the first matter to be considered in any research is 'what is the question?' History may then contribute some background. Ethnography and related approaches attempt to portray how participants themselves see the matters in which they are involved. As we have noted, a return to 'life history' could broaden the context for richer interpretations. Qualitative research is interested in the motives and aims, not just the behavior, of those who are studied. Curriculum criticism, we also have noted, draws on anthropology and aesthetics, which is why we have placed it between those methods and Greene's account of the uses of literature. Finally, not least, but no doubt the result of some researchers focusing single-mindedly on methodology, political and moral considerations are raised in Giroux's account. Other essayists, particularly Edson with history and Greene with literature, consider morality to be pre-eminent. Prior to all these discussions, and for 'focus', in addition to the present essay, is James Giarelli's 'Qualitative Inquiry in Philosophy of Education: Notes on the Pragmatic Tradition', which serves as an introduction. It puts into useful philosophic perspective why qualitative research is coming of age rather than merely coming into vogue, identifies some problems and issues that qualitative inquiry must address, and sketches initial answers to some important questions.

## Qualitative Similarities

From here on we will let the essayists give their own details. But it should be useful to ask about the ways in which different qualitative areas and methods may be similar. Are there similar 'qualitative' concerns no matter where they may be found or what method is employed? Some things stand out in the essays at hand.

One of those things is *context*. Shimahara says that human behavior — experience — is shaped in context and that events cannot be understood adequately if isolated from their contexts. He believes that such isolation, called 'context stripping', is a key feature of science. Giarelli and Chambliss interpret inquiry to be a questioning or searching with an intent or an objective in mind, that is, within some limits. Inquiry is bounded; it cannot be abstracted or approached in general.

The contexts of inquiry are not to be contrived or constructed or modified; they are *natural* and must be taken as they are found. The aim of qualitative research is not verification of a predetermined idea, but *discovery* that leads to new insights. Thus qualitative researchers focus on *natural settings*. (Qualitative research is sometimes called 'naturalistic inquiry'; Lincoln and Guba, 1985.) Nothing is predefined or taken for granted. Shimahara, representing the general view, says that ethnography, for example, is the study of events as they 'evolve in natural settings' or 'contexts in process'.

Another way to make the point is that qualitative researchers want those who are studied to speak for themselves. This appears to be a universal focus, certainly among the essayists in this collection, no matter what their method. The biographer, Jack Campbell, calls this attempt to confront empirical reality from the perspective of those being studied, the 'generic qualitative approach'.

Moreover, experience is to be taken and studied as a *whole*, or holistically. One must attend to all features of experience. The philosophers, Giarelli and Chambliss, remind us that perceptual fields are experienced as wholes. So they say that the researcher must cultivate sensitivity to situations or experience as a whole and to the qualities that regulate them. For example, no biographer would explain his subject as a collection of separate variables. Rather, according to Campbell, biography must 'portray the subject as a whole, in the temporal, geographical, sociocultural context'. Edson even asserts that qualitative inquiry *intends* to make phenomena more complex, for 'complexity, not simplicity, describes life in both the past and the present'. (Marton says that 'researchers cannot take it for granted that subjects always will take a holistic rather than atomistic view of . . . events', but his comment really makes the earlier point that qualitative research presumes nothing, but focuses on the perspective of those being studied. That the researcher, surely, aims at a holistic account is inferred further from Goodson and Walker's campaign to add 'life history' to qualitative studies.) Moreover, *holism* implies *context* (though not vice versa), for to take something as a whole suggests that it has boundaries. To make the point about the whole, or holism, with another word, the aim of qualitative research is to understand experience as *unified*.

Methods of inquiry for carrying out these aims must be appropriate to the aims. It might be expected that the philosophers would remind us of Aristotle's dictum that each 'science' has its appropriate methods which can be found only in its distinctive subject matter. Qualitative researchers take the point seriously. This is not to say that different researchers will not borrow or share features of method, if they are useful. Each of the essayists, and particularly those who build on anthropological and ethnographic bases, describe methods that are similar in some respects and even acknowledge that their inquiries might benefit from other perspectives and approaches.

The point is that qualitative researchers will employ methods and strategies that are consistent with the aims we have generalized here. They will not superimpose a general method on experience, but will be sensitive to the effects of methods on inquiry. (For this reason, ethnographers, for example, are careful to employ *non-interventionist* methods.) The point is often made by contrast with science and the method of science, which intervene in experience and structure and report experience quantitatively. Both Giarelli and Chambliss and Shimahara believe that some interests in experience cannot be measured quantitatively. For the former, philosophers, it is the 'possibilities' in experience, the questions that can be formulated for inquiry, that are important. For the latter, an ethnographer, social–cultural *patterns* of experience or *relationships* among events are the matters of importance, not the quantification of human events. (Marton also focuses on relationships.)

Though these ideas stand out, one still might wonder what the term 'qualitative' means. It was not a requirement that the essayists define the term directly and at the outset of their discussions. To do so might have prevented the discussions from even taking place. A philosopher (Greene, 1971) has observed:

It is part of the popular mythology that we cannot have fruitful . . . discussions unless we first define our terms. It is a common belief that we ought to start with definitions. This point of view is . . . misleading. The object of . . . analysis is to *arrive* at something like a definition; therefore, in principle, it cannot start with one. . . . The search for clarity and precision of thought is an important venture. To suppose that it can get started only by agreement on definitions is to prevent it from starting at all. (pp. 15–16)

But now that we have the discussion in the essays, we can draw them together and *summarize* that 'qualitative' implies a direct concern with experience as it is 'lived' or 'felt' or 'undergone'. (In contrast, 'quantitative' research, often taken to be the opposite idea, is indirect and abstracts and treats experiences as similar, adding or multiplying them together, or 'quantifying' them.) Thus, Giarelli and Chambliss anchor their discussion of qualitative thinking in 'feeling and appreciation' and call it 'aesthetic' activity. (This sense of qualitative also prompts Ross's use of aesthetic criticism and Greene's literary account.) Qualitative research, then, has the aim of understanding experience as nearly as possible as its participants feel it or live it.

In fact, this idea may be a 'test' for qualitative research, whether it be a philosophical discussion, an ethnographic report, a literary account, or an historical study. Ross says that qualitative descriptions 'should transport the reader to the scene, convey the pervasive qualities or characteristics of the phenomenon, and evoke the feeling and nature of the educational experience'. Shimahara agrees and quotes from H. Wolcott (1973) to make the point:

> The test of ethnography is whether it enables one to anticipate and interpret what goes on in a society or social group as appropriately as one of its members. To the extent that the account provided here achieves this objective, the reader should feel that if he were suddenly to find himself in an encounter with staff members, pupils, or parents at the school described, or if he were to attend a meeting with other principals from the school district, he would understand how he might act if he were in the role of the principal. Conversely, if he were to assume the role of some other person in an encounter with the principal, he should feel he would know how the principal might act toward him. (p. ix)

There is another commonality in qualitative research. It is the idea of *judging* or *appraising*. We do not mean that the aim of such research is to approve or disapprove of the behavior that is studied. The aim, rather, is to know or understand it better (though this is not to say that facts and values are sharply separate, and we must take seriously Giroux's concern that understanding should not stand apart from debate over political and moral implications of research). The point here is that *judging* is an *appraisal* of the qualitative situation, the relation of the parts and whole, and an indication of the potentialities that can be sought from the actualities. Judging is a means for keeping inquiry going and for keeping it pertinent to the problem and its solution. Giarelli and Chambliss say that philosophers depend on 'aesthetic judgments' of where difficulties lay in experience and 'on qualitative thinking to bring these difficulties into the form of questions and problems that can be researched'.

Ross also sees a role for appraisal in qualitative inquiry. The function of criticism is to *describe* the essential qualities of phenomena: to *interpret* the meanings and relationships among those qualities; and to give a reasoned *judgment* about the *significance* and *value* of those things. Written appraisals, she says, should indicate if the aims of the curriculum are met and, indeed, if the aims are desirable or worthwhile according to some external criteria. M. Greene believes that 'gaps' in literary accounts, where everything does not 'mesh' and everything is not explained, require the reader's *interpretation* in order to move forward.

Admittedly, some qualitative researchers might shun judgment. Ross acknowledges that social anthropologists generally might avoid evaluation. But we make the point about judgment or appraisal because it may give a clue to why qualitative research is becoming more popular. That is because practitioners, who always have the obligation *to do something* in the situations they are in, have been given little direct help from quantitative research (see Smith, 1983, p. 13). Certainly quantitative research generates abundant information and relationships. But what does it tell the teacher to do? Because that can be determined only in a qualitative context — a real, direct, specific, explicit, and problematic context — the quantitative researcher is — and perhaps must be — mute. The teacher wonders how such researchers can claim to know more and more, and more minutely, and not be able to indicate the significance or use of that knowledge.

## History of Research

An illustration should help to make the point. A person with historical interest might find significance in what has happened to the idea of research in education in the past fifty years. A full study of the subject is worthwhile, but because of space and time we will give only a sketch here. Presume that one wants to know what 'research' in education entails and how it is done. He might consult the *Encyclopedia of Educational Research* (American Educational Research Association, 1941–82) to get the idea. And if he wants to know how the concept and practice may have changed in those years, he has the resource of five editions of the *Encyclopedia* that have been published since 1941.

In the 1941 edition of the *Encyclopedia*, there is no discussion of 'research' (in general) or 'research methods'. But from the heading, 'Research and Philosophy', the reader is advised to see 'Philosophy and Science'. In other words, what was significant about educational research in 1941 is the relationship between science and philosophy. One is told that the successes in the scientific investigation of education should not cause one to overlook the essential role that is played in educational research by other factors. Data are significant, the discussion says, but only as they are interpreted in light of accepted standards and assumptions. In concrete situations, it is not enough to know that 'this will produce that'; we must decide whether or not we want 'that'. Our aim, the article says, is as much a determiner of our course of action as are facts or data. In other words, until a 'should' question is settled by a philosopher, the scientist has no 'problem' to deal with.

The second edition (1950) dropped the discussion of philosophy and science altogether. An article on the 'Science of Education' was added, but it did not mention the theme taken to be important here. In the third edition (1960), 'Philosophy of Educational Science' is but a brief discussion under the larger heading of 'Philosophy of Education'. It begins by saying that 'the philosophical study of educational science is now in an incipient stage', as if in ignorance of the insight given twenty years earlier! This edition includes an article for the first time on 'Research Methods'. It is an extensive discussion, giving a definition and characterizations of research methods and tracing the development of educational research in three historical periods since 1900. In the last period, since 1925, there is a review of four criticisms of the way educational research was going at the time: too little attention is given to the individual; education is more complex than single variable studies show; too little attention is given to the 'less tangible aspects' of education; and educational research is conducted with inadequate theory, for 'scientific research needs a philosophical and historical orientation', that is, an attention to 'goodness', 'worth', and the 'value' of facts.

That is, these criticisms return the discussion of research in education to the relation between philosophy and science and to the concerns that qualitative researchers now address. Presumably in response to the criticisms, the 1960 articles goes on to note that 'refinements' have been made in educational research methodology, and two illustrations are given. But it is suggestive of the trend, and of the human tendency to overlook criticism, that the refinements that are discussed are in data gathering techniques, research design, and statistical analysis — refinements in method, rather than attention to the scope of research.

The 1969 *Encyclopedia* (fourth edition) divides the discussion into 'Research Methods' and 'Research in Education'. The former is in fact a discussion of research approaches and methodologies. The latter is a discussion of the tactics and techniques of science and its use in educational research. The reader is now told that it is *not* the purpose of science to improve the world (i.e., education), though it may in fact do so. Science is not engineering; its task, rather, is to explain. More, scientific research aims not to describe singular phenomena but to seek laws or generalizations; general statements of regularity are of the essence of science. That science has its use or worth within a context of values now has been eliminated deliberately from the discussion of educational research.

The 1982 edition (fifth) of the *Encyclopedia* is so extensive that it is published in four volumes. Yet in all that space, and in spite of its growing popularity, there is no discussion whatsoever of qualitative inquiry or research in education. (There is an article on 'Qualitative Curriculum Evaluation'). Neither is there any longer a general discussion of research 'methods'. Instead, that discussion has been further 'refined' into even more special, and thus more abstract, methodological concerns such as 'measurement', 'experimental methods', 'regression analysis', 'factor analysis', and 'statistical methods'. Someone may think that qualitative research could be tracked through discussions of 'ethnography', 'historiography', 'sociology of education', and 'philosophy of education', which the *Encyclopedia* does contain, but the novice cannot be expected to know that those are representatives of qualitative methodology (there is no cross-reference!) or even to learn from the articles *how* the approaches are representatives of qualitative concern.

The only discussion in the 1982 edition that returns the reader to the concerns voiced over forty years ago (1941), and repeatedly but ever more faintly since that time, can be found under the heading of 'Philosophy of Science in Education' (that is, the relation between philosophy and science as they are used in education). There the point is made that the role of philosophy of science in educational research depends on, among other things, whether one accepts a 'conventional' or 'enlightened' view of educational research. This discussion turns on whether or not the problems of *research* are more important than the problems of *education*. It is safe to say that qualitative researchers will keep their eyes on the latter. The article repeats what was said in 1941, that 'meaning depends on a context of inquiry', and claims that, today, 'the justification of scientific utility is as important an issue as the verification of scientific claims'. It ends with the observation, not recent by any means, that 'educational research, if it is to be enlightened, probably needs to pay closer attention to philosophy of education. . . . Empirical researchers who know these ideas [that philosophy poses] will find apt directions for their inquiries'.

The point of this tracing of the idea of 'research' in education is to show that the present concerns of qualitative researchers have long been part of the educational discussion. But as attention has been turned more and more to methodology, particularly to refinements in logic and quantitative methodology, those concerns have been crowded out. It should be little wonder that so much educational research is of such little help to the teacher today. Much of it does not aspire to be helpful. It has its own agenda. But the issues posed nearly fifty years ago are still with us. Research is not abstract. It exists in a context — we are inclined to say a 'problematic' context — and its aim is to provide a unified sense or grasp of that context, not a piecemeal enumeration of it. It is in this sense that qualitative inquiry is an *appraisal* or judgment; its function is to interpret, or appraise, behavior in relation to contextual circumstances — one circumstance of which is human aims and purposes. And it is because this theme has become urgent again that we believe that qualitative research is becoming ever more popular.

(The *Handbook of Research on Teaching* (American Educational Research Association, 1986) is a more promising resource. Qualitative approaches get considerable discussion in Part I, 'Theory and Method of Research on Teaching'. Erickson's (1986) chapter is wholly about qualitative methods, and qualitative matters are also discussed in Chapters 1, 2, 7, and 8.)

The reader would be mistaken if he thought that we or any of the essayists intend to counterpose 'qualitative' and 'quantitative' forms of research. The error may be due to a manner of speaking. Contrasts between qualitative and quantitative forms of research, and criticism of scientific research in education, may lead someone to believe that one mode and method of research is the only true and useful one. The words in fact are defined in one sense in dictionaries and encyclopedias as contraries. At least one pair of researchers (Smith and Heshusius, 1986) maintain that they are contradictory. But this is *not* our view. Our point, rather, is that educational research today requires a more compehensive perspective in which the considerations that qualitative researchers raise, and the questions about worth and intent posed by philosophy, are as much a part of the discussion as are measurement and analysis.

In other words, the perspective of educational research needs to be broadened. Furthermore, such a perspective should make room for different modes of qualitative and quantitative inquiry. Woods, for example, acknowledges that 'ethnography in itself is not a complete program, nor is it a perfect one. . . . [It should] seek alliance with other related methodologies'. Our late colleague, Robert Curran, made the point astutely when he said, 'The more genuine the problem, the more likely many or all of the modes of inquiry will be required to deal with it. The less genuine the problem — the more abstract and intellectual it is — the more likely the focus will be on a single mode.'

## A Theory of Qualitative Inquiry

In our view, such a perspective is at hand in John Dewey's theory of inquiry. The elements of the theory can be found in many of Dewey's works. The metaphysical basis is set out in *Experience and Nature* (Dewey, 1929a), while the relation of life to art, which seems to express the qualitative most clearly, is found in *Art as Experience* (Dewey, 1934). Our interest is with method, or methods of inquiry, as well as with a general idea of the qualitative; these are discussed in *Essays in Experimental Logic* (Dewey, 1916b), *Logic: The Theory of Inquiry* (Dewey, 1938), and an essay on 'Qualitative Thought' (Dewey, 1930b). Dewey (1938) notes in *Logic* that his ideas were first presented in *Studies in Logical Theory* (Dewey, 1903) and were summarized 'with special reference to education' in *How We Think* (Dewey, 1933).

Commenting on the discussions that appear in *Books That Changed Our Minds*, Cowley (1938) notes the assumptions that underlie John Stuart Mill's essay 'On Liberty', which glorifies reason, and Joseph Wood Krutch's (1929) *The Modern Temper*, which less than 100 years later was a pessimistic attack on science and reason. Cowley says:

That, I think, is a view of mankind justified by the researches of the last eighty years. It is important to note that their effects have not been purely destructive of human ideals. Even the attack on the Reasoning Man was not so much an essay in destruction as the effort to advance another conception, that of man as a living organism in a changing society. Around this conception has been gathered a whole group of studies; indeed the tendency of modern thinking . . . has been to construct a synthesis based on the social sciences, just as the early nineteenth century constructed one that was based on theology. All that is lacking for such a synthesis is a great systematic thinker, a Kant or a Thomas Aquinas of our own time. (pp. 259–260)

At that very moment, Dewey was publishing his *Logic: The Theory of Inquiry*.

In another essay in *Books That Changed Our Minds*, this time directly about Dewey's logic, Clarence E. Ayers (1938) recalled that Dewey had already studied 'the beautiful' (*Art As Experience*; Dewey, 1934) and 'the good' (*Human Nature and Conduct*; Dewey, 1922), and said:

But the beautiful and the good derive from the true. If art and morality are continuous with the whole of life, the essential continuity is that of thought. That idea is the source from which all Dewey's many and various interpretations flow. Given his 'Studies in Logical Theory' [the forerunner of *Logic: The Theory of Inquiry*], somebody else might have done 'Art as Experience', as after a fashion several people have; but the reverse would have been impossible. (p. 119)

Returning to Cowley (1938):

The process of dispersion into specialized fields reached its height in the years preceding the [first] World War. In those same years people began to complain of it. Observing the contrast between the order existing in the separate sciences and the utter confusion in the world outside, they called on the scientists for principles that would serve them as guides through chaos. (p. 252)

Continuity of thought, a conception of distinctive social sciences, and inquiry as a guide for action, among other things, are what Dewey contributes to the idea of qualitative inquiry.

In brief, Dewey believes that all inquiry arises out of actual, or qualitative, life. That is the environment in which humans are *directly* involved. It is the life of 'use and enjoyment of the objects, activities and products, material and [ideal], of the world in which individuals live' (Dewey, 1938, p. 60). The qualitative thus relates to 'concern or interest' (Dewey, 1916a, p. 198); 'values', Dewey says, would be a better word if it were not so open to misconstruction (Dewey, 1916b, p. 4). Inquiry is set in motion when something is in *doubt* about interests or values. Otherwise, use and enjoyment is direct and sufficient. But when a *problem* arises, a different response is necessary.

Inquiry is an attempt to formulate an idea or a plan to remove doubt. It is a mediator between a disrupted and a reconstructed life. Its function (as Giarelli and Chambliss say) is to develop 'possibilities' (or suggestions or hypotheses) for the conduct of life. We are assisted in that formulation not by methods or rules that have been handed over directly from other experience (though these should be considered), but by forms of inquiry that are developed within experience itself with the aim of understanding it more clearly and responding to it more intelligently. Inquiry *mediates* between a given experience and one's intent or aim.

One cannot say prior to experience what forms of inquiry will be more useful than others. That will depend on the assistance they give in formulating or organizing experience. Dewey does not take a side in the debates over theory vs. practice, science vs. art, or quantitative vs. qualitative inquiry. Rather, each mode has its own function in a broader conception of inquiry. What is at issue, according to Dewey (and in the essays in our collection), is that there is no need for or good to come from fitting all inquiry into one mold. Speaking about practical vs. theoretical inquiry, Dewey (1922) says:

> Educators . . . should not try to force one pattern and model upon all. . . . The aim of education should be to secure a balanced interaction of the two types of mental attitude, having sufficient regard to the disposition of the individual not to hamper and cripple whatever powers are naturally strong in him. The narrowness of individuals of strong concrete bent needs to be liberalized. Every opportunity that occurs within practical activities for developing curiosity and susceptibility to intellectual problems should be seized. . . . As regards the smaller number of those who have a taste for abstract, purely intellectual topics, pains should be taken to multiply opportunities for the application of ideas, for translating symbolic truths into terms of everyday and social life. (pp. 228–229)

In spite of Dewey's caution, some recent commentators maintain a dualism — either/or — between qualitative and quantitative research. This is the view of Smith and Heshusius (1986), on one hand, who argue that 'the claim of compatibility and the call for cooperation between quantitative and qualitative inquiry cannot be sustained'; indeed, such claims 'have the unfortunate effect of closing down an important conversation' — about objectivity, values, practical application — crucial to understanding how researchers do their work. The interpretation is an extension of an earlier paper by Smith (1983). Quantitative and qualitative inquiry, according to Smith and Heshusius (1986), come 'close to speaking different languages — a neutral scientific or value-free language versus a value-laden language of everyday discourse' (p. 11). A similar impression is given in a pair of articles by Elliot W. Eisner, who identifies the 'dimensions in which artistic and scientific approaches to qualitative research differ' (Eisner, 1981) and claims that educational research, defined as 'correlational and experimental studies', cannot — sad to say — inform educational practice (Eisner, 1984).

Smith and Heshusius and Eisner simply repeat the dichotomies they describe in others and which Eisner, at least, deplores. They do not consider that other interpretations may be proposed, in which qualitative and quantitative inquiry are not at all in opposition, not because they grasp at an easy synthesis (Smith and Heshusius, 1986, p. 4), but because their conception is not based on dualistic logic. Smith and Heshusius (1986) sense that the debate has to do with 'meanings', but they fail to consider other meanings, such as Dewey's, in which qualitative and quantitative inquiry work together. 'Science' and 'scientific method' have many meanings, even for Dewey — intelligence, reflective thinking, experimental method, even 'inquiry' itself — but, in general, his view is that:

> Science signifies, I take it, the existence of systematic methods of inquiry, which, when they are brought to bear on a range of facts, enable us to understand them better and to control them more intelligently, less haphazardly and with less routine. (Dewey, 1929b, pp. 8–9)

There is no conflict between that conception of scientific study and qualitative life and methods. With due regard for Smith and Heshusius' concern, Dewey's 'middle ground' (Rorty, 1982, p. 206) is perhaps a more powerful stimulus for thinking about our conceptions of objectivity, generalization, the relation of facts and values, and so on, than are any conceptions built on dichotomies.

For Dewey (1938), each perspective, approach, or method, or what he calls 'phase' of inquiry, has potential for clarifying experience and setting it on a course. Each may contribute in its own time and way. Unlike the qualitative, which has 'pretty direct existential application', scientific inquiry seeks significance and meaning through the 'systematic relations of coherence and consistency of [one thing] with . . . another' (p. 65). The goal of science, in fact, depends upon '*elimination* of the qualitative as such and upon reduction to non–qualitative formulation' (p. 65). Further, 'no scientific *proposition* which records the processes and results of observation and experiment is complete unless processes and results are stated in numerical form' (p. 200).

But this is not to say that science is opposed to the qualitative, but only that it has its own work to do. It is the function of science, or inquiry, to construct an 'idea' of things, and it is helped in this task by quantification, logical form, and the like. This is why we say that science is 'abstract', for all *ideas* are 'abstracts' from experience. But the aim always is to get back to experience, back to the qualitative. Dewey speaks repeatedly of 're-qualifying' experience through inquiry. The point to be grasped is that inquiry or research is helped in its course by numerous tactics and techniques, by scientific procedure and logical analysis, quantification and mathematical discourse, historical narration and description, the use of propositions and terms, and different kinds of judgment, to give names to just a few of the resources at hand. Through these devices experience is reconstructed and unified with the aim of directing it toward anticipated experiences. Qualitative life is *re-qualified*.

Certainly a problem arises if numbers and statistics are taken as a substitute for qualitative life. Dewey (1916a) reminds us that numbers only:

> . . . represent qualities and relations of the world in which our action goes on, because they are factors upon which the accomplishment of our purposes depends. [Their] study is effectual in the degree in which the pupil realizes the place of the numerical truth he is dealing with in carrying to fruition activities in which he is concerned. (pp. 134–135)

The function of any statistics in social science, Dewey (1922) says in another place, is as 'a means of stating future results more exactly and objectively and thus of making action more humane' (p. 215). The professional inquirer — the researcher or the scientist — in contrast to the ordinary person, is concerned with developing the tools of inquiry — terms, propositions, logical system, numerical form, and statistical analysis — and so runs the risk of dropping 'from sight the situation in its integrity and treats these instrumentalities of knowledge as objects of knowledge' (Dewey, 1916b, pp. 34–35). But science never wholly gets away from qualitative life. It has its own qualitative background as well as that of 'the world in which the ordinary experience of the common man is lived' (Dewey, 1930b, p. 198). Science grows out of the problems and concerns of qualitative life; it refines, expands, and liberates the content and agencies of that life; and it aims to reconstruct or 're-qualify' that life.

Dewey (1930b) believes that unless qualities are considered, inquiry will be isolated and mechanical (p. 180). Experiences are *wholes* and must be treated as wholes. 'All thought in every subject begins with . . . an unanalyzed whole' (Dewey, 1930b, p. 183). Only when a distinction is made of some element in the total situation, or 'complex whole', is an 'object' thus defined for inquiry. But even then the significance or meaning of the object for inquiry is controlled by continued reference to the total situation. Obvious examples come to mind in the arts (Dewey, 1930b, p. 179; 1934). A painting or a symphony is not a collection of objects or instances, but a whole in which the elements have significance or meaning only in relation to each other and to the whole itself. The whole determines what distinctions may be useful. A more common example is the 'feeling' of anger, which designates not a 'ready-made independent psychical entity', or even the direct presence of quality, but:

> . . . a pervading tone, color, and quality of persons, things, and circumstances, or of a situation. When angry, we are not aware of anger but of these objects in their immediate and unique qualities. In another situation, anger may appear as a distinct term, and analysis may then call it a feeling or emotion. But we have now shifted the

universe of discourse, and the validity of the terms of the latter one
depends upon the existence of the direct quality of the whole in a
former one. (Dewey, 1930b, pp. 182–183)

The role of *judgment* is special in Dewey's conception of qualitative
inquiry. One might be inclined, as we did in an earlier section of this paper
when we summarized the qualitative characteristics marked by the various
essayists, to disavow that judgment implies value judgment. But that would
retain a dualism that is inconsistent with Dewey's idea of qualitative thought.
Judgment is complex (see Thayer, 1952, pp. 63–65). It seems to connote a
termination of inquiry. Dewey himself gives this implication when he speaks
about 'final judgment' as a 'warranted assertion', or the outcome of inquiry.
It is the end or outcome of the inquiry at hand and should move us to action.
Final judgment has *direct* existential import (Dewey, 1938, p. 120). You can
act on it. But 'final' does not mean settled for all time. It is the 'end' only in
the situation that motivated the inquiry. Equally important is the idea that
judgment is ongoing; 'intermediate judgments' are estimates, evaluations, and
appraisals of what to do at any next step of inquiry (Dewey, 1938, p. 174).
Judgment keeps inquiry moving toward a conclusion. Further, Dewey
suggests that judgment which is 'appreciation' is a constituent of value judgment. Having been motivated by some interest, concern, or value, inquiry,
if we are sincere and consistent, terminates in action. Something is done
with our interests and values. Experience is re-qualified; it now functions
satisfactorily as a whole.

We are now in a position to summarize Dewey's theory of the qualitative
and qualitative inquiry. The qualitative is found in *direct* (not disengaged or
abstracted) *experience*. It refers to experience as a direct value. Experience itself
is 'bounded'; it is not anything and everything in the world, but a *context*.
Dewey (1938, p. 66f.) calls this a 'situation'. When the meaning or significance
of experience is 'doubtful' in some way, is unclear or in threat, we turn to
inquiry as a systematic and formal means for restoring its continuity or sense
of *wholeness*. All this implies that inquiry takes place in a *value* context; it is
motivated by a concern for value, and it contributes to settling or restoring
value. Finally, the idea of a *problem* is central in Dewey's theory of inquiry.
It is the focus for inquiry, the thing to be settled and the test for any settlement.
'The problem' unifies theory and practice. Where inquiry is motivated by a
problem, there is no question about the relevance of its product — knowledge
or theory — to practice. The 'reference to experience seems . . . to be the
easiest way of realizing the continuities among subject-matters that are always
getting split up into dualisms' (Dewey, 1916b, p. 71).

For Dewey (1930b), the 'test' for qualitative inquiry, or any inquiry, is
the situation itself, and nothing else:

The underlying quality is itself the test . . . for any particular case.
All that is needed is to determine this quality by indicating the limits

between which it moves [its means or condition and its outcome or end] and the direction or tendency of its movement. (p. 190)

Meaning can be apprehended only by going beyond [symbols], by using them as clues to call up qualitative situations. When an experience of the latter is had and they are relived, the realities corresponding to the propositions laid down may be had. (p. 187)

In his 'Preface' to *Logic: The Theory of Inquiry*, Dewey (1938) suggests that readers who find his discussion too technical:

. . . interpret what is said by calling to mind what they themselves do, and the way they proceed in doing it, when they are confronted with some question or difficulty which they attempt to cope with in an intellectual way. (p. iv)

The test of any theory — and inquiry that leads to it — is practice. And any inquiry — and theory — that is practical is also moral. It makes a difference in life.

In an autobiographical statement written at the age of 70, Dewey (1930a) remarked:

If I read the cultural signs of the times aright, the next synthetic movement in philosophy will emerge when the significance of the social sciences and arts has become an object of reflective attention in the same way that mathematical and physical sciences have been made the objects of thought in the past, and when their full import is grasped. (p. 18)

Recent philosophers (Bernstein, 1960; Rorty, 1982; Sleeper, 1986) have returned to that theme when marking the significance of Dewey's thinking. Their evaluations help us to get the idea of qualitative inquiry.

R. Rorty (1982) makes the point directly and forcefully. Like the essayists in our collection, Rorty believes that the move toward interpretative [read 'qualitative'] social science is a reaction against social policies based on research 'so thin as barely to count as "moral" at all . . .' (p. 196). One of our students said, 'It seems to me that people's attitudes ought to convey some feeling, not just mean scores.' Rorty, following Dewey, recommends that social science return to the use of narratives; they are instruments for 'coping with things', rather than revealing 'essences' or intrinsic nature. Rorty (1982) says, 'It's always wise to ask what the subject *thinks* it's up to before formulating our own hypotheses' (p. 200). That is a qualitative perspective. (It is consistent with Goodson and Walker's recommendation, in our collection, that 'life history' be added to ethnographies.)

The aim of research, of course, is to understand things better. But 'understanding' is ambiguous. It can mean 'explanation' or 'interpretation'. Rorty (1982) believes that we seek explanation when we want to predict and control. But if our aim is to interact with each other, rather than control, social scientists need to act as interpreters, so we can converse more effectively. This, it turns out, is the same expectation we have for poets and other artists. Literature and science come together. Rorty (1982) says:

> If we get rid of traditional notions of 'objectivity' and 'scientific method' we shall be able to see the social sciences as continuous with literature — as interpreting other people to us, and thus enlarging and deepening our sense of community. . . . When the notion of knowledge as representation goes, then the notion of inquiry as split into discrete sectors with discrete subject matters goes. The lines between novels, newspaper articles, and sociological research get blurred. The lines between subject matters are drawn by reference to practical concerns, rather than putative ontological status. (p. 203)

Surely this is what Dewey had in mind with his idea of qualitative inquiry. 'Poetry,' he said, 'is a more competent organ of suggesting [experience] than scientific prose' (Dewey, 1916b, p. 10, n.). But the difference between art and science is not intrinsic.

> It is not because of self-obvious and self-contained traits of the immediate terms that Dante's world belongs to poetry and Newton's to scientific astronomy. . . . The difference in status and claim is made by what we call experience: by the place of the two systems in experience with respect to their generation and consequences. (Dewey, 1916b, p. 63)

Rather, the difference between art and science, and between qualitative and quantitative research, is found in aim and method and moral consequence. Rorty (1982) interprets Dewey's approach as a 'middle ground' which 'inspired the social sciences in America before the failure of nerve which turned them "behavioral" ' (p. 206). He and we, and the essayists in this collection, hope for a return to the middle — and moral — ground.


## To Students

Our discussion of Dewey is not intended to be exhaustive or to convert. It indicates, rather, how we think of qualitative research. The point is that qualitative research, which often is thought to be in competition with quantitative research and with science, is in need of a comprehensive theory that will unify various modes of qualitative research and will unite qualitative and quantitative approaches to research. Dewey is an example; certainly there are others. There is a sense, which our discussion is trying to make plain, in which all research is qualitative. Another one of our students has said that 'all inquiry gets its impetus from quality'. She has learned our lesson well! But there is more. We are tempted to say that all research is qualitative *in origin and outcome*, but even that would be too narrow. The fact is that at every step or phase in its conduct, research has connections with the qualitative situation that set it in motion. As Dewey says, situations have a 'pervasive quality' that focuses or regulates inquiry. Researchers, though they may be conducting a recondite phase of research at the time, should be mindful of these connections and of the qualitative concerns that the writers set forth in the present collection of essays.

We hope the present essays and discussion of qualitative research are helpful to students, especially graduate students. Their own research is the place where they develop attitudes and habits of research. We hope they view the 'qualitative' as life itself, as the interests and concern they have in life, and qualitative (and quantitative) research methods as approaches to understanding and directing that life. Further, we want them to integrate qualitative and quantitative approaches to research in education. Even a study (say a 'dissertation') whose primary purpose may be a quantitative formulation has a qualitative situation or context out of which it grows and to which its conclusions must be put. To do so is to unite theory and practice in the most obvious way, to make research 'relevant', as students used to say. The 'statement of the problem' in such a study calls on philosophy to be made clearly, and the conclusions and suggestions for further research or for practice have philosophical — moral — import. One may even see a 'review of literature' in any study as an historical account of what has been tried in reference to the problem at hand. More, such a review is a continuing attempt to refine and define 'the problem'. Next, an appropriate methodology must be chosen to get at the problem which its careful statement poses. Even references and literary style (Bowersock, 1983–84; Hexter, 1971) contribute to the qualitative treatment of the study. They are not incidentals or merely sugar-coating to get someone to pay attention to the study, but are clues to the qualitative situation. And so on.

Some critics might think that this format for a study (or, correctly, the report of a study) — problem, literature review, method, findings, conclusions — is unique to scientific or quantitative reports. Whether or not the form is characteristic of such reports, our point is that where such a format is used, the qualitative ground of the study can still be revealed if we understand the distinctive function of each phase of inquiry. Though these points are made too simply, they are suggestive of our belief that all research, no matter what methods are employed, is qualitative in aim and must retain a qualitative perspective. If the essays in this collection make these points clear and urgent, they will have been successful.

## References

AMERICAN EDUCATIONAL RESEARCH ASSOCIATION (1941–82) *Encyclopedia of Educational Research*, 5 edns. New York: Macmillan and Free Press.

AMERICAN EDUCATIONAL RESEARCH ASSOCIATION (1986). *Handbook of Research on Teaching* (3rd ed.) M. C. WITTROCK (ed.) New York: Macmillan.

AYERS, C. E. (1938). 'Dewey and his 'Studies in Logical Theory' '. In M. Cowley and B. Smith (Eds), *Books That Changed Our Minds*. New York: Doubleday [Books for Libraries edition, 1970].

BERNSTEIN, R. J. (1960). Introduction. In R. J. Bernstein (Ed.), *On Experience, Nature, and Freedom: Representative Selections [of John Dewey]*. New York: Liberal Arts Press.

BOWERSOCK, G. W. (1983–84). 'The art of the footnote'. *The American Scholar, 53*(1), 54–62.

COWLEY, M. (1938). 'An afterword on the modern mind'. In M. Cowley and B. Smith (Eds), *Books That Changed Our Minds*. New York: Doubleday [Books for Libraries edition, 1970].

DEWEY, J. (1903). *Studies in Logical Theory*. Chicago: University of Chicago Press.

DEWEY, J. (1916a). *Democracy and Education*. New York: Macmillan [Free Press edition, 1966].

DEWEY, J. (1916b). *Essays in Experimental Logic*. Chicago: University of Chicago Press.

DEWEY, J. (1922). *Human Nature and Conduct*. New York: Holt [Modern Library edition, 1930].

DEWEY, J. (1929a). *Experience and Nature*. New York: Norton.

DEWEY, J. (1929b). *The Sources of a Science of Education*. New York: Liveright [1974 edition].

DEWEY, J. (1930a). 'From absolutism to experimentalism'. In R. J. Bernstein (Ed.), *On Experience, Nature, and Freedom: Representative Selections [of John Dewey]*. New York: Liberal Arts Press, 1960.

DEWEY, J. (1930b). 'Qualitative thought'. In R. J. Bernstein (Ed.), *On Experience, Nature, and Freedom: Representative Selections [of John Dewey]*. New York: Liberal Arts Press, 1960.

DEWEY, J. (1933). *How We Think*. Boston: Heath [Gateway edition, 1971].

DEWEY, J. (1934). *Art As Experience*. New York: Minton, Balch.

DEWEY, J. (1938). *Logic: The Theory of Inquiry*. New York: Holt.

EISNER, E. W. (1981). 'On the differences between scientific and artistic approaches to qualitative research'. *Educational Researcher, 10*(2), 5–9.

EISNER, E. W. (1984). 'Can educational research inform educational practice?' *Phi Delta Kappan, 65*(7), 448–452.

ERICKSON, F. (1986). 'Qualitative methods in research on teaching'. In *Handbook of Research on Teaching* (3rd ed.) New York: Macmillan.

GREENE, T. F. (1971). *The Activities of Teaching*. New York: McGraw-Hill.

HEXTER, J. H. (1971). 'The rhetoric of history'. In *Doing History*. Bloomington, IN: Indiana University Press.

KRUTCH, J. W. (1929). *The Modern Temper*. New York: Harcourt, Brace.

LINCOLN, Y. S. and GUBA, E. G. (1985). *Naturalistic Inquiry*. Beverly Hills, CA: Sage.

RORTY, R. (1982). 'Method, social science, and social hope'. In *Consequences of Pragmatism*. Minneapolis, MN: University of Minnesota Press.

SMITH, J. K. (1983). 'Quantitative versus qualitative research: An attempt to clarify the issue'. *Educational Researcher, 12*(3), 6–13.

SMITH, J. K. and HESHUSIUS, L. (1986). 'Closing down the conversation: The end of the quantitative-qualitative debate among educational inquirers'. *Educational Researcher, 15*(1), 4–12.

SLEEPER, R. W. (1986). *The Necessity of Pragmatism: John Dewey's Conception of Philosophy*. New Haven, CT: Yale University Press.

THAYER, H. S. (1952). *The Logic of Pragmatism: An Examination of John Dewey's Philosophy*. New York: Humanities Press.

WOLCOTT, H. (1973). *The Man in the Principal's Office: An Ethnography*, New York: Holt.

*Chapter 2*

# Qualitative Inquiry in Philosophy and Education: Notes on the Pragmatic Tradition

*James M. Giarelli*
*Graduate School of Education*
*Rutgers University*
*New Brunswick, NJ 08903*

I begin this paper with what some of you might think is a problematical claim. From my reading of the critical literature in philosophy, the history of science and social science, and the nature of theory and explanation, I think it is safe to say that the logical positivist intellectual program is over. To be sure, its assumptions continue to dominate the training programs of researchers and policy makers and its detritus remains as topics for the research journals, but its intellectual supports were undermined long ago.

The relevance of this for my present purposes is the bearing it has on the way we think about inquiry and, specifically, about the differences between quantitative and qualitative inquiry. Kenneth Howe in the October 1985 *Educational Researcher*, puts the point this way:

> Although the distinctions between quantitative and qualitative methods and between facts and values do mark important differences, the differences do not constitute sharp, uncrossable dividing lines. . . . Rigid epistemological distinctions between quantitative and qualitative methods and between factual and value judgments exemplified in present thinking about educational research methodology are unsupportable dogmas held over from logical positivism, and . . . the post-positivistic conception of science exemplified by thinkers such as Quine, Kuhn, and Scriven undermines construing the distinctions in this way. (p. 10)

While I have some problems with Howe's account of the features of post-positivistic science and its treatment of the differences between facts and values, I agree with the basic claim of his argument. Put simply, if the logical positivist program is unsupportable, then the typical ways of discussing the differences between quantitative and qualitative inquiry are moribund. I assume that you are all familiar with the usual categories in which these alleged differences are framed, e.g. 'hard' vs. 'soft', 'human' vs. 'natural', 'descriptive' vs. 'evaluative', 'predictive' vs. 'interpretive', and so on. The position I take is that these categories are no longer useful in our attempts to develop an account of rigorous thought. Further, I suggest that what I loosely call the pragmatic tradition gives us a more accurate and enabling perspective on thought, inquiry, and philosophical thinking in education.

If there is anything we have learned from our modern fixation on knowledge it is that all knowing, scientific and otherwise, involves interpretation. By all accounts this seems to be true in all domains of inquiry, even or perhaps especially, in quantitative inquiry. A long account of the varieties of empiricism is really necessary here to support this claim, but it must be omitted. Perhaps a simple, and I think fundamental, point will be at least suggestive of what is at issue. To quantify is to employ a particular symbolic system, chosen from among alternatives, for the purposes of interpreting and expressing observed phenomena. Every move in the process of inquiry away from observation and toward quantification and measurement is an interpretive move. Needless to say, quantitative researchers use other interpretive schemes in the choice of their problems, discussion of results, and so on, but I use this simple example to suggest that even at its most basic level, all inquiry is interpretive.

Now I make this point not because I take some delight in dragging quantitative researchers down into the muck where the qualitative researcher must work. Nor do I think that by saying that all inquiry is interpretive will the problem of rigorous thought be solved. I make the point only to suggest that the problem of rigorous thought is not found in some formal distinction between quantitative and qualitative inquiry, but rather in the nature of interpretation. For if all inquiry is interpretive, then at some point we must face the question of how to judge among competing interpretations.

It is here, of course, where the so-called problem of 'relativism' arises. As it is commonly argued, if all thought involves interpretation, and if there are different interpretations, and if there are no formal and universal benchmarks of truth and falsity to refer to, then everything is relative and the search for knowledge has ended up back in Plato's cave.

Avoiding this supposed fate has consumed the attention of intellectuals for a long time. Dewey called it 'the quest for certainty' and wrote of philosophers who sought solace in their 'barren monopoly of dealings with Ultimate and Absolute Reality' (Dewey, 1920, p. 27). Richard Bernstein (1983, p. 19) writes of the 'Cartesian Anxiety', the 'belief that there are and must be some fixed, permanent constraints to which we can appeal and which are secure and stable' as an 'ontological' condition which lies 'at the very center of our being in the world'. Richard Rorty (1979) satirizes as Sisyphean the self-image of the philosopher who seeks a permanent, neutral matrix for ordering the world through an 'analysis' of the logic of language, mind, or nature. And Alasdair MacIntyre (1981) regards the Enlightenment project of providing a rational account and justification of universal moral principles and rules as an inevitable failure because of its attempt to transcend history, culture, and particularity.

Let us be clear here. These writers and many others in what I call, perhaps arguably, the pragmatic tradition, do not suggest that we embrace relativism. Indeed, they argue, in different ways, that the refutation of objectivism does not imply relativism. More pointedly, they hold that the alleged problem of relativism only occurs when there is the assumption or hope that objectivism is possible. In other words, as Jacques Barzun (1983) writes of William James' pragmatism:

> When the pragmatist says that his truth fits his purpose and may not
> fit others he is not claiming the privilege of being 'subjective' or
> eccentric, he is only pointing to a condition of human thought. (p. 83)

What the refutation of objectivism does, then, is to radically revise or 're-vision' the problem of thought and inquiry. Instead of a concentration on the mechanics (e.g., deduction, decision by formal rule, appeal to abstractions and universals) of an ahistorical closed system, the pragmatic tradition locates the problem of thought and inquiry in the development of the complex rationality of judgment and argumentation necessary for intelligent conduct. While our judgments may not have objective justification and our arguments may be indeterminate and contestable, we still are making judgments and arguing for choices, and thus we are not relativists in any practical sense of the term.

Perhaps I should say more here. In the *Consequences of Pragmatism*, Rorty (1982) following Dewey and the pragmatic tradition, makes the distinction between *philosophical* theories and *real* theories. Pragmatists *are* relativists about philosophical theories, or speculative accounts of the nature of things. For pragmatists, there is no rational way to choose among rival speculative philo-sophical positions. However, pragmatists *are not* relativists about real theories, that is, about concrete proposals for alternative action. These are to be debated, argued over, inquired into, tested, and so on, in terms of their consequences.

Pragmatists are often charged with being relativists because it is believed that if they are philosophical relativists then they must be real or practical relativists. But, of course, they need not be. Indeed, to believe so would mean that people could not make choices or commend certain ways of acting over others on concrete issues until the speculative philosophical issues were resolved. But these issues are never resolved and people, thank goodness, do make complex rational judgments about alternative courses of action all the time. Richard Bernstein (1985) calls this complex rationality of judgment and argumentation the 'choreography of critique', and I think it accurately describes the process which distinguishes any rigorous inquiry, quantitative or qualitative, from both pure fancy and pure fact-mongering.

So far I have argued that the logical positivist program is over and that with its demise the received ways of talking about qualitative and quantitative inquiry, and indeed about inquiry and thought in general, are no longer useful.

In arguing against objectivism and for a view of all inquiry as interpretive, I have suggested that the so-called problem of relativism must be recast. In Dewey, Rorty, Bernstein, MacIntyre and many other contemporary philosophers, we find such an effort and the concomitant portrayal of an account of thought and inquiry rooted not in abstraction, deduction, and formalism, but rather in the dynamics and demands of judgment, argument and lived conduct. It is this last point I wish to develop somewhat further because I believe it has particular relevance for philosophers of education.

To say that thought and inquiry emerge in the dynamics and demands of intelligent conduct is to point to a form of rationality rooted in the analysis of *practices*. To attempt to analyze and understand practices without this form of complex rationality, that is, to impose formalisms, whether methodological, disciplinary, or epistemological, upon subject matter prior to inquiry, is literally thoughtless. This is a point as old as Aristotle, who argues in the *Ethics* that a requirement of any investigation is that the degree of precision and mode of explanation must fit the subject matter in question.

By 'practices', I mean something specific. MacIntyre (1981) puts it this way:

> By a practice I mean any coherent and complex form of socially established cooperative human activity through which goods internal to that form of activity are realised in the course of trying to achieve those standards of excellence which are appropriate to, and partially definitive of, that form of activity, with the result that human powers to achieve excellence, and human conceptions of the ends and goods involved, are systematically extended. (p. 175)

Thomas Green, in his 1984 John Dewey Lecture, makes a similar point, but he is more specific about implications for the professions. As he writes:

> . . . The professions are always practices in response to some fundamental human need or social good *whose advancement is already a moral aim.* . . . The professions, in short, are practices related to the central life giving, life sustaining, and life fulfilling events of human existence. (p. 30)

From this perspective, the defining feature of a practice is its socially established moral aim, and its standards of excellence are derived from this aim. Thus, to prepare people for a professional practice while neglecting to teach them its cultural and moral point is to foreclose the possibility of their achievement of those standards of excellence internal to the activity itself.

There are obvious implications here for the professional preparation of educators, but I believe there are also implications for the conduct of educational and philosophical inquiry or research. If we see inquiry rooted in the analysis of practices, themselves seen as socially established cooperative activities for advancing some human moral aim, then educational inquiry, properly conceived, is the paradigmatic form of complex rational thought. All of the formal epistemological distinctions between quantitative and qualitative inquiry are dissolved in the search for ways of explaining, understanding, and promoting those activities which will advance our most basic human social and moral aims and the standards of excellence that are appropriate to these activities.

This perspective also has implications for philosophical inquiry. In the recent philosophical work that I have cited earlier in this paper, as well as other work in aesthetics and in philosophy of science and social science, we see an effort to base the philosophical study of human phenomena, not in speculation about the nature of mind or the logic of nature, but rather in the historical and phenomenological analysis of lived human conduct. In this view, ethics is not about the nature of the good, but rather involves the study of how human actors settle moral disagreements and attempt to secure cherished values. Aesthetics is not about the nature of beauty, but rather involves the study of our attempts to create quality. Epistemology is not about the nature of truth, but rather involves the study of the social practices by which communities develop a basis for warranted belief and action. It is important to note that this perspective does not merely call for attention to more 'practical' questions. Its radical aim is to overcome the formal theory—practice dualism altogether by rooting all inquiry in a context which admits of no neat separations among meaning, fact, and value.

It is here where the crucial point comes home, for this view leads us to see that *educational* questions are at the core of not only philosophical, but of all complex rational inquiry. When we throw off the quest for metaphysical and extra-experiential foundations of knowledge, and the quest for technical norms and predictive rules, we place the doings and undergoings of people, in their life project to achieve individuality and community, at the center of our attempts at rigorous thought. In short, we make education — our efforts to conserve, criticize, and create culture — the focus of human study in all its varieties.

This, of course, is a Deweyan point, with echoes in Rorty, MacIntyre, Bernstein, Habermas and many others. I suppose that there is some sense in calling this kind of inquiry qualitative, in contrast to quantitative, thought, but I think it would be better to drop these labels altogether and simply get on with the business of developing the multiple ways of inquiring and knowing needed to understand the forms of educational practice central to our existence and to develop their possibilities for excellence.

## References

BARZUN, J. (1983). *A Stroll with William James.* New York: Harper and Row.
BERNSTEIN, R. J. (1983). *Beyond Objectivism and Relativism.* Philadelphia, PA: University of Pennsylvania Press.
BERNSTEIN, R. J. (1985). *Interpretation and its discontents.* Paper Presented at a Conference

on 'Hermeneutic Approaches in Clinical Psychology: Alternatives to Natural Science Modes of Explanation and Understanding', New Brunswick, NJ, October 18.

DEWEY, J. (1920). *Reconstruction in Philosophy*. New York: Holt.

GREEN, T. F. (1984). *The Formation of Conscience in an Age of Technology*. Syracuse, NY: Syracuse University Press.

HOWE, K. R. (1985). *Educational Researcher, 14*, (October), 10–18.

MACINTYRE, A. (1981). *After Virtue*, Notre Dame, IN: University of Notre Dame Press.

RORTY, R. (1979). *Philosophy and the Mirror of Nature*. Princeton, NJ: Princeton University Press.

RORTY, R. (1982). *Consequences of Pragmatism*. Minneapolis, MN: University of Minnesota Press.

*Part II*
# Methods

*Chapter 3*

# Philosophy of Education as Qualitative Inquiry

*James M. Giarelli and J. J. Chambliss*
*Graduate School of Education*
*Rutgers University*
*New Brunswick, NJ 08903*

## Philosophic and Scientific Activity

For much of this century philosophers have tried to emulate scientists. They have thought of their task either as a mimicking of scientific methods and procedures or a servicing of scientific conceptual needs. These tendencies have waned in recent years because of disenchantment over the consequences of scientific thinking for human life and the shaky intellectual grounds on which science alleges to stand. The consequence has been a rethinking of philosophy and its task (Rorty, 1979, 1982; Nozick, 1981; MacIntyre, 1981).

In the late nineteenth and early twentieth centuries, a movement developed based on the conviction that education itself was to be studied as a science. Philosophy of education as a distinct discipline emerged as part of that movement. Three conceptions of philosophy of education stand out in that early period (Chambliss, 1968). The first argued that education could become a science if it too, like the natural sciences, were treated as an inductive science (e.g., Tate, 1885). The second took the position that human reason aims to complete the work of which natural science is not capable, and that reason finds the justification for the conclusions of the sciences (e.g., Rosenkranz, 1886; Horne, 1904). The work of philosophy is to make known the 'invisible whole' from which come the fragmentary experiences of the sciences. The third conception opposed both these tendencies and held instead that the natural place for educational ideas to arise is in educational contexts and that the role of science is to test the meanings of those ideas. Hence, philosophy of education suggests possibilities to be explored further in science (see John Dewey's early writings, in particular, Dewey, 1966; see also MacVannell, 1912).

The appeal of science has endured. In the 1920s and 1930s, for example, an effort was made to equate research in philosophy with the scientific method in its broadest sense (Giarelli and Zimpfer, 1980). Philosophical research was thought to entail the same procedures used by the scientist: identification of problems, generation of hypotheses, collection of evidence, and generalization of findings. It was understood, however, that the philosopher's 'data' were different, that no reliable instruments of measurement of a distinctly philosophical nature were available, and that philosophical problems were not always open to empirical investigation.

This procedure in effect identifies philosophical research with the activity of 'reflective thinking' (Dewey, 1933). Reflective thinking entails the same basic procedures and activities used by the scientist, but acknowledges the differences between the problems, methods, and goals of the philosopher and the scientist. But if reflective thinking is common to all inquiry, it cannot be a distinctive method of philosophical research.

If philosophy is not part of a paradigm of scientific inquiry, what is it? Is there a place for philosophy to stand, apart from, yet related to, science? Is there a way for philosophy to inform science without being merely speculative? Is there a place for rigorous thinking between feeling and fact? The purpose of this essay is to describe the role that philosophy can play.

The modern separation of philosophy and science has come about in a history that would be instructive but is too long to tell here. We may, however, refer briefly to Aristotle (*Nicomachean Ethics*, Book 6, Chapter 2), who has fundamental insights into the story. For Aristotle, there was no hard and fast distinction between the philosopher, who possesses 'wisdom', and the scientist, who possesses 'knowledge'. He does not subordinate one activity to the other, but takes each, in its own way, to be essential to shaping a human being who would be knowledgeable-and-wise, scientist-and-philosopher. He further insists that each science has its own methods which can be found only in its distinct subject matter. Thus, no science is superior to another; each has its own legitimate work to do. Aristotle's view is not 'scientism'; science itself, or any one of the sciences, is not a supreme standard for all other activities. And reason does not stand apart from experience; it works, rather, in the midst of experience, shaping the materials of experience into knowledge. Aristotle shows that the role of rigorous thinking is not to arbitrate between feeling and fact, but to mold feeling and fact into knowledge determined by the subject matter in which thinking goes on.

## Philosophy as Qualitative Thinking

The story is told that as she lay dying, Gertrude Stein, the sponsor of avant-garde culture, turned to her friend Alice B. Toklas and asked, 'What is the answer?' Alice did not reply. Then with her last words Stein asked, 'In that case, what is the question?' This anecdote sets the stage for thinking about the elements from which a view of qualitative inquiry can be constructured. Our emphasis is on philosophy as qualitative inquiry and on the modes of qualitative inquiry in philosophy of education. To this end, our perspective on qualitative inquiry will distinguish among philosophy, science, and art as modes of inquiry and action.

For our purposes, there are two salient points in the Stein anecdote. The first is that before inquiry there is always query, or a question, and, secondly, before query there is aesthetic activity, or feeling and appreciation, which we call 'qualitative thinking'. Thus, one may make a rough distinction among science, philosophy, and art. Where it is the artist's aim to say and represent the world, and the scientist's task to calculate and test what has been said or represented, it is the philosopher's task to ask the unasked question. (This insight is Laura Mindek's (1984). What we call 'qualitative thinking', she calls 'artful thought'. We use the more generic term to avoid a distracting discussion in this essay of the differences between philosophy and art.)

What does it mean to say that inquiry presupposes a query or question and that question-making and asking are aesthetic? To begin, all questions arise from within a perceptual field, a whole, a context, or a situation. Inquiry is the exploration of questions (or queries) that arise and take particular shape *in* a situation. The same may be said for 'research', which word comes from the Latin *re-circere*, 'to go around again'. Research is going *around*, exploring, looking *within* a situation, context, or field. Inquiry, then, is not simply questioning or searching. It is questioning and searching with an intent, with some limits, or with an object in mind.

Perceptual fields are experienced as a whole. Thinking begins in the feeling of an unanalyzed, undetermined qualitative whole. One has a feeling for the dominating quality in the lived world, in the situation as a whole; one notices it but cannot formulate it as a distinction. Thought begins in the 'given' of unmediated quality. John Dewey (1968) writes:

> In truth, 'given' in this connection signifies only that the quality immediately exists, or is brutely there. In this capacity, it forms that to which all objects of thought refer, although, as we have noticed, it is never part of the manifest subject-matter of thought. In itself, it is the big, buzzing, blooming confusion of which James wrote. This expresses not only the state of a baby's experience but the first stage and background of all thinking on any subject. There is, however, no inarticulate quality which is merely buzzing and blooming. It buzzes to some effect; it blooms toward some fruitage. That is, the quality, although dumb, has as a part of its complex quality a move-ment or transition in some direction. It can, therefore, be intellectually symbolized and converted into an object of thought. This is done by statement of limits and of direction of transition between them. . . . Putting the nature of the limits briefly and without any attempt to justify the statement here, the subject represents the persuasive quality as means or condition and the predicate represents it as outcome or end. (p. 107)

Living in a world of habit, thinking is routine, calculative, or representational, and felt quality is elusive. But when a tension or problem arises, the perception of quality becomes intense. Something is wrong, but one does not know how to formulate it. It cannot be put into a question. One does not know how to say it, much less measure it or think representationally about it. But without a formulated question, there can be no inquiry.

'Thought' is the saying of a problem, and 'qualitative thought' is the formulation of a problem in reference to the qualitative elements of the situation as a whole. For Dewey (1968) this kind of thought is 'regulated by qualitative considerations' such that 'the selective determinations and relations of objects in thought is controlled by reference to a situation' where 'the underlying unity of qualitativeness regulates pertinence or relevancy and force of every distinction and relation' (pp. 93, 97, 99). Qualitative thought sets up the conditions for thinking by mediating between unanalyzed wholes and analyzed parts. It makes the phases of experience and inquiry hang together by defining the parts in reference to the pervasive quality of the situation as a whole. Thus, qualitative thought brings rigor to inquiry in that it 'circum-scribes it externally and integrates it internally' (Dewey, 1968, p. 103). While it does not aim at producing direct knowledge or action, qualitative thought provides for the integration of questions and context out of which worthwhile inquiry grows. (Again, we owe this idea to Mindek, 1984.)

The implication is that there are dimensions of experience for which quantitative measures have no utility. To attempt to 'quantify' those dimen-sions of experience is to violate their nature. Such is the case with *possibilities* in experience, as distinct from that which has been actualized in experience. For the teacher, Dewey (1959) says, the '*quality* of activity and of consequence is more important . . . than any quantitative element. . . . Even if it be true that everything which exists can be measured — if only we knew how — that which does *not* exist cannot be measured' (pp. 118–119). Dewey is inter-ested in the possibilities of experience and argues that they are not only different from, but more important than, what has been actualized:

> A progressive school is primarily concerned with growth . . . with *transforming* existing capacities and experiences; what already exists by way of native endowment and past achievement is subordinate to what it may become. Possibilities are more important than what already exists, and knowledge of the latter counts only in its bearing upon possibilities. (Dewey, 1959, p. 119)

Following these views, we believe that the special task of philosophy is the formulation of questions for reflective thought. The philosopher, as a qualitative thinker, tries to cultivate a sensitivity to the situation as a whole and to the qualities that regulate it. In this view, philosophy honors the unanalyzed and precognitive as its origins, but avoids mere speculation by regulating thought in the light of perceived qualities toward worthwhile questions. Philosophy thus also honors science in its aims by making present and possible the questions that scientific inquiry pursues and avoids scientism by insisting upon qualitative determination of the objects of inquiry. For the philosopher, the issue always is, 'What is the *problem*?', which in turn depends on a prior question, 'What is this *all* about?'

## Aims of Qualitative Thinking

Living in the space between feeling and fact, speculation and science, and related to but distinct from both art and science, what does philosophy as qualitative thought hope to accomplish? Not certain knowledge, for its concern is meanings rather than truths. Philosophy does not aim at making the world, for its concern is not action, but qualities. Rather, philosophy serves an educational role. It mediates between immediate experience and experiment and promotes the intelligent development of values. It does this through a concern with clarity, context, and consciousness, among other things.

### Clarity

One aim of philosophy is clarity, which means linguistic and logical accuracy and precision, and also focus, which is the quality that enables the deepening of thought. Focus enables the transition from an unanalyzed whole to analyzed part. Focus without a perception of the whole leads to triviality (only trees, no forest), while a mere feeling for the whole without focus generates no queries and thus no inquiry and knowledge.

### Context

Context is the building up, enriching, and synthesizing of the perceived situation or whole itself. Modern scientific and quantitative methods generally are acknowledged as an intellectual advance over abstract rationality, which was able to put things right in general, but suffered greatly in the particular. Science practiced as technical or instrumental rationality, and hardened into positivist ideology, however, diminishes the significance of the existential condition in which problems arise, fragments and isolates inquiries, and mitigates against the development of valued and meaningful knowledge. The philosopher seeks to restore and awaken a sense of the qualitative whole from which inquiries develop and to which their results must return. A sense of context is a major determinant of a sense of question; that is, one may understand and be able to formulate a question or problem in one context or situation, but not in another. One may be able to respond to a problem of literacy in the context of schooling by stressing the three Rs, but when education is seen as something that also goes on in places other than schools, the response of educating for literacy must go beyond such tutoring. By paying attention to existing contexts and helping to create new ones, the philosopher seeks to promote inquiries that are novel and pertinent.

*Consciousness*

The history of the idea of 'consciousness' is long and attempts at its definition are fraught with difficulties. Nevertheless, the term may be used here in a non-technical way for a heuristic purpose. Where clarity suggests focus within a field or situation, and context suggests the enriching and reinterpreting of the situation itself, consciousness suggests the grasping and awareness of the tensions created by problematic situations and the necessity for choice. Consciousness, rooted in context and intent on an object, enlivens the sense of possibility and enables the movement from habit to reflective thought. Promoting consciousness, philosophy seeks to keep inquiry from becoming mere method and to give experience a means for its own reconstruction.

Boyd H. Bode's (1913) discussion of a 'fringe of consciousness' enables one to see that, while clarity, context, and consciousness are distinct aims of qualitative thought, they must be understood to function together in actual thinking. By 'fringe', Bode referred to that characteristic of objects in experience that is so elusive when one tries to describe and clarify it. Dwelling on the fringe of consciousness means that experience is 'out of focus'; yet its significance *for* consciousness, for clarity, lies in its *possibility* for further consciousness. The aim is to secure a context in which what is suggestive and uncertain may become clarified and focused. When one succeeds in focusing the situation, then something will become 'known' about it.

Thus, the importance of objects on the fringe of consciousness lies in the possibilities they have for future response and experience. The importance of clarifying them in consciousness lies in settling on some choice. Then one may try to unsettle it again by attempting to clarify something else whose possibilities dwell on the fringe of consciousness. Bode (1913) writes, 'We may say of consciousness that its present moment is the darkest . . . that it is always the knower, and not the known, that it is born an owner and dies owned . . .' (p. 237). He means that the fleeting security of consciousness, together with a sense of continuing qualitative possibilities in reflective thought, demonstrate that efforts to find contexts of meaning will, of necessity, have consequences that require one to seek yet another context. In such manner, human experience undergoes qualitative changes. Any philosophy *of* experience, such as philosophy of education, must deal with those qualitative changes.

## Contemporary Approaches to Qualitative Thinking in Philosophy of Education

Though all philosophers of education may have clarity, context, and consciousness as their aims, one may distinguish among contemporary approaches to philosophy of education by the relative emphasis they give to these aims. We will use the terms 'public', 'professional', and 'personalistic–phenomenological' to identify and distinguish the approaches. The distinction among 'public', 'professional', and 'personal' philosophy of education has been forwarded by Jonas Soltis (1979, 1981, 1983). We incorporate and have learned from Soltis' distinctions, but we use the terms here in different ways and for a different purpose.

Soltis is most interested in whether or not philosophy of education should 'go public'. For those we call public philosophers of education, this is not an issue. John Dewey (1920) expresses the sense clearly when he writes that philosophy *is* a civic enterprise whose aim is 'to clarify men's ideas as to the social and moral strifes of their own day. Its aim is to become so far as is humanly possible an organ for dealing with these conflicts' (p. 26). (There are differences among those who call themselves public philosophers. See, for example, Lippman, 1955; Sullivan, 1982; and Bishirjian, 1978.) Similarly, for Soltis a 'personal' philosophy of education refers to a set of personal beliefs or a personal philosophy of life. Our use of the category 'personalitic-phenomenological' intends to suggest not so much an individual or personal philosophy, but a philosophy *of* the individual or person. Whereas a 'personal' philosophy of education refers to someone's beliefs, a 'personalistic–phenomenological' philosophy tries to develop methods and ideas to explore and express the idea of personhood itself.

### Public Philosophy of Education

Public philosophers of education see the context of educational problems to be social and cultural life. Education is a social and historical process which involves the dynamic interaction of many institutions and actors for the purpose of conserving, creating, and criticizing culture. Public philosophers of education focus on developing a context for understanding the process of education as a whole. Their methods are synthetic rather than analytic and aim to integrate and give synoptic meaning to knowledge from all perspectives (e.g., history, sociology, economics, anthropology, psychology, etc.), about all educative institutions (e.g., family, school, workplace, church, community, media, etc.), in order to construct a context or a vision of education in its widest cultural sense. Without such a context, efforts to resolve educational problems will be short-sighted and short-lived.

The literature on public philosophy of education is extensive; we shall point only to certain features. John Dewey's *Democracy and Education*, first published in 1916, is a classic example. Dewey says his endeavor is 'to detect and state the ideas implied in a democratic society and to apply these ideas to the problems of the enterprise of education' (Preface). The critical writings in response to Dewey's work add to the literature of public philosophy of education. Perhaps the most ambitious response is Herman Harrell Horne's (1932) *The Democratic Philosophy of Education*, which was written as an idealist's companion to Dewey's work. Frederick S. Breed's (1932) *Education and the New Realism* criticizes Dewey's educational philosophy from the standpoint of a philosophy of realism. On the other hand, public philosophy of education in the Deweyan tradition includes Boyd H. Bode's (1927) *Modern Educational Theories* and his (1935) *Democracy as a Way of Life* and also John Child's (1931) *Education and the Philosophy of Experimentalism*. Theodore Brameld has criticized the dominant educational philosophies of progressivism, essentialism, and perennialism in his (1955) *Philosophies of Education in Cultural Perspective* and developed an educational philosophy called 'reconstructionism', which is elaborated in his (1956) *Toward A Reconstructed Philosophy of Education*.

Consulting the 1942 and 1955 yearbooks of the National Society for the Study of Education (Brubacher, 1942, 1955), one can make two observations. (1) A characteristic way of doing philosophy of education has been to take positions in philosophy and explore their meanings for philosophy of education. The positions taken in the 1942 yearbook were experimentalism, realism, idealism, catholicism, and neo-scholasticism, and the contributors were philosophers of education. The positions taken in the 1955 yearbook were realism, thomism, Christian idealism, experimentalism, Marxism, existentialism, linguistic philosophy, logical empiricism, and ontological philosophy, while the contributors were from general philosophy. (2) Each contributor, whatever his point of view, wrote what is essentially a *public* philosophy of education. But, as we shall see, this approach has not continued in much of the writing about educational philosophy since the 1955 yearbook.

Indeed, along with the growing professionalization of academic disciplines in the second half of the twentieth century, philosophers of education have turned their attention away from public philosophy. As a result, most recent attempts to develop a broad and generic understanding of education in its public context have come from writers working largely outside the discipline of philosophy of education (see Silberman, 1970; Goodman, 1964; Kimball and McClellan, 1962; Bowles and Gintis, 1976; Freire, 1981). While it is hard to argue that their works are 'philosophical' in a technical or professional sense, their intention to integrate specialized knowledge for the purpose of developing a context for understanding education in its widest cultural sense puts them in the tradition of public philosophy of education.

Most recently, there has been a renewed interest in public philosophy of education. Harry Broudy's (1981) *Truth and Credibility: The Citizen's Dilemma*, Eva Brann's (1979) *Paradoxes of Education in a Republic*, and R. Freeman Butt's (1980) *The Revival of Civic Learning* all seek to integrate ethical, political, and educational contexts and give evidence of the continuing need for public philosophy of education.


*Personalistic–phenomenological Philosophy of Education*

Personalistic–phenomenological philosophy of education puts the individual and questions of being and becoming at the center of qualitative inquiry. Certainly education is a social process and language is bewitching, but fundamentally an education worthy of its name involves the transformation of individual perception and consciousness. Thus, these philosophers of education have sought methods and sources which enable an exploration of individual life-worlds. Many of them use and refer to the arts and literature, since these have always been powerful modes of individual expression. Some of these philosophers use phenomenological methods which they believe will enable direct descriptions of the world as experienced, before it is analyzed and fragmented into social or logical categories. The purpose of such explorations of individual expression and experience is to heighten consciousness, and with it the sense of the possible; to dramatize freedom and choice. They argue that only with a consciousness and empowering of individual choice can authentic education occur — to develop personality and community.

'Contemporary education is filled with the stuff of tragedy' (Benne, 1951). This idea may be taken as the point of departure of a growing body of literature in philosophy of education in which personalistic–phenomenological concerns have addressed questions raised long ago by the ancient Greek tragic poets, Sophocles and Aeschylus; nineteenth-century philosophers Soren Kierkegaard (*Fear and Trembling* and *Sickness Unto Death*) and Friedrich Nietzsche (*Thus Spake Zarathrustra* and *Birth of Tragedy*); and, more recently, twentieth-century writers such as Martin Buber (*I and Thou*), Edmund Husserl (*Phenomenology and the Crisis of Philosophy*), and Jean-Paul Sartre (*Existentialism* and *Being and Nothingness*). Donald Vandenberg (1979) recently has given an historical account and review of the impact of existentialism and phenomenology on philosophy of education since mid-century; we will mention only a few writings in order to give a sense of what has been done. The title of Huston Smith's (1965) *Condemned to Meaning* is taken from the French phenomenologist Maurice Merleau-Ponty's impression of the human predicament. Maxine Greene's (1973) *Teacher as Stranger* describes the teacher's predicament — stranger to one's students, one's subject matter, and to the larger social world. Philo Pritzkau's (1970) *On Education for the Authentic* attempts to show ways in which children's reality is expanded through learning that is personally significant. Donald Vandenberg's (1971) *Being and Education* discusses the need to recover being and children's desires to be someone. Victor Kestenbaum's (1977) *The Phenomenological Sense of John Dewey* considers Dewey's concept of habit from the standpoint of genetic phenomenology. In these works and others, the limitations and possibilities of human beings in quest of meanings in a world filled with tragedy and characterized by 'homelessness' are explored as philosophy of education.

### Professional Philosophy of Education

Professional philosophy of education typically takes as its problems the linguistic and logical muddles arising out of the discourse of educational theorists and practitioners. While not denying that education is a complex social and cultural process, these philosophers of education have assumed the less grand, but important, task of clarifying the ambiguous language and faulty logic which is at the root of many educational problems. Professional philosophers of education have developed linguistic and logical methods and techniques for the clarification of language. Their methods are analytic rather than synthetic, and because their context is educational discourse, their relevant units of analysis are words and concepts.

The literature in professional philosophy of education, like the other approaches, is extensive. General introductions may include Jonas Soltis' (1978) *An Introduction to the Analysis of Educational Concepts*; D. J. O'Connor's (1959) *An Introduction to the Philosophy of Education*; and James McClellan's (1976) *Philosophy of Education*. Professional literature also has developed around central educational concepts, for example: Thomas F. Green's (1971) *The Activities of Teaching*; C. J. B. Macmillan and Thomas W. Nelson's (1968) *Concepts of Teaching*; B. O. Smith and Robert H. Ennis' (1961). *Language and Concepts in Education*; B. Paul Komisar and C. J. B. Macmillan's (1967) *Psychological Concepts in Education*; Robert H. Ennis' (1969), *Logic in Teaching*; Israel Scheffler's (1976) *Reason in Teaching* and his (1960) *The Language of Education*; Jane R. Martin's (1970) *Explaining, Understanding and Teaching*; Donna H. Kerr's (1976) *Educational Policy*; Kenneth Strike's (1982) *Educational Policy and the Just Society*; and Richard Pratte's (1977) *Ideology and Education*.

Professional philosophy of education has largely been an outgrowth of the Anglo-American analytic movement; thus another main source of literature has come from such philosophers of education as R. S. Peters, (1973), *The Philosophy of Education* and (1966) *Ethics and Education*; R. F. Dearden, P. H. Hirst, and R. S. Peters, (1972) *Education and Reason*; I. A. Snook (1972) *Indoctrination and Education*; and, in general, the series in the International Library of the Philosophy of Education, under the general editorship of R. S. Peters.

Other sources as well can give the idea of professional philosophy of education. Perhaps the best for understanding the scope, methods, and aims of professional philosophy of education are the periodic *Proceedings* of both the American and British Philosophy of Education Societies.

## Qualitative Thinking: Unifying the Ways of Doing Philosophy

The categories discussed above do not suggest hard and fast distinctions within the practice of philosophy of education. Rather, there is a steady and vital interplay of aims, methods, and problems among scholars working within each approach. Some philosophers exhibit all three approaches in their writings on education. To show these things, we turn, finally, to a brief discussion of two classic writers on philosophy of education — Plato and Rousseau.

Plato's way of doing philosophy clearly unifies the public, professional, and personalistic approaches. The investigations in which Socrates engages himself and others in attempting to find the meaning of such virtues as justice, courage, and friendship, and even virtue itself, involve public, professional, and personalistic dimensions of philosophy. In the dialogues *Protagoras* and *Meno*, for example, the question, 'Can virtue be taught?', is pursued. In that pursuit, logical clarity is sought (professional), the ways in which young people are educated in a social context are examined (public), and the possibility of shaping the moral character of the participants in the dialogues is explored (personalistic). In trying to understand what Plato means by the claim that 'virtue is knowledge', one must consider technical matters (what do 'virtue' and 'knowledge' *mean*?), and, yet, the answer is to be found in the public realm. At the same time, the quest is personal. Werner Jaeger (1943) neatly summarizes the point: 'Socrates' politics are "looking after one's soul". Anyone who looks after his soul is thereby looking after "the polis itself" (p. 410, n. 32). The essential point for philosophy of education as qualitative inquiry is that such strivings constitute a quality of experience.

Another classic educational theory that joins professional, public, and personalistic philosophies is Rousseau's (1979) *Emile*. In describing Emile's education, Rousseau portrays the limitations of existing social life while recognizing the inescapable fact that Emile is a social creature who must be educated to moral and rational maturity. Rousseau's professional philosophizing is shown dramatically more than it is argued discursively; in *Emile*, the 'meanings' of the technical arguments in which philosophers engage are found in the life which Emile leads as he is educated. As the drama ends, Emile himself declares that he must work out his destiny in a social context whose moral conflicts are unsettled and yet remain very much with him. This is an 'existential predicament': to be well educated is to learn that one is 'homeless' — estranged from the world in which he has been educated. Emile finds that he is unable to bring the best kind of world into existence; his reason is unable to transcend experience when demonstrating better possibilities for experience. In terms of the distinctions between philosophy and science made earlier, Rousseau shows that philosophy's own limits are revealed as we learn the limits of our knowledge. What remains, or rather stands out, is the aim to gain a quality of experience in the face of the limitations of philosophy and science.

Modern philosophers who have demonstrated the kind of qualitative unity we seek are the idealist, Josiah Royce; the realist, George Santayana; and the pragmatist, John Dewey. William James and Alfred North Whitehead are others who can be mentioned.

As a heuristic device, we hope the distinctions we have made will be helpful. Although all philosophers of education are concerned with clarity, context, and consciousness, different emphases in the field have arisen in the last forty years, with professional philosophers of education stressing clarity, public philosophers of education concerned with context, and personalistic-phenomenological philosophers of education emphasizing consciousness. But perhaps more important than these different emphases is the understanding that all are examples of qualitative thinking. All take as their first task the identification of the fundamental problems of education, and, though they consider the field and the problems differently, they all depend on an aesthetic judgment of where the difficulty is and on qualitative thinking to bring these difficulties into the form of questions and problems that can be researched.

## References

BENNE, K. (1951). 'Education for tragedy'. *Educational Theory, 1* (November–December), 199–210, 217, 274–283.

BISHIRJIAN, R. J. (Ed.). (1978). *A Public Philosophy Reader*. New York: Arlington House.

BODE, B. H. (1913). 'The definition of consciousness', *Journal of Philosophy, 10 Psychology and Scientific Methods* (9), 232–239.

BODE, B. H. (1927). *Modern Educational Theories*. New York: Macmillan.

BODE, B. H. (1935). *Democracy as a Way of Life*. New York: Macmillan.

BOWLES, S. and GINTIS, H. (1976). *Schooling and Capitalist America*. New York: Basic Books.

BRAMELD, T. (1955). *Philosophies of Education in Cultural Perspective*. New York. Dryden.

BRAMELD, T. (1956). *Toward a Reconstructed Philosophy of Education*. New York: Dryden.

BRANN, E. (1979). *Paradoxes of Education in a Republic*. Chicago: University of Chicago Press.

BREED, F. S. (1932). *Education and the New Realism*. New York: Macmillan.

BROUDY, H. (1981). *Truth and Credibility: The Citizen's Dilemma*. New York: Longman.

BRUBACHER, J. S. (Ed.). (1942). *Philosophies of Education*. 41st Yearbook of the National Society for the Study of Education. Chicago: University of Chicago Press.

BRUBACHER, J. S. (Ed.). (1955). *Modern Philosophies and Education*. 54th Yearbook of the National Society for the Study of Education. Chicago: University of Chicago Press.

BUTTS, R. F. (1980). *The Revival of Civic Learning*. PDK Educational Foundation.

CHAMBLISS, J. J. (1968). *The Origins of American Philosophy of Education: Its Development as a Distinct Discipline, 1808–1913.* The Hague: Martinus Nijhoff.

CHILDS, J. (1931). *Education and the Philosophy of Experimentalism.* New York: Century.

DEARDEN, R. F., HIRST, P. H. and PETERS, R. S. (1972). *Education and Reason.* London: Routledge and Kegan Paul.

DEWEY, J. (1916). *Democracy and Education.* New York: Macmillan.

DEWEY, J. (1920). *Reconstruction in Philosophy.* New York: Holt.

DEWEY, J. (1933). *How We Think.* Lexington, MA: Heath.

DEWEY, J. (1959). 'Progressive education and the science of education'. In M. S. Dworkin (Ed.), *Dewey on Education.* New York: Teachers College.

DEWEY, J. (1966). *Lectures in the Philosophy of Education: 1889* (R. D. Archambault, Ed.). New York: Random House.

DEWEY, J. (1968). *Philosophy and Civilization.* Gloucester, MA: Peter Smith.

ENNIS, R. H. (1969) *Logic in Teaching.* Engelwood Cliffs, NJ: Prentice Hall.

FREIRE, P. (1981). *Pedagogy of the Oppressed.* New York: Continuum.

GIARELLI, J. M. and ZIMPFER, W. D. (1980). 'What is research in philosophy of education?' *Review Journal of Philosophy and Social Science, 15,* 52–64.

GOODMAN, P. (1964). *Compulsory Miseducation.* New York: Vintage.

GREENE, M. (1973). *Teacher as Stranger.* Belmont, CA: Wadsworth.

GREEN, T. F. (1971). *The Activities of Teaching.* New York: McGraw-Hill.

HORNE, H. H. (1904). *The Philosophy of Education,* New York: Macmillan.

HORNE, H. H. (1932). *The Democratic Philosophy of Education.* New York: Macmillan.

ILLICH, I. (1970). *Deschooling Society.* New York: Harper and Row.

JAEGER, W. (1943). *Paideia: The Ideals of Greek Culture* (Vol. II., G. Highet, Trans.). London: Oxford University Press.

KERR, D. H. (1976). *Educational Policy.* New York: McKay.

KESTENBAUM, V. (1977). *The Phenomenological Sense of Dewey.* New York: Humanities.

KIMBALL, S. and MACLELLAN, J. E. (1962). *Education and the New American.* New York: Vintage.

KOMISAR, B. P. and MACMILLAN, C. V. B. (Eds). (1967). *Psychological Concepts in Education.* Chicago, IL: Rand McNally.

LIPPMAN, W. (1955). *Essays in the Public Philosophy.* Boston: Little, Brown.

MACINTYRE, A. (1981). *After Virtue.* Notre Dame, IN: University of Notre Dame Press.

MACMILLAN, C. J. B. and NELSON, T. W. (Eds). (1968). *Concepts of Teaching.* Chicago, IL: Rand McNally.

MACVANNELL, J. A. (1912). *Outline of a Course in the Philosophy of Education.* New York: Macmillan.

MARTIN, J. R. (1970). *Explaining, Understanding and Teaching.* New York: McGraw-Hill.

McCLELLAN, J. (1976). *Philosophy of Education.* Engelwood Cliffs, NJ: Prentice Hall.

MINDEK, L. (1984). *Art as a Paradigm for World-making: The Pragmatic–Phenomenological Perspective as a Synthesis of the Work of Dewey and Heidegger.* Unpublished doctoral dissertation, Rutgers University.

NOZICK, R. (1981). *Philosophical Explanations.* Cambridge, MA: Harvard University Press.

O'CONNOR, D. J. (1957). *An Introduction to the Philosophy of Education:* London: Routledge and Kegan Paul.

PETERS, R. S. (1966). *Ethics and Education.* London: Routledge and Kegan Paul.

PETERS, R. S. (1973). *The Philosophy of Education*. Oxford: Oxford University Press.

PRATTE, R. (1977). *Ideology and Education*. New York: McKay.

PRITZKAU, P. (1970). *On Education for the Authentic*. Glasgow: International Textbook.

RORTY, R. (1979). *Philosophy and the Mirror of Nature*. Princeton, NJ: Princeton University Press.

RORTY, R. (1982). *Consequences of Pragmatism*. Minneapolis, MN: University of Minnesota Press.

ROSENKRANZ, J. K. F. (1886). *The Philosophy of Education* (A. C. Brackett, Trans.). New York: Appleton.

ROUSSEAU, J. J. (1979). *Emile, or, On Education* (A. Bloom, Trans.). New York: Basic Books.

SCHEFFLER, I. (1960). *The Language of Education*. New York: Thomas.

SCHEFFLER, I. (1976). *Reason in Teaching*. London: Routledge and Kegan Paul.

SILBERMAN, C. E. (1970). *Crisis in the Classroom*. New York: Random House.

SMITH, B. O. and ENNIS, R. H. (Eds.) (1961). *Language and Concepts in Education*. Chicago, IL: Rand McNally.

SMITH, H. (1965). *Condemned to Meaning*. New York: Harper.

SNOOK, I. A. (1972). *Indoctrination and Education*. London: Routledge and Kegan Paul.

SOLTIS, J. (1978). *An Introduction to the Analysis of Educational Concepts* (2nd ed.). Wokingham: Addison-Wesley.

SOLTIS, J. F. (1979). 'Philosophy of education since mid-century'. *Teachers College Record, 81* (Winter), 127–129.

SOLTIS, J. F. (1981). Introduction. *Philosophy and Education* (J. F. Soltis, Ed.). 80th Yearbook of the National Society for the Study of Education. Chicago: University of Chicago Press.

SOLTIS, J. F. (1983). Perspectives on philosophy of education. *Journal of Thought, 18* (Summer), 14–21.

STRIKE, K. (1982). *Educational Policy and the Just Society*. Urbana, IL: University of Illinois Press.

SULLIVAN, W. M. (1982). *Reconstructing Public Philosophy*. Berkeley, CA: University of California Press.

TATE, T. (1885). *The Philosophy of Education; or, The Principles and Practice of Teaching*. New York: Kellogg.

VANDENBERG, D. (1971). *Being and Education*. Englewood Cliffs, NJ: Prentice Hall.

VANDENBERG, D. (1979). 'Existential and phenomenological influences in educational philosophy'. *Teachers College Record, 81* (Winter), 166–191.

# Chapter 4

# Our Past and Present: Historical Inquiry in Education

*C. H. Edson*
*College of Education*
*University of Oregon*
*Eugene, OR 97403*

## Introduction

Qualitative inquiry in education connotes a subjective process of understanding and assessing educational phenomena. It would be contradictory to argue that what follows represents an accurate description of *the* qualitative method or details the exact nature of history as a form of qualitative inquiry. Indeed, if we view the purpose of qualitative inquiry as a quest to gain understanding, there is no qualitative method *per se*, only methods to gather information with which we construct our qualitative understanding.

This essay is exploratory. The intent is to examine some of the concerns that characterize qualitative inquiry in general and to relate these concerns to historical inquiry in education in particular. First, a note of caution. To label a range of concerns as hallmarks of qualitative inquiry merely suggests that those committed to qualitative inquiry share a concern for some of the same issues; it does not imply agreement as to the resolution or understanding of those issues. Thus, although this essay draws extensively on ideas of other scholars, the understandings presented here are personal.

## Qualitative Inquiry

In *Habits of The Heart*, a trenchant critique of individualism in American life, Robert Bellah (1985) and his colleagues argue that we have largely lost the language necessary to make moral sense out of our private and public lives. Only older forms of moral discourse — forms that see the individual in relation to a larger whole, a community and a tradition — can provide what the authors describe as 'communities of memory', that is, those things that will sustain and nurture both private and public life (see also Shils, 1981).

Qualitative inquiry may be seen as a form of moral discourse. By qualitatively exploring 'communities of memory' we learn to understand ourselves in relation to the larger world; we learn that we are inexorably entwined with both the past and the present. Thus, qualitative inquiry leads to qualitative understanding. Qualitative understanding, in turn, serves to condition the range and quality of human thought and may help to restore those moral dimensions of thought and practice that Bellah and his colleagues find so absent in American life today.

Qualitative inquiry plays an important role in educational research by assisting us in raising new questions, by leading us to question assumptions, by cultivating an appreciation for complexity, and finally, by expanding our frames of reference. In short, qualitative inquiry enhances the critical and intellectual dimensions of human thought and enables researchers to view themselves in relation to the larger world.

Consider the issue of asking new questions. We undertake qualitative inquiry not so much from our recognition that we do not know all the answers to our problems but rather from an appreciation of the fact that we do not know all the questions. It is not surprising that there is widespread agreement with the truism that the world is full of the right answers to bad questions, for not only are good questions hard to raise, but it is even harder to question that which is the most obvious. Qualitative inquiry offers an antidote to this pathology: by making the familiar strange, by turning familiar facts into puzzles, qualitative inquiry can, in the words of Herbert Kliebard and Barry Franklin (1983), 'serve to heighten our critical sensibilities and thereby help us to reformulate our problems in fresh and constructive ways' (p. 153).

Qualitative inquiry also expands our understanding of research by making us conscious of our assumptions and by fostering an appreciation for complexity. Everyone operates from assumptions, and educational researchers are no exception. The danger, however, lies not in having assumptions but rather in not being aware of them. One hallmark of a qualitative approach is that it causes us to acknowledge our assumptions so that we can suspend beliefs in these familiar convictions and examine evidence in a new and productive manner. From an enlarged awareness of how our own assumptions may limit our understanding comes a growing appreciation of complexity. Qualitative inquiry seeks to make phenomena more complex — not simpler — for complexity, not simplicity, describes life in both the past and the present.

Finally qualitative inquiry informs our understanding of educational research by expanding our frames of reference. Qualitative approaches to research, for example, provide a means of counteracting the extreme rationalization of researchers in the logical–positivist tradition and helps us to question the search for universal and eternal generalizations. By changing the set of lenses through which we view the world, we come to recognize, in the words of Kenneth Burke, that 'a way of seeing is always a way of not seeing' (quoted in Tyack, 1976). By raising questions, challenging assumptions, embracing complexity, and expanding our frames of reference, qualitative inquiry provides educational researchers with an important lesson: knowledge that our understanding as individuals and our ability to understand as researchers is limited.

Given the important role that qualitative inquiry plays in expanding our understanding of research, it remains to explore certain common concerns or hallmarks of qualitative approaches that allow us to group a range of research methodologies under the rubric of 'qualitative' (see Sherman *et al.*, 1984). One shared concern is the importance of context. Qualitative research is context-specific, that is, it posits that ideas, people, and events cannot be understood if isolated from their contexts. Unlike researchers in the physical sciences and in some of the social sciences, researchers employing qualitative methods do not seek to examine phenomena in ways that are context-free or context-independent.

In addition to context, a second common concern of qualitative methodology is that research should take place in natural settings as opposed to abstract or theoretical settings. Although theoretical contexts or models assist researchers to relate previously unrelated phenomena, actual experiences in natural settings have too many variables to be susceptible to singular models of explanation.

A third hallmark of qualitative approaches to research is that experience is studied as a whole, not in isolation from the past or the present. Qualitative researchers seek to understand as closely as possible experience as it was actually lived and understood and attempt to discern relationships between those experiences. Being concerned with the wholeness of experience, however, does not mean that qualitative research merely attempts to document all that can be known about an event or an individual in relation to the larger world. Rather, such experiences become 'relevant only when interpreted in terms of a frame of reference that can encompass them and give form and shape to a conception of the whole' (Bellah *et al*, 1985, p. 300).

The fourth hallmark of qualitative approaches to research, therefore, is a shared concern for interpreting experience and explaining its significance. Put simply, experiences do not speak for themselves; likewise, there is no pre-existing or determinate order that encompasses all experience. Qualitative researchers must employ an interpretive frame of reference in order to bring meaning to experience. In this sense, qualitative inquiry is not merely a search for knowledge for knowledge's sake, but a search for the significance of knowledge.

Thus, defined in the terms expressed in Bellah's *Habits of The Heart*, qualitative inquiry shares some of the same understandings with what the authors label 'moral discourse'. In short, moral discourse and qualitative inquiry 'allow us to connect our aspirations for ourselves and those closest to us with the aspirations of a larger whole and see our own efforts as being, in part, contributions to a common good' (Bellah *et al.*, 1985, p. 153).

## History as Qualitative Inquiry

Carl Becker defined history as 'the memory of things said and done' (quoted in Sherman, 1984, p. 80). Just as memory is qualitative (in the sense that it is human, limited, interpretive, and judgmental), so too is history qualitative. Becker, however, was referring to history itself — the past as we know it — not to the process of historical inquiry or the ways in which we come to know about the past. Because our concern is with history as a qualitative mode of inquiry, we shall limit the scope of discussion to an analysis of the discipline of history or the practice of doing history. As a discipline, history is a mode of qualitative inquiry for, along with other qualitative approaches to research, history shares a concern for context, for undertaking research in natural settings, for the wholeness or integrity of experience, and for interpreting and explaining the significance of experience.

First, historical inquiry is context-specific. As the English social historian E. P. Thompson stated, 'the discipline of history is, above all, a discipline of context; each fact can be given meaning only within an ensemble of other meanings' (quoted in Kammen, 1982, p. 19). Thus, a common understanding of historical approaches to research is that people, events, and ideas cannot be understood apart from their historical contexts. Moreover, the contexts must be precise rather than general or theoretical, for, as Lawrence Stone (1981) argues, history 'deals with a *particular* problem and a *particular* set of actors at a *particular* time in a *particular* place' (p. 31; emphasis in original).

The context of historical inquiry, however, is not only the past — as many erroneously assume — but the present as well. Because written history communicates what historians think they know about the past, we must, if we are to understand the continuity between past and present, understand that historians in their present contexts are a part of the whole they are examining. Historical inquiry, therefore, is concerned with two contexts and is, in the words of E. H. Carr (1962), 'a continuous process of interaction between the historian and his facts, an unending dialogue between the present and the past' (p. 35).

In addition to being context-specific, historical inquiry shares with other qualitative approaches a concern for natural settings. Contrived settings, usually designed to test abstract or theoretical models, may help historians to classify evidence and challenge them to see interrelationships not visible in natural settings. On the other hand, theoretical models may deceive as well as illumine. In seeking to document theoretical relationships, historians who use these models may overlook other relationships and will always run the danger of becoming reductionist by only selecting evidence that fits the particular thesis. 'The historian who puts his system first,' remarked one observer, 'can hardly escape the heresy of preferring the facts which suit his system best' (quoted in Tuchman, 1981, p. 23).

Natural settings are central to historical inquiry, for history is not a quest to validate concepts or theories; rather, it broadens our understanding of ourselves by helping us to understand past experiences. Theoretical settings, according to Lawrence Stone (1981), 'reduce the study of man . . . to a simplistic, mechanistic determinism based on some preconceived theoretical notion of universal applicability' (p. 42). Because historical inquiry raises questions that are recalcitrant to empirical demonstration, historians must arrive at theory by way of natural settings, not the other way around.

The third shared concern of qualitative research — the need for understanding the wholeness of experience — is clearly manifested in historical inquiry. Tempered by knowledge that no historian can ever discover or communicate the whole truth about a person, an event, or a place in the past, historians seek to reconstruct as closely as possible the past as earlier participants experienced and understood it. With an appreciation of the wholeness of experience, historians strive to know the real past (the past as it actually happened) as well as the mythical past (what people believed happened), for both influenced the course of events. Gaining such knowledge about the past requires imagination and a tolerance for ambiguity. Historians must seek to imagine themselves in the past with all of its foibles, beliefs, and assumptions and realize that the participants of history ascribed different meanings to the events they witnessed.

Historical inquiry that seeks to reconstruct the wholeness of past experiences must be written in terms of what was known and believed at the time; however, historians know how things turned out. According to David Tyack and Elizabeth Hansot (1982):

> This is both an advantage and a disadvantage. It is an advantage, because hindsight makes it easier to distinguish between the basic, underlying forces of change and the ephemeral. The disadvantage is that concentrating on developments that *later* become crucial may obscure the mainstream of past experience as seen through the eyes of contemporaries. (p. 19; emphasis in original)

Finally, historical inquiry seeks to interpret and explain the significance of past experiences, not merely to document them. As historical facts do not speak for themselves, the past becomes relevant to the present only through interpretation and evaluation. Without these shared concerns of qualitative inquiry in general, historians' preoccupation with the past becomes mere antiquarianism. Interpretation and evaluation of past experiences enable historians to fashion arguments designed to bring meaning to experience. History means interpretation; interpretation implies argument. As Theodore White (1978) explained, 'Good reporters organize facts in "stories", but good historians organize lives and episodes into "arguments" ' (p. 2).

Because we can never know the whole truth about the past, historical interpretations will always be partial and incomplete. On the other hand, historians recognize that in some cases they know more about the past than contemporaries did. The task of historical interpretation, therefore, requires historians to seek an understanding not only of what contemporaries saw and understood but also of those things that contemporaries could not or chose not to see.

Interpretation involves judgment, but a particular kind of judgment. It is not the historian's task to pass value judgments when interpreting the past, because moral assessments of the past in terms of good or bad inevitably reflect the moral conventions of the present rather than those of yesteryear. The type of judgments central to historical interpretations are ones that seek to explain *how* things could have happened — not whether they were good or bad. Historians interpret the past, therefore, in terms of the contemporaneous standards and conditions then prevailing, not in comparison with the present day.

*History and Curriculum Inquiry: An Example.*

As a mode of inquiry that is context-specific, that examines the wholeness of experience in natural settings, and that seeks to interpret and explain, the discipline of history is qualitative. History may inform our understanding of research by counteracting the empiricism and quantification that dominates educational research today. By ignoring the concerns of qualitative research, non-qualitative approaches often limit our ability to ask questions, fail to unmask common assumptions, deny the complexity of experience, and restrict our frames of reference.

Take, for example, the field of curriculum inquiry. Most researchers acknowledge that schools are not the only institutions that have curricula that seek to educate youth; however, few researchers seriously examine the explicit nature of these curricula or explore how these various curricula affect school curriculum. Likewise, researchers realize that what is intended by the curriculum is not necessarily what is internalized, yet they continue to devote their major attention to the physical manifestations of school curriculum rather than to how children actually experience curricula in wide variety and form. The result, according to one observer, is that we know:

> . . . next to nothing about where anything in particular has been learned, about the relation between what is learned in one institution and what is learned in another, about how different individuals synthesize what they have learned in various institutions, and about what might be the best possible combinations of institutions for teaching particular kinds of knowledge or skills. (Cremin, 1976, p. 89)

Historical inquiry expands our understanding of these persistent issues that appear so resistant to other modes of curriculum inquiry. In *American Education: The National Experience, 1783–1876*, the second of a projected three-volume study of American education, Lawrence Cremin (1980) illustrates how the concerns of qualitative inquiry, manifested in a particular historical work, may broaden our understanding of curriculum research. First, Cremin considers curriculum in a context-specific manner, viewing curriculum comprehensively and relationally. He examines not only what was taught in nineteenth-century schools but also explores a comprehensive range of others institutions that had deliberate curricula, including families, churches, newspapers, workplaces, voluntary associations, custodial institutions, lyceums, fairs, and museums. By appreciating contextual complexity, Cremin is also able to inquire about interrelationships among various curricula, for example, how the curricula of Sunday schools, Bible and tract societies, and missionary organizations may have affected the content and pedagogy of school offerings.

Second, Cremin's research reflects a concern for natural settings. By grounding his analysis of curricula and their relationships in natural settings, he avoids the danger of subordinating historical evidence to fit a theoretical setting. Eschewing attempts to provide universal or eternal generalizations derived from abstract models, Cremin discusses his research findings about curriculum in the nineteenth century in specific natural settings. Relationships between curricula, whether complementary or contradictory, Cremin (1976) argues, 'must be ascertained in their particularity rather than assumed in some kind of generality' (p. 32). Thus, although places such as Lowell, Massachusetts; Sumter District, South Carolina; Macoupin County, Illinois; and New York City (to cite Cremin's examples) shared some common characteristics, each reflected particular patterns or configurations of curriculum unique to their natural settings. Therefore, to broaden our understanding of how curriculum was actually experienced, it is imperative to focus on natural settings — ones strictly defined by time and location.

In addition to an appreciation for context and for natural settings, Cremin's research also demonstrates a concern for the wholeness of experience — the third hallmark of qualitative approaches to research. Seeking to understand the past as it was actually lived and understood requires curriculum researchers to appreciate that different individuals experience curriculum in different ways with different outcomes. Thus, in addition to examining curriculum in natural contexts, Cremin explores individual life histories in an attempt to understand how individuals interacted with a range of curriculum in a particular place. Returning to the natural settings of Lowell, Sumter District, Macoupin County, and New York City, Cremin re-examines the curriculum configurations of these communities in terms of how they were actually experienced by seven nineteenth-century Americans. Employing individual life histories in an attempt to recreate the wholeness of past experience:

> . . . illustrates both the extraordinary variegation of nineteenth-century American education and the striking range of human character that always issues, to greater or lesser extent, from any particular set of educational arrangements, whatever the time or the place in human history. (Cremin, 1980, p. 451)

Finally, Cremin shares the qualitative concern for interpreting and explaining the significance of past experience. Broadly interpreting education as 'the deliberate, systematic, and sustained effort to transmit, evoke, or acquire knowledge, values, attitudes, skills, or sensibilities', Cremin (1980, p. ix) redirects the focus of curriculum inquiry away from the physical manifestations of school curriculum toward an appreciation of the multiplicity of institutions that deliberately educate. He labels his interpretive framework 'an ecology of education' (Cremin, 1976, pp. 27–53). Designed to bring meaning to the gathered educational experiences of the past, not just merely to report them, his ecological approach views curricula comprehensively, relationally, and individually. By illustrating the scope and complexity of curriculum, Cremin's framework suggests that researchers today must understand that families, churches, synagogues, Girl Scouts, Little Leagues, television networks, peer groups, and day-care centers all have curricula that intentionally educate (or mis-educate) youth every day. Curriculum inquiry that remains blind to the interrelationships among various curricula and which fails to explore how individuals actually experience these curricula will be unlikely to reformulate curricular issues and problems in new and constructive ways.

## The Varieties and Limits of Historical Research

There is no single, definable method of historical inquiry. Historians employ a method (or a variety of methods) to deal with evidence about the past; however, history, which is a matter of understanding or bringing meaning to past events, has no particular method. History is inevitably the product of a subjective interaction between present-day historians and an incomplete record of past events. Although most historians share a concern for some of the same qualitative issues discussed earlier in the essay, they often disagree as to their resolutions or applications; consequently, the varieties of history are as infinite as the varieties of historians. Comprehensive description of historical variety is clearly impossible; even if it were possible, it would be of dubious value. Selective illustration of some of that variety, however, may provide general direction that will assist researchers to select a historical topic, to deal with historical evidence, to undertake historical explanation, and to write a historical study.

### Selecting a Topic

Choosing a topic for historical inquiry exposes researchers to the myriad varieties of history. It is inappropriate to call these varieties 'schools' (which denotes a group of people held together by the same or congruent beliefs, methods, and understandings such as the 'structural–functional school of sociology'). On the other hand, specialization and compartmentalization of history during the last century has led to grouping historians according to their areas of interest: intellectual history, diplomatic history, military history, political history, and women's history, to name a few. Many historians transcend these artificial, if convenient, lines of demarcation. For example, a historian interested in studying nineteenth-century school experiences of daughters of Irish Catholic working class immigrants in Boston might be alternately labeled an educational historian, a women's historian, an ethnic historian, a religious historian, a social historian, an immigration historian, and an urban historian — not to mention a nineteenth-century historian, an institutional historian, a family historian, a historian of childhood, and so on. Again, the point is not to document all the areas of historical inquiry but rather to suggest a wide variety of interests from which historians select specific topics for research.

Given many areas of historical inquiry, how do historians formulate specific topics that give focus and direction to their research? Some begin with available source materials in a search for questions that might be asked — for example, what can an examination of the collected writings of Horace Mann tell us about the origins of free public schools in mid-nineteenth-century Massachusetts? Others begin by asking questions — for example, did the working classes favor or oppose free public schools? Both methods of refining a topic should be approached with caution. In the first case, historians who let the date dictate the topic run the danger of escalating the importance of the subject or of examining subjects that are trivial and insignificant. In the second case, historians may choose topics and develop questions regardless of the availability or the reliability of the data. Because historical records are notoriously faulty and incomplete, historians who focus on topics for which we have inadequate records run the danger of becoming novelists rather than historians. When choosing a topic, therefore, historians must initially establish the significance of the subject and insure the adequacy of surviving records.

After selecting a topic and developing some initial questions to guide their research, historians establish limits to their investigations. As the investigation proceeds, these limits often change because of the availability and reliability of the data. Despite their tentative nature, initial limits must be set, for subjects under historical investigation have no inherent limits and can be expanded infinitely depending on source materials. Take the example of mid-nineteenth-century school reform. Because historical inquiry is context-specific, historians cannot study school reform apart from the broader context of mid-nineteenth-century social and religious reform. On the other hand, historians clearly cannot study the entire context, which means that they must arbitrarily impose limits. Setting limits always implies choice. What should be included? What should be omitted? Which questions are central? Which questions are peripheral? Unfortunately, historians find few of these choices completely satisfying.

Just as there are many varieties of history, there are many varieties of evidence and modes of explanation. Limited space precludes detailed description of the vast array of sources historians employ in conducting their research, the numerous methods they use to record and organize their data, and the different manners in which they explain their evidence. A few general observations, however, can be made.

After selecting a topic and establishing initial limits, historians undertake an examination of evidence relevant to their chosen subject. Because the standard of judgment for a historical work is extrinsic (in the sense of whether it is congruent or compatible with the surviving record), historians, unlike novelists, must possess an overriding commitment to the available evidence. The historical record, however, is notoriously incomplete, fragmentary, ambiguous, and even faulty. It would be a mistake, therefore, to accept passively and uncritically all that has been preserved about the past. Rather, historians confirm their allegiance to evidence by actively subjecting historical records to analysis, validation, comparison, and criticism.

Because historians must interact with the evidence they gather, interpretation is inescapable. Although historians seek to suspend beliefs in familiar convictions and to become aware of their assumptions, they cannot escape all preconceived notions and theories. If historians cannot be purely objective in their treatment of sources, they can approach historical evidence with an open mind. For example, evidence that may appear to be trivial to the researcher may be or might have been of great importance to others. Historians who do not approach evidence with an open mind are often unable to recognize that sources are sometimes mute or ambiguous concerning the questions that interest them most, and thus they are liable to shape or subordinate that evidence to fit their own understandings. In their interaction with evidence, therefore, historians are committed to objectivity as a value or an ideal, not as a product or an attainment.

After examining the evidence, historians have the duty of explaining it. Historians view the past with the same eyes they use to understand the present; however, when explaining historical evidence, they must avoid what are known as the 'perils of presentism' — superimposing present-day understandings and answers on the past. Because historical explanation is undertaken to gain perspective, not to provide prescription, historians must be careful not to elevate their beliefs into facts or to inflate partial insights into truths.

In the past decade, it has become fashionable in the historical profession to make sharp distinctions between two modes of explanation: narrative, the 'old' history; and structural, the 'new' history (Himmelfarb, 1984; Berkhofer, 1983; Stone, 1981, pp. 74–96; Tuchman, 1981, pp. 13–64). While the debate serves to heighten our awareness of important epistemological issues concerning the nature and limits of historical inquiry, it often obscures a functional understanding of historical explanation by polarizing explanatory modes through the use of extreme examples. Briefly, the debate suggests that structural history (as opposed to narrative history) is analytical rather than descriptive, thematic rather than chronological, concerned with circumstances rather than with individuals, and focuses on the collective and statistical rather than on the particular and specific. These characterizations must be viewed skeptically, for most historians combine narrative and structural modes of explanation.

Historical narrative is the most common form of explanation. Proponents of narrative history argue that there is no historical explanation in the scientific sense, only comprehensive description of what happened in the past. As description, narrative history seeks to understand how we have gotten from the past to the present. Historians never accurately replicate the past as it really was, for 'any historical writing perforce does violence to the kaleidoscopic surface and hidden dynamics of everyday life' (Tyack, 1974, p. 4). In this sense, a narrative mode of explanation can only seek to offer the best and the most likely account of the past that can be sustained by surviving records.

Narrative history seeks to make events intelligible, not to fit them into a general law. A narrative historian's conclusions are generally intuitive — the result of a systematic but unstructured examination of the evidence. Because of this lack of structure, narrative history is often criticized as being anti-theoretical for failing to employ more powerful theoretical models of understanding. On the other hand, 'this lack of theoretical prescription guards against the premature exclusion of data and the fallacy of self-fulfilling prophecy' (Warren, 1983, p. 158).

Historians favoring structural modes of historical explanation — ones, for example, which posit the material bases of human existence or describe psychological states of human development — usually employ models of understanding in their search to reconstruct the past (Braudel, 1981–84; Erikson, 1958). In formulating their theses, structuralists go beyond the narrativist's concern to describe *what* happened in order to consider the question of *why* it happened. Recognizing that causality in history is difficult if not impossible to ascertain, most historians do not discuss causes in the same fashion as physical scientists. Rather, they employ explanatory models to structure their inquiry, to discover relationships among previously unrelated phenomena, to suggest what is general and what is particular in history, and, in the case of statistics, to make historical comparisons more exact and explicit. Structural modes of explanation help to extend our historical imagination by challenging us to think about historical evidence in new and different ways.

Although structural modes of explanation have much to contribute to our historical understanding, they can also lead us astray. History must remain sensitive to complexity, for human behavior has too many variables to be susceptible to singular, causal models of explanation. Injudicious use of structural modes of explanation expose historians to the temptation of ignoring or neglecting evidence that does not fit their explanatory model. Likewise, too great a reliance on methodologically-specific models may narrow and trivialize history by limiting the scope of inquiry to subjects and sources that lend themselves capable of analysis by that particular mode of investigation. As Lawrence Stone (1981) reminds us, 'The historical context is all-important, and cannot be ignored or brushed aside in order to fit the data into some overarching social science model' (p. 31).

Without denying that real differences exist between narrative and structural modes of explanation, recent debates magnifying their differences tend to obscure important similarities between the two. It is important to recognize that both methods of explanation seek to ask important questions of the past. That they ask different questions and consult different sources of evidence appropriate to the questions posed should suggest that each approach can inform the other. No one form of explanation is superior in an absolute sense, nor can any one approach claim to be the 'total history'. In short, historians both describe and analyze — they seek to understand as well as to explain the past.

*Writing History*

In his Presidential Address to the American Historical Association in 1912, Theodore Roosevelt stated: 'Writings are useless unless they are read, and they cannot be read unless they are readable' (quoted in Tuchman, 1981, p. 56). Along with many others before and since, Roosevelt pointed to the inseparability of doing history and communicating or writing history. Whether or not we agree that 'in the long run the best writer is the best historian', even the most enlightening historical explanation is useless if it cannot be understood by others (Tuchman, 1981, p. 39).

Attention to language and to how it influences our ability to think is as important to historical inquiry as gathering evidence. In a frequently quoted passage, George Orwell (1968) warns that language 'becomes ugly and inaccurate because our thoughts are foolish, but the slovenliness of our language makes it easier for us to have foolish thoughts' (p. 128). When undertaking historical inquiry, therefore, individuals must be rigorously attentive to language and be careful not to subordinate their writing to their research. As Barbara Tuchman (1981, p. 21) reminds us, 'Research is endlessly seductive; writing is hard work'.

Oftentimes the sheer volume of evidence militates against closer attention to writing history. Writing and research should not be viewed as separate tasks — one following the completion of the other. Historians who wait until the last fact is found before commencing to write seldom put pen to paper. Likewise, historians cannot be 'content to throw words down on a page and let them lie there, like cow-flops in a field, on the grounds that since history is a science, it needs no art to help it along' (Stone, 1981, p. 75). History is an art, and if historians are to realize the qualitative goals of historical inquiry, they must make themselves understood by writing clearly and carefully. As one observer cautions: 'Let us beware of the plight of our colleagues, the behavioral scientists, who by the use of a proliferating jargon have painted themselves into a corner — or an isolation ward — of unintelligibility' (Tuchman, 1981, p. 55). Jargon merely serves to make the simple complex and the obvious obscure.

When historians write history, their use of corroborative detail gives 'artistic verisimilitude to an otherwise bald and unconvincing narrative' (Tuchman, 1981, p. 33). Historians, however, are always faced with the problem of just how much detail to include. The amount of detail necessary for one audience may 'simply clutter the text for another audience and stultify their imaginations' (Hexter, 1971, p. 46). Regardless of the amount of detail incorporated in their writing, historians should not interrupt their prose with excessively long quotations. For example, reproducing the entire text of Horace Mann's 5th Annual Report may be relevant to increase our understanding of Mann's influence on common schools, but it would interfere with the historian's task of describing and explaining to the reader what actually happened. Part of the art of writing history, therefore, lies not only in understanding that different audiences have different needs but also in recognizing that not all the details historians collect will appear in their written research.

## Imperatives For Historical Inquiry

Qualitative research in education serves to militate against the extreme rationalization that characterizes so much of what we do in education today. By examining phenomena from a rational, social–scientific perspective, researchers tend to view the past as an obstacle to progress, fail to see the continuity between the past and the present, and are unable to understand themselves as a part of the whole they seek to examine and understand. As a mode of qualitative inquiry, history serves as an important corrective for researchers by counseling that our understanding as individuals and our ability to understand as researchers is limited. Although our society encourages us to escape our past and to define ourselves in our own individual ways, history teaches the opposite. One message contained in *Habits of The Heart* (Bellah *et al.*, 1985) is that historical inquiry may aid us, as educators and individuals, to restore a form of 'moral discourse' that can sustain and nurture both our private and professional lives. Studying history and participating in history are inseparable. As Robert Bellah (1985) and his colleagues conclude:

> If our high culture could begin to talk about nature and history, space and time, in ways that did not disaggregate them into fragments, it might be possible for us to find connections and analogies with the older ways in which human life was made meaningful. (p. 283)

## References

BELLAH, R. N., MADSEN R., SULLIVAN, W. M., SWIDLER A. and TIPTON, S. M. (1985). *Habits of the Heart: Individualism and Commitment in American Life*. Berkeley, CA: University of California Press.

BERKHOFER, R. F., Jr. (1983). 'The two new histories: Competing paradigms for interpreting the American past'. *OAH Newsletter, 11* (May), 9–12.

BRAUDEL, F. (1981–84). *Civilization and Capitalism: 15th-18th Century* (Vols 1–3; S. Reynolds, Trans.). New York: Harper and Row.

CARR, E. H. (1962). *What is History?* New York: Knopf.

CREMIN, L. A. (1976). *Public Education*. New York: Basic Books.

CREMIN, L. A. (1980). *American Education: The National Experience, 1783–1876*. New York: Harper and Row.

ERIKSON, E. (1958). *Young Man Luther: A Study of Psychoanalysis and History*. New York: Norton.

HEXTER, J. H. (1971). *Doing History*. Bloomington, IN: Indiana University Press.

HIMMELFARB, G. (1984). 'Denigrating the rule of reason'. *Harpers 268* (1607), 84–90.

KAMMEN, M. (1982). 'Vanitas and the historian's vocation'. In S. I. Kutler and S. N. Katz (Eds), *The Promise of American History: Progress and Prospects*. Baltimore, MD: Johns Hopkins University, Press.

KLIEBARD, H. M. and FRANKLIN, B. M. (1983). 'The course of the course of study: History of curriculum'. In J. H. Best (Ed.), *Historical Inquiry in Education: A Research Agenda* (pp. 138–157). Washington: American Educational Research Association.

ORWELL, G. (1968). 'Politics and the English language'. In S. Orwell and I. Angus (Eds), *The Collected Essays*. New York: Harcourt, Brace.

SHERMAN, R. R. (1984). *Understanding History of Education* (2nd ed.). Cambridge, MA: Schenkman.

SHERMAN, R. R., WEBB, R. B. and ANDREWS, S. D. (1984). 'Qualitative inquiry: An introduction'. *Journal of Thought, 19* (Summer), 24–33.

SHILS, E. (1981). *Tradition*. Chicago: University of Chicago Press.

STONE, L. (1981). *The Past and the Present*. Boston: Routledge and Kegan Paul.

TUCHMAN, B. (1981). *Practicing History*. New York: Knopf.

TYACK, D. B. (1974). *The One Best System: A History of American Urban Education*. Cambridge, MA: Harvard University Press.

TYACK, D. B. (1976). 'Ways of seeing: An essay on the history of compulsory schooling'. *Harvard Educational Review, 46* (August), 355–389.

TYACK, D. B. and HANSOT, E. (1982). *Managers of Virtue: Public School Leadership in America, 1820–1980*. New York: Basic Books.

WARREN, D. (1983). 'The federal interest: Politics and policy study'. In J. H. Best (Ed.), *Historical Inquiry in Education: A Research Agenda* (pp. 158–179). Washington, DC: American Educational Research Association.

WHITE, T. H. (1978). *In Search of History: A Personal Adventure*. New York: Harper and Row.

## Further Reading

BARZUN, J. and GRAFF, F. Henry. (1977). *The Modern Researcher* (3rd ed.). New York: Harcourt Brace Jovanovich.

BERKHOFER, R., Jr. (1969). *A Behavioral Approach to Historical Analysis*. New York: Free Press.

COMMAGER, H. S. (1965). *The Nature and Study of History*. Columbus, OH: Merrill.

DANIELS, R. V. (1981). *Studying History: How and Why* (3rd ed.). Englewood Cliffs, NJ: Prentice Hall.

FREIDEL, F. (Ed.). (1974). *Harvard Guide to American History* (rev. ed., Vols 1–2). Cambridge, MA: Belknap.

GOTTSCHALK, L. M. (1969). *Understanding History: A Primer of Historical Method* (2nd ed.). New York: Knopf.

HANDLIN, O. (1979). *Truth in History*. Cambridge, MA: Belknap.

*History of Education Quarterly* (formerly *History of Education Journal*), 1949–.

HUGHES, S. H. (1975). *History as Art and as Science*. Chicago: University of Chicago, Press.

KAMMEN, M. (1980). *The Past Before Us: Contemporary Historical Writing in the United States*. Ithaca, NY: Cornell University Press.

OAKESHOTT, M. (1983). *On History and Other Essays*. Totowa, NJ: Barnes and Noble.

VEYNE, P. (1984). *Writing History: Essay On Epistemology* (M. Moore-Rinvolucri, Trans.). Middletown, CT: Wesleyan University Press.

WINKS, R. W. (Ed.). (1968). *The Historian as Detective: Essays on Evidence*. New York: Harper and Row.

# Chapter 5

# Inside Lives: The Quality of Biography

*Jack K. Campbell*
*College of Education*
*Texas A&M University*
*College Station, TX 77843*

The biographer's fancy has always turned to the vision of seeing the world through the subject's frame of reference. The biographer can track the public path of the subject through a paper trail of documents, but how can the biographer walk in the subject's shoes, look out of the subject's eyes, or see through the subject's own interpretations and intentions? And how much of the biographer is in the biography? These questions of life writing have now become the questions of human life sciences. The point of view of the actor has become the critical point of the new 'qualitative' sociology, and the bias and interference of the observer a new stumbling block (Schwartz and Jacobs, 1979; Overend, 1983; Bloor, 1984).

Autobiographies, and even self-reported questionnaires, come from the inside. They are drawn out of the subject's own privileged perspective, but they cannot be trusted to expose the whole self. The biographer and the qualitative sociologist must turn their subjects inside out and discover the private as well as the public selves. How can the unobservable be revealed by empirical science or even by written personal documents? What rights of privacy must be preserved? Should the quest for the 'inside life' of others lift away every fig leaf?

Somewhere between the pressure of objective social facts and the vacuum of subjective interpretation, a new force with alternative ways of knowing is manifesting itself. Somewhere between the humanistic and scientific modes of inquiry, this new multidisciplinary force is in dynamic tension with the powers of mechanism, standardization, abstraction, and statistical and quantitative analysis. Appearing in various forms, this new force has revealed itself as 'qualitative sociology', 'metasociology', 'phenomenology', 'symbolic interactionism', 'ethnography', 'ethnomethodology', 'naturalistic inquiry', or 'grounded theory', but these are only labels for a generic 'qualitative' approach, or 'different attempts to confront empirical reality from the perspective of those who are being studied' (Denzin, 1970, p. 28; Owens, 1982).

Penetrating or getting inside other lives is no longer the fancy of the biographer or the prerogative of the novelist's omniscient perspectives. It has become the reality which must be sought for explaining and predicting human behavior. While the present study sees getting 'inside lives' as the essence of qualitative biography, the related characteristics of qualitative research will not be neglected. These characteristics have been noted as '*context; natural settings; holistic experience*, or the *unity* of experience; *meanings, interpretation, patterns*, or *relationships* within experience; experience as *process*; and *judging*, or *appraising*, the *significance* or *value* of experience' (Sherman and Webb, 1986).

This new qualitative force, with its developing modes of 'reflexivity' for looking through the eyes of the observed, could be of immense value to the biographer, while the qualitative researcher could benefit from the biographer's long association with the attempt to get inside other lives. Moreover, this new qualitative force is really grounded in biography. It takes for its life-text the intertexture of the individual and the concrete world view of the individual and the intersubjectivity of the observer and the observed.

While it has been suggested that biography and behavioral sciences could merge into a new discipline, called 'sociobiography' (Campbell, 1984), the present study will honor their traditional boundaries. It will examine the life crisis in social science, the biographic foundations of qualitative inquiry, and the qualitative foundations of biography. It will suggest, in the end, the interbiographical foundation of teaching and learning.

## Paradigm Lost

The affair between the methods of the natural sciences and the humanities has produced a number of offspring known as social sciences. Since the nineteenth century these sciences have searched for the promised land of eternal human laws. No Moses has come down from the mountain of empirical data with laws that can command the behavior of all individuals in all times and places. By 1985, when *The Chronicle of Higher Education* announced that researchers were now 'questioning the Science in Social Science' (Winkler, 1985), it was no longer news. The human being, as a part of nature rather than apart from it, could hardly be a neutral observer. Even the popular press has satirized the behavioral scientist who pretended to be indifferent to himself but was always trying to catch a glimpse of himself when no one was looking (Allen, 1980; see also, Alexander, 1983).

The fall of empirical science from its supremacy among the paradigms of knowing had for its cause the fatal flaw of an arrogant belief in human objectivity. (Edmund Husserl believed the 'objectivist, naturalistic attitude was the original sin for which the West was being driven into cultural exile' (Dupré, 1976); but, for a different view that positivism's death is exaggerated, see Phillips, 1983.) Objectivity, the critical attitude in the eye of the scientist, has become a blind spot. Objectivity has collapsed into relativity and uncertainty in the universe of physics. Social scientists are even farther removed from the world of objectivity when they observe the behaviors of others as well as their own. It now appears that it is as impossible to view social behavior with a detached eye as it is to see with a detached retina.

There was a time when knowledge was not thought to be outside the knower and thus 'objective'. The Platonic claim to knowledge did not rest on the evidence and data provided by others. Its foundation was the autobiographic essence of innate ideas. One looked within the self for truth. Descartes could not be certain of anything except his autobiographic thinking self. It was only after the social sciences monopolized social inquiry that the 'inner' life was exiled to the province of religion and metaphysics (Dupre, 1976, p. 3). Science ruled the public domain, the world of surfaces and exteriors. Introspection was the bane of behaviorists. Sociology located the source of human behaviour 'outside of the individual and in the various social institutions and structures' (Scimecca, 1980, p. 5). Human beings functioned as social actors and played given roles at different stages of development.

The tragedy in the recent fall of empirical social science is the human banishment from a world of determined laws and relationships. Is truth, as well as beauty, now in the eye of the beholder? Is the human being condemned to wander in a world of rank relativity, where perspectivism rules and unresolved points of view clash? It would seem evident that the individual's interpretation of the events of experience, whether truly perceived or not, determine that individual's responsive behavior. Words and actions take their meanings out of the perceiving individual's personal field of experience, a construct of the individual's particular biographical store of episodic memories. Just as all biographies are different in some detail, there is no way of predicting how any situated individual will respond to thought or deed unless one can look through that person's point of view or biographical background.

It is easier to predict the behavior of waves or particles of matter than the behavior of a cognitive and sensing person. Individuals do not respond on cue like billiard balls. Thus, the physiomathematical methods of studying atoms are not always appropriate for studying the sons and daughters of Adam.

No biographer would approach a subject of investigation as though the person were an inanimate object or a collection of separate variables that could be isolated and manipulated. The biographer must approach the subject as another human being and as a whole person. The biography must portray the subject as a whole, in the temporal, geographical, socio-cultural context. This is the 'qualitative' approach to human behavior. No quick survey of numerous individuals on a few isolated variables will suffice for an in-depth, qualitative investigation. The qualitative investigation, like biography, is difficult to quantify and display in abstract graphics and tables. Like a biography, it is not possible to replicate exactly, and it does not claim to be generalizable. It may, however, be much closer to reality as individuals perceive it.

Anthropology once held up a *Mirror for Man* (Kluckhohn, 1961), but a generation later, 'qualitative' investigators in anthropology and sociology were reporting *A Crack in the Mirror* (Ruby, 1982). The mirror reflected the observer. Is there no way to get through the looking-glass, to get inside the lives of others? Qualitative investigators are looking for a two-way mirror between the observer and the observed. They are exploring many ways of knowing and how to 'indwell' in others. For the moment, objective, impersonal truth is a disembodied ghost. 'Personal knowledge', in Michael Polanyi's sense, is what the biographer and the qualitative researcher seek. Such knowledge is dependent on the 'contribution of the person knowing what is being known' (Polanyi, 1962, p. viii). This is an element of what will be called the 'interbiographical dialogue' between the knower and the known, but the basic elements of biography as qualitative inquiry must be analyzed first.

## Qualitative Biographic Analysis

In the chemistry of human action and reaction, there are many elements, in countless combinations, that make up the complicated matter of human behavior. The unique combination of biographical experience for each individual makes it difficult to formulate rules of human understanding. The sociologist, Alfred Schutz (1962), writes that 'another's existence transcends mine as mine does his. We have in common only a small section of our biographies'. We come by our uniqueness, Schutz argues, because we are 'born of mothers and not concocted in retorts', and our formative periods are shaped in different ways (pp. xxvii–xxx). How can the scientist transcend his own 'biographical situation' to interpenetrate another?

When the methods of natural science were applied to human study in the nineteenth century by Auguste Comte, social alchemists began trying to turn human subjects into objects. The stream of positivism, with its absolute reliance on a science of objective human observation, flowed out of the 'social physics' of Comte and whirled into the Vienna Circle of Logical Positivists in the twentieth century. There was, however, a qualitative undercurrent from the very source of positivism. A generation after Comte promised 'positive' certainty through the methods of natural science, Wilhelm Dilthey (1833–1911), from the German side of the Rhine, poured out a polemic against positivist sociology. Dilthey, and a host of other neo-Kantians of the 'Baden' school (Willey, 1978), such as Wilhelm Windelband and Heinrich Rickert, deplored the scientific approach to human study. Dilthey's student, Martin Buber (1978) called his teacher the father of philosophical anthropology and carried his idea of the 'I in the Thou' into the human relationship of the 'I–Thou' (Buber, 1958). (Dilthey, 1969, argued that 'understanding is a rediscovery of the 'I in the Thou'.') The science of objectivity had reduced human relationships to the 'I–It'.

Dilthey had argued that the 'human studies' arise out of 'lived experience' by way of 'autobiography, biography, and history'. These studies rested first on self knowledge and then the knowledge of others. Thus, Dilthey believed autobiography was the most instructive form of study for understanding life, but autobiography had the disadvantage of being 'a one-sided view'. Biography was the next step in developing human knowledge, for it offered a 'double focus', a possible stereoscopic view. Biography must provide insight into the subject from the subject's own perspective. (In this respect, Dilthey already anticipated the qualitative point of view which has come into focus in the late twentieth century.)

Dilthey thought the study and writing of biography was the most appropriate mode for learning about oneself and others, but biography should also focus on the subject from a greater distance. Biography required a far-sighted and more objective focus, as well as the near-sighted and subjective focus of autobiography. The study of the human being had to be from the inside *and* the outside. This study was but two sides of the same process, though Dilthey believed the human being was 'determined from within', not from without (Dilthey, 1969, p. 124). In this respect he was on the wrong side of the skin in the development of mainstream sociology. (For an idea of how wholes can be comprehended in terms of parts and parts in terms of wholes, or the concepts of 'connectedness of life' and the 'hermeneutic circle', see Rickman, 1976, pp. 10–14, 212–214; see also Bleicher, 1982.)

But Dilthey did influence one of sociology's greatest pioneers, Max Weber, in the next generation of sociological thinkers. Although Weber believed the 'person of the thinker must not intentionally obtrude itself in the realm of scholarship but should withdraw behind the subject', he did hold to the idea of the actor's 'subjectively meant meaning', and he attempted a federation between the humanities and their realm of 'freedom' and the material sciences and their domain of casual determinants and necessity (Marianne Weber, 1975, pp. 309, 313, 677; see also Schwartz and Jacobs, 1979, pp. 17–21; Smith, 1983).

Following the German succession of neo-Kantians, Edmund Husserl turned his inheritance into 'phenomenology', with its 'pure sphere of transcendental subjectivity'. Now it was the mind, receiving impressions from the outside world, that was the starting point. 'Meaning' is inside. Husserl's method for getting around the world of appearances to pure phenomena was to 'bracket' the 'ego' by a process of reduction which is so much like the 'pure consciousness' of Zen Buddhism that a long period of Zen training might be required for its ultimate understanding and application (Husserl, 1962; Sekida, 1975; Ames, 1962).

Phenomenology seems elusive to the Western mind. Harold Garfinkel (1967), who introduced 'ethnomethodology' into the arena of qualitative research, borrowed from Husserl the phenomenological position that an 'auditor' of language cannot make sense out of another person's words and actions without 'knowing or assuming something about the biography' of the speaker, as well as the circumstances of the utterance (pp. 4, 11).

The study of language thus becomes a vital element in the analysis of qualitative inquiry and antipositivism. Unlike the behavior of most natural phenomena, human behaviour is symbolic-dependent, caught up in a web of language. Not all human experience is 'sense-perception'. Much of living involves a process of 'abstraction', or what Charles Sanders Peirce called 'abstractive observation' through the medium of language and verbal imagination (Buchler, 1950, pp. 88, 98). Peirce also challenged the positivism of empirical science with his doctrine of 'fallibilism'; 'our knowledge,' he said, 'is never absolute but always swims, as it were, in a continuum of uncertainty and indeterminacy' (Hartshorne and Weiss, 1931, p. 70). The human being lived in two worlds, according to Peirce. There was the external world of fact and the inner world of fancy. The inner world was always veiled or clothed by a 'garment'. This garment was spun out of symbolic strands of signs and might be penetrated by the human being's study of the logic of signs. A 'sign,' Peirce said, is 'something which stands to somebody for something' and may relate to its object as an *icon, index,* or *symbol* (Buchler, 1950, pp. 88, 99, 102). The *icon,* such as a painting, is a sign that signifies a definite resemblance to its object. The *symbol,* of course, is the most abstract of signs, while the *index* is a sign that is affected by its object. It cannot be understood out of context. (See Hartshorne and Weiss, 1931; Hawkes, 1977, pp. 123–150; Copeland, 1984.)

There is a long but discernible line of thought connecting Peirce's sign of the *index* to the 'indexical properties of natural language' and context-bound 'indexical actions' which became a sociolinguistic base to what Harold Garfinkel (1967) terms 'ethnomethodology' (see also Garfinkel and Sacks, 1970, pp. 338–353). The indexical expression, in language as well as in human action, is always context-sensitive. Subjects must be studied in their natural habitats. The indexical properties of their language can be understood through observations of the consequences that follow the words. The linguistic concept of 'reflexivity' has become the expression for fusing the knower with the known itself. It means to be reflective and to be sensitive to the arts and all forms of human communication in order to understand the point of view of those who made the words or the forms of expression. Reflexive perspectives in anthropology have been described as 'the withdrawal from the world, bending back toward thought process itself' (Ruby, 1982, p. 2). (Schwartz and Jacobs, 1979, pp. 51–52, 218–223, 360, clarify the relation of the reflexive to the indexical. There is obviously a connection between reflexivity and the relativity of knowledge. The reflexive approach is more of a subject–subject than a subject–object study.)

The symbolic situations in which we live inspired a 'new key' to philosophy for Susanne K. Langer (1957). It is important to consider that a study of signs reveals their use to 'confuse and inhibit, warp and misadapt' as well as communicate between individuals. Thus, intentionality, or getting 'inside' the lives of others, is the object of qualitative inquiry, and to see within their words and behind their actions. Langer (1957) says, 'a book is like a life: all that is in it is really of a piece' (p. xi).

The emphasis on biography has always had its defenders in anthropology and sociology, especially in their use of the life history or life story (Denzin, 1970). Long on 'thick descriptions' (Geertz, 1973) by the participant–observer, the life history was considered as short on generalizability by mainstream social scientists. Still, ethnologists always relied on the interview and case study of what they thought were 'representative' figures. Pure biography, on the other hand, concentrated on the exceptional person, which for statistical designs would be discarded as outliers by the social scientists.

A whole literature has developed about the relation between biography and society (Bertaux, 1981; Langness and Frank, 1981; Langness, 1965). It may be considered to be the basic structure underlying the qualitative study of life and society.

Alfred Schutz, who helped transmit phenomenology to American sociology, thus challenging the structural functionalist domination of that discipline, stressed that the origin of all reality lay in what he called the 'biographically determined situation'. All actions, as well as symbols, are interpreted always in what Schutz (1962) said was the 'unique biographical situation in which I find myself within the world at any moment of my existence' (pp. 9, 18, 312). The 'biographical situation' thus became a basic unit of human understanding. Individuals 'locate' themselves in a particular biographical manner. At any given moment in life, the individual brings to the situation the 'sedimentation of all his previous subjective experiences' (p. xxviii), a kind of 'stockpiling' of typifications that have been amassed since childhood to serve as 'recipes' for working out various social situations. In face-to-face relationships, Schutz said, we are mutually involved in 'one another's biographical situations' (p. xxxix). (In commonplace meetings and conversations, do we not recall and share similar biographical experiences?)

## The Quality of Biography

Qualitative inquiry, with its techniques for looking within, has an important element of biography, and biography itself has a qualitative mode. The quality of biography suggests, like the quality of life itself, a matter of style and form. The Peckham view of human ethology holds that the 'quality of life' depends on the physical, mental, and emotional needs of the living individual being fully integrated into the environment as a whole (Pearse, 1979). The qualitative approach to inquiry considers the total context of the human subject in the natural environment. If a written biography is to be more than two-dimensional, it must situate the subject in the historical context and embody it with life. The biographer of quality is a creator as well as a recreator.

In the beginning was the flesh, and the flesh was made word, so to speak, by the biographer. The biographer, coming out of many disciplines, must form life out of the dust of documents, breath life into the subject of study, and get inside the private and personal parts of another living, thinking, and feeling being. Taking a life for one's text and weaving it into its proper context, past or present, the writer must find and reveal the truth.

But the form of biography may be as important as its content. What form should a biography take? Should a biographer take life the way it comes or bring some poetic license to it? Should a theme be sought, or a plot? Should the biographer plunge into the middle of things, *in medias res*, create suspense, flashbacks, flow into streams of consciousness, or take liberties with little details in order to frame a greater truth? Such is the 'craft and calling' of the biographer, according to Catherine Drinker Bowen (1969). (For the relationship among autobiography, biography, and the novel, see Bakhtin, 1981; and between the novel and social science, see Berger, 1971, and Burns, 1973.)

Biographies, like the lives they represent, come in many shapes and forms and belong to various tribes, some popular, some scholarly, some closer to fiction and story than truth and history, some more art or science, some mere 'silhouettes', and some ponderous tomes. Harold Nicholson (1933) divides the genre into 'pure' and 'impure' forms. The pure biography is historical, truthful, and well constructed. It is individualized and is art. The 'impure' biography is not the truth. It is created to celebrate the dead, to distort, or to compose a life in order to ilustrate a theory or principle or moral.

James L. Clifford (1970) categories biographic forms on a continuum from objectivity to subjectivity. Clifford cites Edward Nehls' (1959) *D. H. Lawrence: A Composite Biography* as an example of 'objective' biography, which aims at getting inside the subject and revealing everything from that perspective. Nehls' attempt is to bring 'together in chronological order the relevant available evidences, not only from others but from Lawrence himself, and [allow] it to speak for itself, with no narrative and sketchy "factual" notes' (p. xi). While this appears 'objective' to Clifford, it appears to be qualitative to an ethnographer who gathers data and makes no effort to intervene or impose interpretations. Clifford (1970) moves away from this idea of objective biography toward a 'scholarly–historical' model, where there are no fictional devices, no attempts to interpret the subject's personality, and no unacknowledged sources or guesswork by the biographer (p. 85). The scholarly–historical biography abounds in university presses.

Next in the line toward subjectivity comes the 'artistic–scholarly' biography, which combines 'exhaustive research' with 'an imaginative creative artist' who presents the research in an interesting manner. This kind of biographer is imaginative but does not imagine the facts. Clifford considers his own work to be in this category.

Moving toward the subjective, Clifford describes 'narrative' biography, in the mode of Catherine Drinker Bowen, who creates dramatic scenes to carry the story along. Finally, Irving Stone comes to mind as a master of the 'biographical novel', the most subjective and imaginative biography of all.

Clifford finds no place on his continuum for the 'ironical, sometimes vindictive' Lytton Strachey, whose 'miniatures' formed the beginning of modern biography, or for Virginia Woolf's *Orlando*, which only pretends to be a biography. The latter possibly may be a separate kind of biography (Clifford, 1970, pp. 87–89). (It is interesting that Virginia Woolf was an intimate of Lytton Strachey and the English biographer Harold Nicholson (Lehman, 1975).) And where would he put the *Life of Johnson*? James Boswell surely was the archetypical participant–observer and biographer (Dowling, 1978). And what of the novels which literary critics take apart in search of their author's own biographical experiences? Vladimir Nabokov (1966) discusses the 'autoplagiarism' of the novelist. He filled his novels by stealing from his own life, and though he wrote 'fictitious biographies' in which 'reality is a very subjective affair' and the 'inner knowledge' of his characters is a vital device, he had a dim view of critics who searched for biographical substance in his novels (Grabes, 1977, pp. 7, 16).

These questions of form and style suggest Elliot Eisner's idea of qualitative evaluation. The distinction Eisner (1981) draws between qualitative and non-qualitative research is a matter of style. All research must consider qualities as well as quantities. (For example, the qualitative biography might count the days of a subject's life or the hairs on the head, and intensity of feeling is sought in every Likert scale of human activity.) For Eisner, the difference between qualitative and non-qualitative forms of research lies not in what is studied but in how it is studied, whether by a scientific mode or an artistic mode. Artistic, for Eisner, has no single meaning, be it form, truth, beauty, or good, but it does differ from science in its representation. Where science extols the standardized form, the artistic form strives for individualization. The artistic form is more concerned with meaning than with the discovery of truth (see also Eisner, 1985, 1979).

A novel could provide as much, if not more, meaning as an encyclopedia. Form or style is a virtue, and perhaps the message is too. At least it seems useful to speak of an artistic way of knowing as well as a scientific way. How does one know about the life of another? Imagination and empathy are ways of knowing. Indeed, the attempt to reconstruct reality is based on the ability to imagine (Schwartz and Jacobs, 1979; Frye, 1964). Without imagination, the human being would be a 'captive of actuality', much like an animal (Kwant, 1963). Eisner (1981) argues that the only way to make sense of the 'non-observable' is to 'indwell' or to 'empathize', that is, 'to imaginatively participate in the experience of others' (p. 6).

There is danger in projecting the self into others and of generalizing from the particular, but the qualitative mode in biography, history, and science does not rest on generalization and statistical abstractions. It rests on the reactive modes of interviewing and the non-reactive modes of 'unobtrusive' sources of personal documents, even myths, legends, folklore, and children's literature, as well as written documents and physical remains (Schwartz and Jacobs, 1979, pp. 37–103).

There are psychological modes as well. Leon Edel (1984) considers Freudian 'transference' in the biographer's personal involvement with the subject. (Would this not apply also to the ethnographic investigator and the respondent?) Freud described the biographer's role as possible hero-worshiping, or the opposite, of fulfilling certain self needs through the subject. Such transference must be recognized and dealt with by the biographer.

Freudian methods of psychoanalysis have been used by biographers. Psychobiography was part of the biographical tradition by the 1920s, when many biographies were beginning to be couched in Freudianism. Even a form of 'pathography' surfaced as a way to discredit notable individuals as emotionally disturbed (Hoffman, 1984). Again, the biographer's motives need to be examined. The biographer and the biography are interconnected, just as the social researcher and the persons being researched are connected.

In addition to the usual historical method of researching sources, criticizing their authenticity and reliability, and providing corroboration, biographers have used all sorts of psychological instruments, not just Freudian, for getting inside their subjects. G. W. Allport's (1942) *The Use of Personal Documents* shows how the researcher can use written documents and reflections of their writer's personalities and psychological make-up.

Graphology, the study of handwriting, has also been suggested as a way of getting inside the subject. Handwriting is 'brainwriting', it is said (Garraty, 1957). Content analysis of writers' work can be used to note the number of adjectives or verbs used. The kinds of words one uses, the images, can give outward hints of inward perspectives. It even may be that the more qualitative words (adjectives) are used, the more emotionally unstable the writer may be. Semanticists have argued that bad semantic habits are a sign of a 'cranky, jumpy, even paranoid personality' (Garraty, 1957, pp. 224–225).

With the sources available for getting inside another, there remains the important question of how much of what is found should be revealed. Qualitative and quantitative researchers try to preserve the anonymity of respondents. But biographers cannot. There are biographers who, like Sherlock Holmes and Sigmund Freud, expose the whole truth and insert all of the facts into the biographic message (Edel, 1973). But some would not (Vandiver, 1983). 'Do we really have to know of some famous person that wet his pants at age six?', asks Barbara Tuchman. What purpose would it serve? Tuchman (1979) argues that 'biography is a prism of history', and it should be used to 'illumine history, voyeurism has no place' (p. 147). Yet voyeurism to one biographer might be illumination to another.

Biography has found many uses, as a mode of inquiry as well as a subject-matter or genre of literature and history. It has been used for instruction, as a form of therapy, and as a popular entertainment. In 1981, the Biographical Research Center published a survey of leading biographers on the future directions of biography. Biographers predicted a move toward 'group biography', 'biography of the common man', and biography which mixes historical with fictional figures (Friedson, 1981). There may also be an impact of biography on teaching and learning, the future of which might be called 'biographic interactionism'.

## Biographic Interactionism

The passion for one person to know another is as old as time. Historians and social scientists are moved by this passion and make it their life work. It is the profession of biographers. The study of humanity might be biography writ large. Whether biographer or social scientist, or even doctor, lawyer, or Indian Chief, all we really know about the world is grounded in the consciousness of what might be called our Autobiographic Self. Others write their laws and opinions into our consciousness and behaviors, and all we really know about them is what we read into their words and actions. Therefore, an attempt to understand anyone else in particular or human behavior in general is a common quest for what might be called the Biographic Other. Studying the lives of others is the life study of every human being. As the child studies its mother's face, so it must also study every feature, action, and reaction of others in the lifelong struggle to anticipate the actions of others and one's own actions on the reactions of others.

Between the Autobiographic Self and the Biographic Other stand volumes of studies which have tried to bind together the knower (the subject of knowing) and the known (the object of knowing), but there always is space in between, because of the ambiguity of language and the intersubjectivity of differing experiences, perceptions, and personal meanings. This space may make all the difference in the explanation and prediction of human behavior. Though the Autobiographic Self and the Biographic Other may be bound together in the same cultural context and even touch, as pages in a book, they cannot interpenetrate and see through the eyes of each other.

The lives of others, in written form as well as the flesh, interact with us, keep us company, and tell us about ourselves. We interact with written lives as we interpret the words of the biography and compare notes between ourselves and the others in the biography. We find ourselves in the society of others. And we find ourselves in the biographies we read. Much of our Autobiographical Self is written by others, as we write ourselves into the Biographic Other.

All of this suggests George Herbert Mead's (1934) theory of the 'I–Me', in which the self finds 'itself' as the object of others. The developmental self, through the medium of language and socialization, is the objective 'me', created by one's 'significant others'. History, Mead (1934) says, is 'but biography, a whole series of biographies' (p. 36). 'What happens to an individual can have no other locus than in his biography,' Mead (1938, p. 59) says. The sociologist looks for unity in the lives 'presented by biographies which follow a man from his birth to his death, showing all that belongs to the growth of the individual and the changes that take place in his career' (Mead, 1934, p. 84). This unity is like a melody. It is a common theme, a parallelism between the organism and the objects interacting with it. The 'reflective self' is a dialogue between the subject 'I' and the social object 'Me'.

Herbert Blumer (1969) took Mead's work, and that of John Dewey, William James, and others, and formed 'symbolic interactionism', which has become a distinctive approach to qualitative methodology. Symbolic interactionism has three simple premises. First is the belief that humans act on the basis of meanings that things have for them. Secondly, meaning is derived from the social interaction between a person and others. Thirdly, meanings are modified through an interpersonal process (pp. 1–5, 8). Thus, interpersonal meanings may be brought forth and shared by a process of interbiographical dialogue, or what will be called 'biographic interactionism'.

As one comes to know another in verbal and nonverbal interaction, there is a sharing of biographical names, places, and events. We come to know each other through sharing lived experiences. We come to understand what we hear and read by processing it through cognitive structures that have been constructed out of our past or biographical experience. The greater our biographical experience, the greater our capacity to learn and retain new information (Anderson *et al.*, 1977). Information that has no relation to our biographic framework is meaningless.

If we follow the theory of 'symbolic interactionism', the self we call our own is compounded from the bits and pieces of other lives, or the Biographic Other. In a sense we are cannibals, internalizing the expectations and demands of others; we are what we devour. So biographic inquiry into the lives of others is in a sense an inquiry into ourselves. The study of the self is the study of others, and vice versa.

Informal education teaches the necessity to study the behavior of others, or 'significant others', especially the Gatekeepers. Formal education also has its biographical advocates. John Dewey (1966) recommends the 'biographical method' as the 'natural mode of approach to historical study' (p. 214). Series of biographies have been written for children (Norton, 1984). Robert W. Johns (1984) has explored 'Biographical History: Microcosm of Meaning and Mankind' through the theories of Karl Marx, Arnold Toynbee, Jose Ortega y Gasset, Max Weber, and Wilhelm Dilthey. He found some common themes related to 'meaning', or some sense of connectedness between oneself and the world. The emphasis is still on the study of lives for a better understanding of oneself.

The curriculum 'reconceptualists', in proposing alternatives to the traditional and the empirical conceptions of curriculum, have suggested that 'the autobiographical mode of inquiry is a way to help students discover their own relation to school and language. They may see the ways in which the texts of everyday life such as family, peer relations, and mass culture are not merely activities or institutions "out there" but become fragments of that praxis by which we form ourselves' (Aronowitz, 1981, p. 464). Biography and autobiography have been used in curriculum research and in critiquing the teaching process (Berk, 1980; Grumet, 1980; Pinar, 1980, 1981).

Biographical interactionism implies more than the use of biographies and autobiographies. It is a basic teaching–learning relationship in which the events of learning are matched with the biographical events of the students. It implies a greater sharing, even study, by teachers and students about their own lives, experiences, interests, and abilities.

Louise M. Rosenblatt (1978) suggests the necessity for every text to be studied in terms of the author's biography — as well as the reader's. The reader makes an important contribution in what Rosenblatt (1978) calls a two-way 'transactional' relationship with the text (see also Rosenblatt, 1968). Literary critics have been concerned with the writer's biography. Except for the 'New Criticism', which proposed that literary works stand on their own, without reference to their authors, times, or places, the background of the author has been a hallmark of literary interpretation and criticism (Webster, 1979; Glicksberg, 1970; Sontag, 1966). The 'New Criticism' now is getting old. Once again the reader's biography appears to be essential for understanding the text.

Fiction and nonfiction are filled with 'perspectives'. So are readers. Let us study perspectives and teach each other about our own perspectives. Some perspectives are better than others, despite the cultural relativism of anthropologists, because they are more wide-angled, and thoughtful, and examined. But all perspectives are interpretations of the world. There may be many realities to be found, or simply many perspectives of reality, but whatever views there are begin in the Autobiographical Self.

The teacher, at almost any level of education, could ask students what they know about themselves. When and where were they born, and what were the basic life experiences of their parents, grandparents, spouses, children, and friends? Do they know what they were like at critical periods in their life cycle? Do they know about their appearances and health? Can they describe their formal education, their interests, their competencies, and decisions on their career paths?

The teacher also could ask if the students would tell the truth to their biographer and whether the biographer would interpret correctly what they said. What things have the students left behind that could tell biographers about them? In fact, how can we know about others? Does all knowledge depend on our own perception and interpretation, which is determined by our biographical experience? Must one study the lives of others in order to survive in a society of others? Is my Autobiographical Self written by others, and do I help to write the biography of others?

These are the questions that represent 'biographic interactionism'. They prompt the writing as well as the study of biography. It seems self-evident that all we really know about the world is grounded in our consciousness of it, and that our consciousness is slanted by the perspectives developed out of our particular life history, our Autobiographic Self. Getting inside the lives of others must be the object of the student-centered educator. Getting inside the lives of others is the object of the qualitative researcher, who cannot understand the acts of others except from the perspectives of the actors. Getting inside the lives of others is the object of every human being in the lifelong negotiations with others. Getting inside the lives of others always has been the aim of biographers.

Whatever the methods of the biographer (e.g., Geraldine Clifford, 1983), any prolonged study of another person is a better way of getting inside that person than through quick and impersonal quantitative surveys. In order to get the bearings of others, one must have more than one reference point, including one's own, and more than one method. This is what Norman K. Denzin (1970) calls 'triangulation' (pp. 260–261). Interpretations of oneself and others, through many sources and through qualitative as well as quantitative methods, may close the triangle between the Autobiographic Self, the Biographic Other, and the situation at hand.

### References

ALLEN, W. (1980). 'Remembering Needleman'. In *Side Effects*. New York: Ballantine.

ALLEXANDER, J. C. (1983). *Theoretical Logic in Sociology* (Vols. 1–4). Berkeley, CA: University of California Press.

ALLPORT, G. W. (1942). *The Use of Personal Documents in Psychological Science*. New York: Social Science Research Council.

AMES, Van M. (1962). *Zen and American Thought*. Honolulu, HI: University of Hawaii Press.

ANDERSON, R. C., REYNOLDS, R. E., SCHALLERT, D. L. and GOETZ, E. T. (1977). 'Frameworks for comprehending discourse'. *American Educational Research Journal*, *14* (Fall), 367–381.

ARONOWITZ, S. (1981). 'Politics and higher education in the 1980s'. In H. A. Giroux, A. N. Penna and W. F. Pinar (Eds.), *Curriculum and Instruction: Alternatives in Education*. Berkeley, CA: McCutchan.

BAKHTIN, M. M. (1981). *The Dialogic Imagination* (M. Holquist, Ed. and Trans.). Austin, TX: University of Texas Press.

BERGER, M. (1971). *Real and Imagined Worlds: The Novel and Social Science*. Cambridge, MA: Harvard University Press.

BERK, L. (1980). 'Education in lives: Biographic narrative in the study of educational outcomes'. *The Journal of Curriculum Theorizing*, *2* (Summer), 88–212.

BERTAUX, D. (Ed.). (1981). *Biography and Society: The Life History Approach in the Social Sciences*. Beverly Hills, CA: Sage.

BLEICHER, J. (1982). *The Hermeneutic Imagination: Outlines of a Positive Critique of Scientism and Sociology*. London: Routledge and Kegan Paul.

BLOOR, D. (1984). 'A sociological theory of objectivity'. In S. C. Brown (Ed.), *Objectivity and Cultural Divergence*. Cambridge: Cambridge University Press.

BLUMER, H. (1969). *Symbolic Interactionism: Perspectives and Method*. Englewood Cliffs, NJ: Prentice Hall.

BOWEN, C. D. (1969). *Biography: The Craft and the Calling*. Boston, MA: Little, Brown.

BUBER, M. (1958). *I and Thou*. New York: Scribner.

BUBER, M. (1978). *Between Man and Man*. New York: Macmillan.

BUCHLER, J. (Ed.). (1950). *The Philosophy of Peirce: Selected Writings*. London: Routledge and Kegan Paul.

BURNS, T. (1973). *Sociology of Literature and Drama*. Harmondsworth: Penguin.

CAMPBELL, J. K. (1984). 'Sociobiography: A new discipline'. *Vitae Scholasticae, 3* (Spring), 221–250.

CLIFFORD, G. J. (1983). 'The life story: Biographic study'. In J. H. Best (Ed.), *Historical Inquiry in Education: A Research Agenda*. Washington: American Educational Research Association.

CLIFFORD, J. L. (1970). *From Puzzles to Portraits: Problems of a Literary Biographer*. Chapel Hill, NC: University of North Carolina Press.

COPELAND, J. E. (Ed.). (1984). *New Directions in Linguistics and Semiotics*. Houston, TX: Rice University Press.

DENZIN, N. K. (1970). *The Research Act: A Theoretical Introduction to Sociological Methods*. Chicago: Aldine.

DEWEY, J. (1966). *Democracy and Education*. New York: Free Press.

DILTHEY, W. (1969). *Wilhelm Dilthey: An Introduction* (H. A. Hodges, Ed.). New York: Howard Fertig.

DOWLING, W. C. (1978). 'Boswell and the problem of biography'. In D. Aaron (Ed.), *Studies in Biography*. Cambridge, MA: Harvard University Press.

DUPRÉ, L. (1976). *Transcendent Selfhood: The Loss and Rediscovery of the Inner Life*. New York: Seabury Press.

EDEL, L. (1973). *Literary Biography*. Bloomington, IN: Indiana University Press.

EDEL, L. (1984). 'Transference: The biographer's dilemma'. *Biography: An Interdisciplinary Quarterly*, 7 (Fall), 283–291.

EISNER, E. W. (1979). *The Educational Imagination*. New York: Macmillan.

EISNER, E. W. (1981). 'On the difference between scientific and artistic approaches to qualitative research'. *Educational Researcher, 10* (April), 5–9.

EISNER, E. W. (1985). 'Aesthetic modes of knowing'. In E. W. Eisner (Ed.), *Learning and Teaching the Ways of Knowing*. 84th Yearbook of the National Society for the Study of Education, Part II. Chicago: University of Chicago Press.

FRIEDSON, A. M. (Ed.). (1981). *New Directions in Biography*. Honolulu, HI: University Press of Hawaii.

FRYE, N. (1964). *The Educated Imagination*. Bloomington, IN: Indiana University Press.

GARFINKEL, H. (1967). *Studies in Ethnomethodology*. Englewood Cliffs, NJ: Prentice Hall.

GARFINKEL, H. and SACKS, H. (1970). 'On formal structures of practical actions'. In J. C. McKenny and E. A. Tirakian (Eds.), *Theoretical Sociology: Perspectives and Developments*. New York: Appleton.

GARRATY, J. A. (1957). *The Nature of Biography*. New York: Knopf.

GEERTZ, C. (1973). 'Thick description: Toward an interpretive theory of culture'. In *The Interpretation of Culture*. New York: Basic Books.

GLICKSBERG, C. I. (1970). *Modern Literacy Perspectivism*. Dallas, TX: Southern Methodist University Press.

GRABES, H. (1977). *Fictitious Biographies: Vladimir Nabokov's English Novels*. The Hague: Mouton.

GRUMET, M. (1980). 'Autobiography and preconceptualization'. *The Journal of Curriculum Theorizing, 2* (Summer), 155–158.

HARTSHORNE, C. H. and WEISS, P. (Eds.). (1931). *Collected Papers of Charles Sanders Peirce: Vol. 1. Principles of Philosophy*. Cambridge, MA: Harvard University Press.

HAWKES, T. (1977). *Structuralism and Semiotics*. Berkeley, CA: University of California Press.

HOFFMAN, L. E. (1984). 'Early psychobiography, 1900–1930: Some reconsiderations'. *Biography: An Interdisciplinary Quarterly, 7* (Fall) 341–357.

HUSSERL, E. (1962). 'Consciousness and natural reality'. In W. Barrett and H. D. Aiken (Eds), *Philosophy in the Twentieth Century: An Anthology* (Vols 1–3). New York: Random House.

JOHNS, R. W. (1984). 'Biographical history: Microcosm of meaning and mankind'. *Theory and Research in Social Education, 12* (Fall), 35–60.

KLUCKHOHN, C. (1961). *Mirror for Man*, Greenwich, CT: Fawcett.

KWANT, R. C. (1963). *The Phenomenological Philosophy of Merleau-Ponty*. Pittsburgh, PA: Duquesne University Press.

LANGER, S. K. (1957). *Philosophy in a New Key: A Study in the Symbolism of Reason, Rite, and Art*. Cambridge, MA: Harvard University Press.

LANGNESS, L. L. (1965). *The Life History in Anthropological Science*. New York: Holt.

LANGNESS, L. L. and FRANK, G. (1981). *Lives: An Anthropological Approach to Biography*. Navato, CA: Chandler and Sharp.

LEHMAN, J. (1975). *Virginia Woolf and Her World*. New York: Harcourt Brace Jovanovich.

MEAD, G. H. (1934). *Mind, Self, and Society: From the Standpoint of a Social Behaviorist* (C. W. Morris, Ed.). Chicago: University of Chicago Press.

MEAD, G. H. (1938). *The Philosophy of the Act* (C. W. Morris, Ed.). Chicago: University of Chicago Press.

NABOKOV, V. (1966). *Speak, Memory. An Autobiography Revisited*. New York. G. P. Putnam.

NEHLS, E. (Ed.). (1959). *D. H. Lawrence: A Composite Biography: Vol 3. 1925–1930*. Madison, WI: University of Wisconsin Press.

NICHOLSON, H. (1933). *The Development of English Biography*. London: Hogarth.

NORTON, D. E. (1984). 'Centuries of biographies for childhood'. *Vitae Scholasticae, 3* (Spring), 113–127.

OVEREND, T. (1983). *Social Idealism and the Problem of Objectivity*. London: University of Queensland Press.

OWENS, R. G. (1982). 'Methodological rigor in naturalistic inquiry: Some issues and answers'. *Educational Administration Quarterly, 18* (Spring), 1–21.

PEARSE, I. H. (1979). *The Quality of Life: The Peckham Approach to Human Ethology*. Edinburgh: Scottish Academic Press.

PHILLIPS, D. C. (1983). 'After the wake: Postpositivistic educational thought'. *Educational Researcher, 12* (May), 4–12.

PINAR, W. F. (1980). 'Life history and educational experience'. *The Journal of Curriculum Theorizing, 2* (Summer), 159–212.

PINAR, W. F. (1981). 'Life history and educational experience, Part Two'. *The Journal of Curriculum Theorizing, 3* (Winter), 259–286.

POLANYI, M. (1962). *Personal Knowledge: Towards a Post-critical Philosophy*. Chicago: University of Chicago Press.

RICKMAN, H. P. (Ed.). (1976). *W. Dilthey: Selected Writings*. New York: Cambridge University Press.

ROSENBLATT, L. M. (1968). *Literature as Exploration*. New York: Noble and Noble.

ROSENBLATT, L. M. (1978). *The Reader, the Text, The Poem: The Transactional Theory of the Literary Work*. Carbondale, IL: Southern Illinois University Press.

RUBY, J. (Ed.). (1982). *a Crack in the Mirror: Reflective Perspectives in Anthropology*. Philadelphia, PA: University of Pennsylvania Press.

SCHULZ, A. (1982). *Collected Papers: Vol. 1. The Problem of Social Reality* (M. Natanson, Ed.). The Hague: Marinus Nijhoff.

SCHWARTZ, H. and JACOBS, J. (1979). *Qualitative Sociology*. New York: Free Press.

SCIMECCA, J. A. (1980). *Education and Society*. New York: Holt.

SEKIDA, K. (1975). *Zen Training*. New York: Weatherhill.

SHERMAN, R. R. and WEBB, R. B. (1986). Preface. [Special issue: Qualitative Research.] *Journal of Thought, 21* (Fall), 5–6.

SMITH, J. K. (1983). 'Quantitative versus qualitative research: An attempt to clarify the issue'. *Educational Researcher, 12* (March), 6–13.

SONTAG, S. (1966). *Against Interpretation*. New York: Dell.

TUCHMAN, B. W. (1979). Biography as a prism of history. In M. Pachter (Ed.), *Telling Lives: The Biographer's Art*. Washington, DC: New Republic Books.

VANDIVER, F. E. (1983). 'Biography as an agent of humanism'. In J. F. Veninga (Ed.)., *The Biographer's Gift: Life Histories and Humanism*. College Station, TX: Texas A and M University Press.

WEBER, M. (1975). *Max Weber: A Biography* (H. Zohn, Trans. and Ed.). New York: Wiley.

WEBSTER, G. (1979). *The Republic of Letters. A History of Postwar American Literary Opinion*. Baltimore, MD: Johns Hopkins University Press.

WILLEY, T. E. (1978). *Back To Kant*. Detroit, MI: Wayne State University Press.

WINKLER, K. J. (1985). 'Questioning the science in social science, scholars signal a "Turn to Interpretation".' *The Chronicle of Higher Education, 30* (17), 5–6.

Chapter 6

# Anthroethnography: A Methodological Consideration

*Nobuo Shimahara*
*Graduate School of Education*
*Rutgers University*
*New Brunswick, NJ 08903*

## Introduction

In the past decade ethnographic research has gained popularity in education. Until the early 1960s, however, educational researchers considered ethnographic methods to be an instrument of inquiry exclusively employed by cultural anthropologists. A few anthropologists pioneered ethnographic studies of schooling in the 1950s (see Spindler, 1955, 1963b; Brameld, 1959; Brameld is a philosopher by training, but he did anthropological research extensively in the 1950s and the 1960s). The anthropology of education became a formally recognized applied discipline in the 1960s, and it came of age in 1968, when the American Anthropological Association established a new division, the Council of Anthropology and Education.

George Spindler (1963a, p. 3) has suggested three typical types of ethnographies: anthroethnography, socioethnography, and psychoethnography. The distinction among their methodologies is often obfuscated, though their topical areas and scopes may widely differ. Also, field sociologists have had a sustained interest in qualitative research, although they have rarely called it 'ethnography'. Sociologists such as Robert and Helen Lynd, William F. Whyte, and Lloyd Warner, among others, have produced outstanding studies of communities and education based on the methodology of participant observation. Probably the best known is August B. Hollingshead's (1949) *Elmtown's Youth*.

As ethnography steadily attracted interest among educational researchers, it began to suffer from faddism. Spindler (1963a) warned:

It is not surprising that some work called 'ethnography' is marked by obscurity of purpose, lax relationships between concepts and observation, indifferent or absent conceptual structure and theory, weak implementation of research method, confusion about . . . hypotheses . . . (p. 2)

The warning suggests that ethnographers must have proper training in cultural anthropology and familiarity with methodological and theoretical knowledge of the discipline.

The purpose of this paper is to delineate anthroethnography in education (shortened hereafter to ethnography). Its main emphasis is on methodology, in Pelto's (1970) sense of methodology as 'the "logic-in-use" involved in selecting particular observational techniques, assessing their yield of data, and relating these data to theoretical propositions' (p. 4).


## Development of Ethnology and Ethnography

Ethnology is generally defined as the comparative study of cultures; it emphasizes the generation of concepts and theories based on crosscultural field data, seeks patterns of cultural regularities (see Clifton, 1968), and emphasizes the interpretation of field data (Hymes, 1980). Hence, traditionally it has been the domain of cultural anthropology. The development of anthropology, like other disciplines, was based on a special theory of reality and 'causal' explanation, and is dependent on a distinctive methodology (Voget, 1975, p. 3). The origin of anthropology as the science of culture is often traced to Edward Tylor, whose *Primitive Culture* (1929, originally published in 1871) is an effort to make what he called 'ethnography' into a science of culture (Voget, 1975, p. 136). Tylor (1929) identified the objects of ethnographic study in his definition of culture:

> Culture or civilization, taken in its wide ethnographic sense, is that complex whole which includes knowledge, belief, art, morals, law, custom, and any other capabilities and habits acquired by man as a member of society. The condition of culture among the various societies of mankind . . . is a subject apt for the study of laws of human thought and action. (p. 1)

The further development of ethnology, however, demanded greater refinement and precision in ethnographic methodology. Ethnologists in the early twentieth century began to stress field investigation and emphasize systematically collected field data, instead of relying upon secondary data available in the library. Among these ethnologists, most noted are Franz Boas in the United States and Bronislaw Malinowski in Britain. (Rosalie Wax, 1971, pp. 35–38, refers to Malinowski as the first anthropologist who conducted participant observation.)

One may examine Boas' (1940) work to illustrate the dominant concern of ethnologists with methodology. Boas set out to destroy evolutionary ethnology as speculative and unscientific and devoted himself to advancing the 'historical method' of controlled investigation to study the complexity of cultural development. He emphasized concrete descriptions of cultural phenomena in particular times and places, contending that only on such a basis was a controlled comparison of different cultures possible. He further argued that the field investigation must yield substantive data that shed light upon 'the sociopsychological nexus of form and meaning', and that the validity of such data depended upon the degree to which ethnographers were capable of describing the views of the natives studied (Voget, 1975, p. 333).

Having established 'historical methods', Boas' (1940) research orientation was directed toward a gamut of problems, including cultural dynamics, the integration of culture, and the interaction between the individual and society (pp. 305–311). Students trained under his guidance, such as Ruth Benedict, Alfred Kroeber, Edward Sapir, Margaret Mead, and Melville Herskovitz, carried forward work in these areas.

## Anthroethnography

Historically, anthropologists' ethnographic research consisted of case studies of small-scale societies, such as pastoral tribes, and their primary interest was to compare such societies to gain general knowledge of various cultures. Generally the social sciences have a two-fold endeavor: the observation and explanation of human behavior. For anthropologists, the domain of observation is culture as manifested in people's verbal and nonverbal behavior. In the most generic sense, ethnography consists of the process of observing human behavior in a holistic cultural context. An ethnography is expected to offer a detailed and comprehensive description of culture — an account of the behaviors, beliefs, attitudes, and values of the people under study. It is 'the science of cultural description', as Wolcott (1975, p. 112) aptly phrased it.

The general scope of ethnography defined by anthropologists is broad and covers major aspects of the culture of a given society or a culture-bound group most relevant to understanding its functions. As Berreman (1968) suggested, '. . . the aim of ethnography is to report the culture studied in sufficient depth and breadth to enable one who has not experienced it to understand it' (p. 338).

Ethnography, however, must be understood in terms of not only its products but also its strategy. As a strategy it is an inclusive research endeavor usually involving anthropologists as residents of different societies over an extended period of time, as participant observers interacting with natives in accordance with their customs and communicating with them in their languages. Such inclusive participation in the cultures studied is requisite to obtain first-hand knowledge of their organizations and functions. Anthropologists' main research tools are their own senses, sensitivities, and ability to communicate with native informants. Ethnography requires them to be perceptive observers, sensitive inquirers, and skillful participants (a good example is Lewis, 1951).

When ethnography is applied to specific problems and areas in education, such as a given school and a pattern of school desegregation, the scope and focus of ethnography are quite different from those of ethnography in anthropology proper. Anthroethnography in education has come to mean intensive and in-depth studies of relatively limited and specific problems and topics, the scope of which varies considerably from a school system to an individual school administrator. For example, Ianni's research team studied three high schools simultaneously to examine the social organizations of schools (see Horace Mann — Lincoln Institute, 1975; Ianni was director of this project). In contrast, Wolcott (1973) observed the behavioral pattern of a single principal over an extended period of time.

Three selected aspects of an ethnographic paradigm that underlies ethnography in education may be noted. The methodological orientation of ethnography is embedded in what Kuhn (1970, p. 22) called a paradigm, a 'model of coherent traditions' followed by a group of adherents. It is not a set of rigid rules shared by all anthropologists, but a research perspective, assumptions about culture, and an epistemological orientation that are adhered to by ethnographers.

*Contextual Orientation*

One of the insights anthropology has for education is the fact that human behavior is shaped in the context of a sociocultural milieu and that every human event is culture-bound. That context consists of 'value premises' — a 'configuration' that shapes individual cognitive orientation. Kluckhohn (1943), for example, believes that common value premises, or the configuration of each culture, 'unconsciously' guides and sustains the conventional way of life.

In my own study of Japanese society, which reflects Kluckhohn's emphasis on covert cultural context, I noted a remarkable continuity in Japanese social relations over the past two centuries and concluded that central to understanding this continuity is the concept of value premises, which I called 'cultural orientations' (Shimahara, 1979). The core of Japanese cultural orientation is group orientation, which influences formal and informal social relations, the organizational decision-making process, socialization, schooling, and the pattern of social mobility. Although Japan has similar social, educational, and organizational problems as Euro-American societies, it adapts to such problems differently from the ways displayed by Euro-American societies. Japanese adaptation is governed by group orientation.

Culture-and-personality studies begun in the 1930s by Kardiner (1939), Linton (1945), Mead (1936) and Kluckhohn and Murray (1948), among others, abundantly demonstrated the linkages between the individual and culture. As Kluckhohn (1949) has phrased it, culture is 'the mirror for man'. Meanwhile,

Brameld (1957) translated these anthropological insights into a coherent theoretical framework of educational concepts and questions to be investigated.

Studying human behavior and events in a cultural context entails two methodological aspects. The first requires observation of not only events relevant to the framework of an immediate research setting but also of their relationships to a broader sociocultural milieu, which remains the background of the immediate setting. Ogbu's (1974) study of schools in California, Gans' (1965) observation of schooling and socialization of Italian-Americans in Boston, and Gearing and Epstein's (1963) study of classroom interaction in a school in upper New York State aptly illustrate this aspect. The second aspect was succinctly stated by Spindler (1963b):

> Sociocultural knowledge held by social participants makes social behavior and communication sensible to oneself and to others. Therefore a major part of the ethnographic task is to understand what sociocultural knowledge participants bring to and generate in the social setting being studied. (p. 7)

Schofield's (1982) investigation of a desegregated middle school illuminates the effect of teachers' sociocultural knowledge on the pattern of social relations between blacks and whites. She observed that teachers consistently took the 'ideological stance' — one form of sociocultural knowledge — that reference to race is illegitimate in dealing with children's academic, social, and personal problems, despite the apparent divisiveness prevailing in the school. Likewise, in her own analysis of data, other research participants' sociocultural knowledge was brought to bear upon their behavior.

All ethnographers study events as they evolve in natural settings — the 'contexts in process' in which human experience takes place. The aim is to view events holistically. Some events may be anticipated, but others may be totally unexpected. Nevertheless, the ethnographic commitment is to study ongoing realities without affecting their process. An event cannot be isolated from the context in which it originates, for to do so will destroy the full meaning of experience. In contrast, Mischler (1979) has pointed out that 'context stripping' is a key feature of our standard methods of experimental design, measurement, and statistical analysis.

### Qualitative Orientation

Three paradigmatic premises underlie the qualitative orientation of ethnography. First, anthropologists are interested in sociocultural patterns of human behavior rather than the quantification of human events. Cultural phenomena are more susceptible to qualitative description and analysis than to quantification (Voget, 1975, p. 388). According to Kluckhohn (1959), the relevance of anthropological information is found not simply in the account of incidence and distribution, but in the *description of the pattern of behavior* or various ways the pattern is manifested. He believes statistics obscure the qualitative dimensions of pattern and suggests that informants should be viewed not as actors whose behavior must be measured, but as documents that reflect the culture of which they are the bearers (pp. 259–260).

Ethnographic research emphasizes the integration of particular events into a coherent and qualitatively meaningful pattern where the relationship of events is established. A good example of this approach is Wolcott's (1973) study, *The Man in the Principal's Office*. What is important in the study is not only the detailed account of principalship, but the culturally governed pattern of the principal's behavior emerging from the description of his behavior in his particular social context. Wolcott (1973) says:

> The test of ethnography is whether it enables one to anticipate and interpret what goes on in a society or social group as appropriately as one of its members. To the extent that the account provided here achieved this objective, the reader should feel that if he were suddenly to find himself in an encounter with staff members, pupils, or parents at the school described, or if he were to attend a meeting with other principals from the school district, he would understand how he might act if he were in the role of the principal. Conversely, if he were to assume the role of some other person in an encounter with the principal, he should feel he would know how the principal might act toward him. (p. xi)

The second premise holds that cultural events are understood and categorized in terms of the cultural actor's definition of human events. The epistemological assumption of this approach is that the perspective of people under study is crucial to understanding their behavior. Accordingly, it is assumed that cultural investigation can be accomplished by actively participating in their life. Attention is focused upon how they define their reality, often called 'emic': the classification of objects, the definition of the situation in which they act, the assumptions on which activity takes place. (The terms 'emic' and 'etic' — to be discussed later — were introduced by Kenneth Pike, 1954.)

At this point, it is relevant to review the anthropological background leading to the idea of 'emic' inquiry. Boas (1943) elucidates the emicist orientation: 'If it is our serious purpose to understand the thoughts of a people the whole analysis of experience must be based on their concepts, not ours' (p. 314). That paradigm was followed by Boas' students. It was further articulated by anthropological linguists and cognitive anthropologists in the 1950s and 1960s (Pike, 1954; Goodenough, 1956; Frake, 1980). And it led to the development of what has been called the 'New Ethnography', directly confronting the 'eticist' approach, which stresses the observer's rather than the actor's perspective.

Eticists believe that the conceptual categories of cultural reality must be determined by the researchers, based on their identification of the causes of cultural phenomena. This idea is articulated best by Harris (1979):

> Etic operations have as their hallmark the elevation of observers to the status of ultimate judges of the categories and concepts used in descriptions and analyses. . . . Frequently, etic operations involve the measurement and juxtaposition of activities and events that native informants may find inappropriate or meaningless. (p. 32)

Pelto (1970) characterizes the debate between emicists and eticists as 'the single most important theoretical disagreement [in anthropology] — one which involves the foundations of all our methodological procedures' (p. 82). Nevertheless, the main stream of ethnography follows the emic approach, though there are sometimes varying degrees of eclecticism that incorporate both approaches.

The third premise involves the ethnographer's focus on ongoing settings in sociocultural contexts, such as communities, educational institutions, and classrooms, where events occur as human interaction takes place. These settings are often characterized as 'natural' in the sense that they are not contrived or modified by the observer. The ethnographer attempts to understand holistically the cultural meanings of behavior observed. This approach requires that observers attend to all features of behavior as they constitute a pattern in a given setting. Paramount is their interest in the qualitative character of the setting, involving the coherence and durability of relationships among behavioral features as they are manifested in a multitude of forms. Accordingly, researchers must avoid the use of strategies that may influence the integrity of the entire setting studied.

To appreciate the ethnographer's qualitative orientation, it may be contrasted with conventional quantitative research methods in the social sciences. Quantitative methods aim to formulate general 'laws' free of specific sociocultural constraints. Hence, the subjects of research are removed from the natural sociocultural setting by either placing them in a laboratory situation or by manipulating them to respond to questions arbitrarily formulated by the researcher. This is done to eliminate qualitative responses so as to avoid contamination by variables other than those specifically predetermined for research. By comparison, the ethnographer seeks the full meanings of behavior and its patterns shaped in the actual matrix of a given sociocultural environment, rather than causal relationships among predetermined variables subjected to rigid measurement.

### Ethnographic Questions and Hypotheses

Questions and hypotheses are formulated to guide the process of inquiry. In quantitative research, the observer's role is defined independent of the observed events. Accordingly, hypotheses are generated prior to data collection. Quantitative social science research employs a linear sequence model of research (Spradley, 1980, p. 27). It begins with the definition of a problem, followed by the formulation of hypotheses, and proceeds to the designing of instruments to test the hypotheses; subsequently, it involves data collection and analysis, followed by the drawing of conclusions.

In contrast, the ethnographic paradigm defines the role of the observer in relation to the observed. The observer is not able to formulate questions or hypotheses prior to starting fieldwork. The guiding questions are typically formulated after the orienting phase of fieldwork, and such questions are generally regarded as tentative hypotheses, continuously subjected to refinement as research proceeds. The linear social science approach — quantitative research — not only predetermines what inquiry is to take place, it also forecloses other researchable problems inherent in a natural context. In ethnography, the perspectives of the observer and the observed are intertwined in the generation of questions and hypotheses.

Spradley (1980, pp. 28–29) viewed ethnographic inquiry as cyclical instead of linear. It begins with the selection of an ethnographic project and proceeds to asking ethnographic questions, followed by data collection and analysis. This cycle is repeated as research progresses, but the research questions are modified as the inquiry progresses from 'descriptive', to 'structural', to contrast questions. Descriptive questions are general and broad, appropriate particularly in the orienting phase, and structural questions are formulated in the phase of focused observation to concentrate on more articulately defined domains of inquiry. Subsequently, contrast questions are generated in the phase of 'selective' observation, in which contrasting behavior is studied.

For ethnographers, fieldwork is a context in which questions are generated and modified. In Spindler's (1963a) words, 'Hypotheses and questions for study emerge as the study proceeds in the setting for observation' (p. 6). All ethnographers do not espouse the same views concerning how questions and hypotheses are generated. There are two views, however, which are fundamentally in agreement with the central orientation of ethnography.

Bogdan and Taylor (1975), who define a 'phenomenological' approach to fieldwork, suggest that while the observer formulates hypotheses throughout research the central phase of generating hypotheses comes in the process of data analysis:

> . . . *'Data analysis' refers to a process which entails an effort to formally identify themes and to construct hypotheses (ideas) as they are suggested by data and an attempt to demonstrate support for those themes and hypotheses. By hypotheses* we mean nothing more than propositional statements that are either simple . . . or complex . . . (p. 79; italics in the original)

On the other hand, Erickson (1977, p. 62), advocated 'focused strategies of primary data collection', which actively and consciously direct inquiry. He urged researchers to develop hypotheses in the field, along a line of theoretical orientation derived from both fieldwork and 'substantive theory' in social science. He suggested:

Research questions come from interaction between experience and some kind of theory, substantive or personal. It is extremely important that qualitative researchers make that interaction as explicit as possible to their audience in reporting and to themselves in the field. (p. 22)

I personally favor the Erickson approach and have used it in my own work (Shimahara, 1969, 1979).

## Ethnographic Method

Unlike the linear, quantitative research in social science, ethnography has no standardized procedures of investigation that all ethnographers use (see Wax, 1971; Powdermaker, 1966; Pelto, 1970, pp. 34–35). This reflects the fact that ethnographic research is the craft of participant observation. Ethnographers often combine different methodological techniques, some of which are devised personally, in such a way as to facilitate their data collection in particular field situations. For example, Lewis (1966) employed methods in his study of a Puerto Rican family quite different from those suggested by Spradley (1980). Similarly, Ogbu's (1974) investigation of schooling in Stockton, California, used methods of data collection dissimilar from Brameld's (1969) procedures for studying schooling in Japan. Nevertheless, one can discuss methodological components employed by ethnographers in general.

### Research Problems

The problems that ethnographers study emerge from their substantive and theoretical interests. A substantive interest is an awareness of problems that arise in ongoing inquiry. Theoretical interests arise from established theories that constitute researchers' theoretical frames of reference. Thus, the first strategy of inquiry entails a broad examination of the historical, social, and cultural contexts of problems, and an identification of the relation of the problems to pertinent theories and literature.

Problems may differ in scope. Anthropological research is often categorized into micro- and macroethnographies depending on the scale of the study (see Ogbu, 1981). Spradley's (1980, p. 30) typology of ethnography involves seven social units studied at differential levels: single and multiple communities, and a complex society. In educational ethnographies, research dealing with the first two or three units is usually viewed as microethnography, and studies encompassing the other units are regarded as macroethnographic.

## Choosing Research Settings

After problems for inquiry are decided, the next task is to determine a research setting. Perhaps this is the most difficult task in research. Gaining access to an organizational site or a community (that is, getting the cooperation of the 'gatekeepers' who have the power to grant access) is time consuming and often frustrating. Novice ethnographers should not be disheartened when they are denied access once or twice to the organizations chosen for study. They must be patient and continue to seek cooperation from alternative organizations. Normally, an organization chosen for ethnographic study wants to review the outline of the study. Thus, the researcher must have a generally framed study proposal before the site is chosen.

## Descriptive Observation

The first observations that researchers do may be called 'descriptive observation' (Spradley, 1980, pp. 32–33). The observation is governed by a general question, 'What is going on here?' (Spradley, 1980, p. 73). The intent of the observation is to gain insight into researchable problems when researchers have little knowledge of the culture to be studied. Researchers make field notes that provide a detailed, narrative description of what has been observed with particular attention to activities, actors, space, physical objects, and the sequence of activities and events.

Subsequently, by reviewing their field notes, researchers identify and analyze domains of the phenomena observed. Spradley (1980, pp. 85–99) called this process 'domain analysis' (it may be compared with the concept of category used by Glaser and Strauss, 1967). The primary purpose of domain analysis is to identify categories — for example, activities and actors — and their relationships, leading to a taxonomy of domains. Categories should be flexible, so that they can be modified as research proceeds. Domain analysis is helpful in outlining the general boundary of a problem and its internal dimensions.

## Guiding Questions/Hypotheses

Guiding questions and hypotheses emerge only after the orienting phase of inquiry. The use of 'hypothesis' here indicates a propositional statement — such as 'Adolescent peer groups influence formal learning in school' — intended to sensitize the researcher to the nature of a social situation under study (Bogdan and Taylor, 1975, pp. 79–80). Though guiding questions/hypotheses develop continuously, they are especially useful in guiding research in its early stages. They are framed in general terms to allow other questions to evolve later.

### Participant Observation

Participant observation is a major method of ethnographic data collection. The researcher becomes an instrument of inquiry by playing dual roles — by being present in the situation but by standing aside to observe it. The ethnographers' commitment is to immerse themselves in the 'host' culture, to strive 'to understand and enter into "the world of morals and meanings" of the hosts' (Wax and Wax, 1980, p. 30). In Berreman's (1968) words, participant observation is 'the practice of living among the people one studies, coming to know them, their language, and their lifeways through intense and nearly continuous interaction with them in their daily lives'. At the same time, researchers remain detached, intense observers inquiring into cultural phenomena. Their role is to observe events at which they are physically present but to refrain from participating in those events so that they will not affect the activity being studied.

The intensity and duration of participant observation varies with research units. It usually involves ethnographic interviews in order to complement data gathered through observation (Spradley, 1979). Participant observation employed by microethnographers is not as comprehensive as that employed in macroethnographies (e.g., Singleton, 1967). Microethnographers conduct participant observation as 'scheduled visitors' rather than as participating residents.

### Validity and Reliability

Validity and reliability of research are crucial in all social research regardless of disciplines and the methods employed. Collected data must be accurate, authentic, and represent reality. Also, intersubjective replicability of research enables investigators to produce cumulative findings.

Ethnographic validity refers to the degree to which participant observation achieves what it purports to discover, i.e., the authentic representation of what is happening in a social situation. Ethnographic reliability refers to the repeatability of a given study by researchers other than the original participant observer; the extent to which independent researchers discover the same phenomena in comparable situations (Pelto, 1970; LeCompte and Goetz, 1982). It is the reliability of ethnographic research (and validity to a degree) that more often than not is criticized (LeCompte and Goetz, 1982, p. 32; Rist, 1977, p. 45).

In participant observation, validity indicates the ethnographer's understanding of the meanings of the observed sociocultural experience. Therefore, to attain a high degree of validity, the observer must repeat observation through prolonged involvement in the culture studied. It is because of this that establishing residence among the participants is an essential factor in research. The participant observer must maintain neutrality and have a multi-

dimensional vision for both observing and interacting with research participants. This suggests that the researcher has to focus on the entire group and
a wide range of informants (a stratified sample, if possible) representing the
group. Also, the observer must guard against ethnocentrism and perceptual
biases. Still another strategy is to involve participants in reconstructing the
events recorded by the observer. This contributes to reducing the researcher's
perceptual biases.

Measures to enhance reliability, on the other hand, involve a complete
description of the research process, so that independent researchers may replicate the same procedures in comparable settings. This includes a delineation
of the physical, cultural, and social contexts of the study; a statement of the
ethnographer's roles in the research setting; an accurate description of the
conceptual framework of research; and a complete description of the methods
of data collection and analysis. Special attention must be given to what
LeCompte and Goetz (1982, pp. 41–43) call 'internal reliability', agreement
among descriptions of observed phenomena in the same study. Measures to
insure internal reliability, suggested by LeCompte and Goetz involve low-
inference description and what Spradley (1980, p. 67) terms 'the verbatim
principle', stressing verbatism accounts of events; confirmation of findings by
informants; team observation, involving multiple researchers; peer examination by researchers working on the same problem in different settings; and
the use of audio-visual instruments. Internal reliability is closely related to
validity; hence these measures may also be used to maximize ethnographic
validity.

## Summary

Ethnographic research has its roots in the tradition of anthropological fieldwork. It is characterized by its qualitative and contextual orientations. It
emphasizes the integrity of natural settings and the 'emic' approach to studying
problems. Participant observation as an ethnographic method integrates these
methodological considerations into fieldwork. To elevate participant observation to the level of scientific research, special attention must be given to
strategies that maximize ethnographic validity and reliability.

## References

BERREMAN, G. D. (1968). 'Ethnography: Method and product'. In J. A. Clifton (Ed.),
*Introduction to Cultural Anthropology: Essays in the Scope and Methods of the Science
of Man.* Boston, MA: Houghton Mifflin.
BOAS, F. (1940). *Race, Language and Culture.* New York: Macmillan.
BOAS, F. (1943). 'Recent anthropology'. *Science, 98* (October 8), 311–314; (October
15), 334–337.

Bogdan, R. and Taylor, S. J. (1975). *Introduction to Qualitative Research Methods: A Phenomenological Approach to the Social Sciences.* New York: Wiley.

Brameld, T. (1957). *Cultural Foundations of Education: An Interdisciplinary Exploration.* New York: Harper.

Brameld, T. (1959). *The Remaking of a Culture: Life and Education in Puerto Rico.* New York: Harper.

Brameld, T. (1969). *Japan: Culture, Education, and Change in Two Communities.* New York: Holt.

Clifton, J. A. (Ed.). (1968). *Introduction to Cultural Anthropology: Essays in the Scope and Methods of the Science of Man.* Boston, MA: Houghton Mifflin.

Erickson, F. (1977). 'Some approaches to inquiry in school-community ethnography'. *Anthropology and Education Quarterly, 8* (May), 58–69.

Frake, C. O. (1980). *Language and Cultural Description.* Stanford, CA: Stanford University Press.

Gans, H. J. (1965). *The Urban Villagers: Group and Class in the Life of Italian-Americans.* New York: Free Press.

Gearing, F. and Epstein, P. (1963). 'Learning to wait: An ethnographic probe into the operations of an item of hidden curriculum'. In G. Spindler (Ed.), *Doing the Ethnography of Schooling: Educational Anthropology in Action.* New York: Holt.

Glaser, B. G. and Strauss, A. L. (1967). *The Discovery of Grounded Theory: Strategies for Qualitative Research.* Chicago: Aldine.

Goodenough, W. (1956). 'Componential analysis and the study of meaning'. *Language, 32,* 195–216.

Harris, M. (1979). *Cultural Materialism: The Struggle for a Science of Culture.* New York: Random House.

Hollingshead, A. B. (1949). *Elmtown's Youth.* New York: Wiley.

Horace Mann–Lincoln Institute. (1975). *Social Organization of the High School Study.* (ERIC Document, ED 129 711.)

Hymes, D. (1980). Educational ethnology. *Anthropology and Education Quarterly, 11* (Spring), 3–8.

Kardiner, A. (1939). *The Individual and His Society.* New York: Columbia University.

Kluckholn, C. (1943). 'Covert culture and administrative problems'. *American Anthropologist, 45,* 213–227.

Kluckholn, C. (1949). *The Mirror for Man: The Relation of Anthropology to Modern Life.* New York: McGraw-Hill.

Kluckholn, C. (1959). 'Common humanity and diverse cultures'. In D. Lerner (Ed.), *The Human Meaning of the Social Sciences.* Cleveland, OH: Meridian.

Kluckholn, C. and Murray, H. (1948). *Personality in Nature, Society, and Culture.* New York: Knopf.

Kuhn, T. S. (1970). *The Structure of Scientific Revolutions* (2nd ed.). Chicago: University of Chicago Press.

LeCompte, M. D. and Goetz, J. P. (1982). 'Problems of reliability and validity in ethnographic research'. *Review of Educational Research, 52* (Spring), 31–60.

Lewis, O. (1951). *Life in a Mexican Village: Tepoztlan Restudied.* Urbana, IL: University of Illinois Press.

Lewis, O. (1966). *La Vida: A Puerto Rican Family in the Culture of Poverty.* New York: Vintage.

Linton, R. (1945). *The Cultural Background of Personality.* New York: Appleton.

MEAD, M. (1936). *Coming of Age in Samoa*. New York: Blue Ribbon Books. (First published in 1928).

MISCHLER, E. G. (1979). 'Meaning in context: Is there any other kind?' *Harvard Educational Review, 49* (February), 2–10.

OGBU, J. U. (1974). *The Next Generation: An Ethnography of Education in an Urban Neighborhood*. New York: Academic Press.

OGBU, J. (1981). School ethnography: A multi-level approach. *Anthropology and Education Quarterly, 12* (Spring), 3–29.

PELTO, P. J. (1970). *Anthropological Research: The Structure of Inquiry*. New York: Harper.

PIKE, K. (1954). *Language in Relation to a Unified Theory of the Structure of Human Behavior* (Vol. I). Glendale, CA: Summer Institute of Linguistics.

POWDERMAKER, H. (1966). *Stranger and Friend: The Way of an Anthropologist*. New York: Norton.

RIST, R. C. (1977). 'On the relations among educational research paradigms: From disdain to detente'. *Anthropology and Education Quarterly, 8* (May), 42–49.

SCHOFIELD, J. W. (1982). *Black and White in School*. New York: Praeger.

SHIMAHARA, N. K. (1969). *Burakumin: A Japanese Minority and Education*. The Hague: Martinus Nijhoff.

SHIMAHARA, N. K. (1979). *Adaptation and Education in Japan*. New York: Praeger.

SINGLETON, J. (1967). *Nichu: A Japanese School*. New York: Holt.

SPINDLER, G. (Ed.). (1955). *Education and Anthropology*. Stanford, CA: Stanford University Press.

SPINDLER, G. (1963a). General Introduction. In George Spindler (Ed.), *Doing the Ethnography of Schooling: Educational Anthropology in Action*. New York: Holt.

SPINDLER, G. (Ed.). (1963b). *Education and Culture: Anthropological Approaches*. New York: Holt.

SPRADLEY, J. (1979). *The Ethnographic Interview*. New York: Holt.

SPRADLEY, J. (1980). *Participant Observation*. New York: Holt.

TYLOR, E. B. (1929). *Primitive Culture*. London: J. Murray. (Published originally in 1871.)

VOGET, F. W. (1975). *A History of Ethnology*. New York: Holt.

WOLCOTT, H. (1973). *The Man in the Principal's Office: An Ethnography*. New York: Holt.

WOLCOTT, H. (1975). 'Criteria for an ethnographic approach to research in schools'. *Human Organization, 34* (Summer), 111–127.

WAX, R. H. (1971). *Doing Fieldwork: Warnings and Advice*. Chicago: University of Chicago Press.

WAX, M. L. and WAX, R. H. (1980). Fieldwork and the research process. *Anthropology and Education Quarterly, 11* (Spring), 29–37.

*Chapter 7*

# Educational Ethnography in Britain

*Peter Woods*
*School of Education*
*The Open University*
*Milton Keynes, MK7 6AA, England*

Over the past fifteen years there has been an upsurge of ethnographic work in British educational research, making ethnography the most commonly practiced qualitative research method. This interest in ethnography was sparked by the advent of the 'new sociology' (M. F. D. Young, 1971), which concentrated on the taken for granted categories of everyday life and the social construction of human reality. Though the new sociology employed many theoretical approaches, symbolic interactionism soon dominated the field.

Symbolic interactionism holds that human beings act toward things on the basis of the meaning that things hold for them. The attribution of meaning to objects is a continuous process which takes place in social contexts. Thus, symbolic interactionists focus on the *perspectives*, through which people make sense of the world; the *strategies* people employ to achieve their ends; the different contexts and *situations* in which they define their goals; their group *cultures* in which they interact; and their subjective, as opposed to objective, *careers*.

The research technique most favored by symbolic interactionists has been ethnography, with its characteristic emphasis on participant observation. In truth, however, there has been little 'participation' in the sense of a researcher taking a recognized role within an institution (Bruyn, 1966). Most researchers have observed in school settings over long periods of time (on the average, one to two years) and have frequently used unstructured interviews (Hammersley and Atkinson, 1983).

Rather than attempt to give an exhaustive account of findings. I will focus on what I consider to be the strengths of the approach, illustrating from research studies. This approach retains an emphasis on method while capturing the flavor of British ethnographic research.

## Illumination

Much ethnographic work describes and illuminates the fine-grained details of school life. But ethnographic description differs from ordinary description in that the researcher's aim is to penetrate beneath surface appearances and reveal the harder realities there concealed. Such realities are illuminated over time and often contrast sharply with official accounts of the schooling process.

Consider, for example, the matter of teaching methods and teacher strategies. It is popularly thought that schools reward students for their 'knowledge' and 'ability', but Edwards and Furlong (1978, p. 121) show that often pupils are rewarded for accepting 'the teacher's system of meanings, which either confirms or extends or replaces [their] own'. Hammersley (1974, 1976, 1977b) demonstrates how teachers enforce their definitions of the school situation by organizing pupil participation in lessons. Teachers arrange classrooms, define rules of conduct, manage pupil turn-taking, and control and develop discussion topics. Teacher control, in fact, is built into the very fabric of classroom language: 'O.K., now listen all of you!'; 'Colin, what were you going to say?' Stubbs (1976) calls such language 'metacommunication' because it not only tells students what the teacher wants them to do but silently carries the more important message that the teacher is in control.

Even 'progressive' and 'child-centred' teaching contains traditional structures of teacher control. Atkinson and Delamont (1977), for example, show how guided 'discovery science' does not entail 'discovery' in naturally occurring situations, but is in fact a teacher-dominated and carefully 'stage-managed recapitulation of already known "facts"' (p. 141). Edwards and Furlong (1978) argue that resource-based teaching represents a change in the technology of teaching rather than a shift from the knowledge-transmission role of traditional instruction (see Ball, 1981; Barnes, 1976; Goodson, 1975; A. Hargreaves, 1977; and Corbishley et al., 1981). In another study, Woods (1979) questions whether teachers were really 'transmitting knowledge' or merely 'surviving' in a difficult job. Teachers in his study appeared caught between irredeemable commitment to the job on the one hand (they had families, mortgages, etc.) and intractable discontent on the other (they suffered from low school morale, poor student motivation, etc.). In such circumstances, teachers developed 'survival strategies' which mimicked teaching but did little to enhance learning. Teachers absented themselves mentally, and sometimes physically, from the classroom; mechanically went through the motions of teaching; or devoted themselves to a therapeutic role which passed classroom time agreeably and minimized teacher–student conflict. Studies such as these offer descriptions of teaching that differ fundamentally from the official definitions of the teacher role. Yet when researchers bring their findings back to their subjects, teachers often report that they 'ring true'.

With pupils, too, things are not always what they seem. For example, apparently straight 'conformist' pupils strategically 'work the system'. Much pupil activity is not devoted to learning but simply to 'pleasing the teacher'.

Six- and 7-year-olds have been observed hiding ignorance behind a knowledgeable mask or searching for answers to teacher questions through the facial expressions, body language, and behavior of teachers (Tuckwell, 1982). Older pupils become adept at anticipating questions and duping teachers by using 'impressive language' that is not backed by knowledge (D. Hargreaves, 1972).

Pupils may 'please teachers' only as long as it furthers their own interests. Delamont's (1976) girls, for example, pleased teachers in return for grades, jobs, or peace and quiet. Without such payoffs, disruptive behavior increased (Turner, 1982). Pupils bent on good examination results for career purposes were likely to misbehave in classrooms of incompetent teachers. Classroom disruption was likely in situations when the sanctions of peers were more important to students than the sanctions of teachers (Turner, 1982; Birksted, 1976 a, b).

In some instances of such conflicting pressures, youngsters have been observed using 'knife-edge strategies' (Measor and Woods, 1984). For example, a deviant boy placed in the bottom ability group worked hard to gain promotion to a middle group because he did not want to appear 'really thick'. Once there, he did not work to go higher because he did not want to be considered a 'goody-goody' by his peers, and in fact presented a more deviant appearance to emphasize the point.

These are some of the ways in which ethnographers have discovered things that one might not have expected to find. In the process, they have been obliged to classify their findings under such headings as 'metacommunication', 'survival strategies', or 'knife-edge strategies' that give currency to their ideas and facilitate further investigation and refinement.

### Breadth of View

The ethnographer, writing the limits of his or her own perceptions and ability, aims to give a thorough description of the relationship between all the elements characteristic of a single human group. This holistic character is another distinctive feature of the approach.

One example of comprehensive ethnographic knowledge is found in studies of 'good teachers' from the perspective of students. A number of studies suggest that pupils use three principles to guide their evaluations of teachers: whether teachers can control the class, whether they can teach, and whether they are human enough to let their personalities extend beyond the boundaries of their official role. 'Good teachers' must be skilled in all three areas.

Pupils told Marsh *et al.*, (1978) that some teachers interpreted their role too literally. Such instructors were defined as 'straitlaced' and were criticized for 'putting us down . . .' and 'not knowing who pupils were' (p. 36). Woods (1979) found pupil opposition to depersonalized relationships, the growing institutionalization of school, and ultra-rule conscious teachers. Students preferred evidence of humanity from teachers and appreciated classroom humor. Jokes ease situational tensions, make relationships more intimate (Walker and Goodson, 1977), develop common frameworks of meaning (Walker and Adelman, 1976), and relieve the tedium of lessons (Stebbins, 1980).

However, students are seldom satisfied with mere 'fun and games' within classrooms. They expect to work in school. In Delamont's (1976) study of an all-girl private school, students respected the good teacher who 'makes you learn' (p. 75; see also Furlong, 1977). Davies (1982) found that in junior school 'the constant concern of the children is that work should be done' — but not just any work, for good teachers also 'explained lessons clearly, made them interesting and helped students understand the material'.

Controlling the classroom is also important to students. They disapproved of unthinking authoritarianism but respected quiet strength and teachers who ordered events to keep classes interesting and lessons comprehensible. Marsh *et al.* (1978) found that pupils felt 'insulted by weakness on the part of those in authority who they expected to be strong' (p. 38). Furlong's (1976) pupils harassed 'soft' teachers mercilessly. But students also disliked teachers who were 'too strict', 'unfair', and those who 'picked on' students (Marsh *et al.*, 1978) or 'showed them up' in class (Woods, 1979).

The general principles guiding students' evaluation of teachers are widely distributed across student populations. Another comprehensive property of student culture has to do with pupil identity. Three elements appear to affect identity: friendship, status and competence. Friendships form the structural basis of pupil life. Without close friends, one is outside the pale of student society. Friends help pupils through awkward moments in status transitions (Bryan, 1980; Galton and Delamont, 1980; Measor and Woods, 1983). Indeed, friendships are so important that some students line up 'contingency friends' to support them just in case their main allies are not available or fail them (Davies, 1982). For some, friendships are the best thing about school (Woods, 1979; Meyenn, 1980) and friendship patterns can affect students' career choices after school (Willis, 1977).

Pupils' concern with status manifests itself in several ways. Conformist pupils find status in grades and will compete with others to come out on top. Such competition even exists within 'progressive' classrooms (Sharp and Green, 1975; Denscombe, 1980b; Ball, 1981). Pupils with anti-academic values compete for status in other areas. Within 'delinquent' groups, status rests on fighting ability, skillful teacher baiting, and courage in the face of punishment (D. Hargeaves, 1967; Willis, 1977; Grundsell, 1980; Measor and Woods, 1984).

'Competence' has to do with the successful appropriation of one's preferred identity as a 'high achiever', 'one of the boys', 'ace deviant', or whatever. Students act out these parts, sometimes in exaggerated style, sometimes purely experimentally. Appearance is closely tied to identity maintenance. Battles over school uniforms and dress codes, for example, are struggles to see who controls the actual identity of students: teachers, peer groups, or individual pupils (Stone, 1962).

Without claiming that everything is known about pupil perspectives on teachers or pupils' cultural values (an unattainable state, to be sure), I would argue that we have achieved a useful breadth of view of such matters. Ethnographers continue to seek to expand such views.

## Balance

In the early 1970s, at the beginning of the new sociology movement, it was customary to do ethnographies within individual institutions. There was so much to discover that it mattered little where one began. There was concern, too, not to 'take but to make problems', that is to say, not to predefine a problem to be studied but rather allow interesting problems to emerge from within the social setting. In time, however, it became clear that some areas of school life were receiving more attention than others. As ethnographies accumulated, it became possible to spot lacunae and imbalances. Armed with this knowledge, ethnographers addressed neglected areas and redressed imbalances, insuring fuller descriptions of school life and enabling theory construction to begin.

For example, Lacey (1977) became concerned that there was within the literature an implication that teacher behavior was largely determined by external structures and situational forces. He found in Becker's (1977) work, for example, little sign of individual volition. Lacey wondered if teachers were really hapless puppets or were just being made to appear so because of the direction of studies. Lacey therefore proposed a three-part model of teacher adaptation, which included elements of teacher volition, that he hoped would stimulate research on a broader front. Further studies of teacher socialization will allow a refinement of Lacey's model, thus insuring a healthy interaction between data analysis and model construction.

Another example of how ethnography is attempting to find its own balance and maintain an interaction between data analysis and model construction is found in the area of pupil adaptation. Here we are customarily faced with broad dichotomies such as 'conformists' vs. 'non-conformists' or 'deviants'. Detailed work within schools has revealed the inadequacy of such categories. One attempt to broaden the range of pupil adaptation choices drew on the work of Merton (1957), who proposed five major models of adaptation to the social order based on combinations of acceptance and rejection of official goals and means for achieving those goals. These ranged from conformity (accepting both means and goals), through innovation (acceptance of goals, rejection of means), ritualism (rejection of goals, acceptance of means), retreatism (rejection of both goals and means), and finally to rebellion (rejection of goals and means but with the replacement of both).

Merton's functionalist model was given an interactionist twist by Wakeford (1969) and was further extended by Woods (1979). The latter linked adaptation to the personal goals of teachers and pupils and to the means available to them. As a result, Merton's categories were broadened and new attention was given to the volition of teachers and pupils in school situations.

The development of interactionist models, based in part on empirical studies and in part on hypotheses, has drawn researchers' attention to a wide range of previously ignored possibilities. Such models will inform other ethnographic work and promote theory development. It is to the latter topic that I now turn.

## Theory

Critics contend that ethnographic findings are insubstantial and trivial and provide only an 'endless description and a sequence of plausible stories' (Eldridge, 1981, p. 131). Of course, the ethnographer's interest in their subjects' perceptions necessitates the descriptive emphasis of qualitative work. However, as Denzin (1978, p. 58) warns, ethnographers must not stop at description because 'the major goal of their discipline is the development of theory'.

While it may be true that much early ethnography stopped at the level of description, it is not an inevitable consequence of the approach. Of necessity British ethnographers gave primacy to first order, rather than second order, constructs (Schutz, 1967), and worked largely on their own in discrete case studies. This last point was partly a product of the belief that all situations are unique and we can only work towards understanding each one better, as opposed to constructing generalizations that cover a number of cases — though eventually most came to be more interested in the latter. There was pressure, too, in the early stages for detailed descriptions of school process simply because they had been so neglected.

There are signs, however, that qualitative researchers are now coming to grips with the full theoretical potential of the ethnographic approach (A. Hargreaves, 1980; Hammersley, 1980; Delamont, 1981; D. Hargreaves, 1981; Woods, 1984b, 1984c). Certain areas of inquiry such as 'negotiation' and 'deviance' (Woods, 1984b) have already reached the 'saturation' point that Glaser and Strauss (1967) have shown is necessary for successful theory development. We might note that much of the work already discussed in this article is theoretical in orientation. For example, the models discussed in the previous section do not constitute full-blown explanations in themselves, but certainly facilitate explanation by providing heuristic frameworks.

Opportunities to move from what Glaser and Strauss (1967) call 'substantive' to 'formal theory' abound. For example, relationships, status, and competence are major features of teacher and pupil life (D. Hargreaves, 1980). These substantive categories have formal properties and thus applicability beyond the roles of teachers and pupils alone. They illuminate many aspects of human adaptation to institutional roles. Such adaptations have implications for identity formation and maintenance. Such insights increase the potential for a useful interplay of theory and data collection at both the substantive and formal levels.

Occasionally ethnography contributes to a theoretical tradition or line of study in both cumulative and competitive ways. An instructive example is found in the study of pupil cultures. In two early studies, D. Hargreaves (1967) and Lacey (1970) posited models of two different conflicting pupil subcultures, one pro- and one anti-school. Furlong (1976) later criticized these models for overestimating the power of subcultural norms and underestimating individual pupils' ability to define and redefine what happens in their schools. Furlong observed that pupil groups were often unstable, and those he observed he termed 'interaction sets' to emphasize their transient nature. Groups formed when pupils agreed on a particular definition of a situation and could communicate their agreement. 'The fact that different pupils take part in [different] interaction sets at different times,' says Furlong (1976, p. 169), 'simply illustrates . . . that they do not always agree about what they know. Teachers, subjects and methods of teaching mean different things to different pupils. . . .' Furlong, in turn, has been criticized for not investigating the reasons why pupils define things differently and for not relating pupils' perspectives to their goals or values or to the structure of the school (Hammersley and Turner, 1980).

Some see the work of D. Hargreaves, Lacey and Furlong as having contributed competing explanations to the prolonged debate over determinism and volition in sociology. But if we deny this polarity and see determinism and volition as different ends of a single dimension, the work of these three ethnographers may be regarded as cumulative and as an encouraging reach for balance. Studies of pupil culture may not all be concerned with the same aspect, or pitched at the same level. The fact that pupils participate in variably constituted 'interaction sets' for a multitude of different purposes does not preclude the possibility of more firmly based and durable groups associated with the internal organization of the school or social structural factors (such as social class, gender, ethnicity) without.

Ethnography is implicated in another sociological debate, namely that over the relationship between macro and micro spheres and approaches. Some critics of ethnography have claimed that it is hopelessly mired in situationalism and idealism. Again this may be true of some studies, but by no means all. An important contribution here has come from the awakening of interest in Marxism. Marxists claimed that ethnography and interactionism, did not offer satisfactory explanations on their own, but would have to take into account forces external to the school. While some Marxists abandoned ethnography altogether, others attempted to incorporate the method with dialectical theory. For example, Sharp and Green (1975), in contrasting the progressive doctrine of child-centeredness with the anti-progressive reality of much classroom life, argued that progressivism had become a rhetoric that justified the perpetuation of inequality through schooling. Well-intentioned teachers they maintained, were deeply, and often unconsciously, influenced by the wider system of control and differential opportunities endemic to capitalist society. Interactionists in their turn have criticized Sharp and Green for inadequate exploration of teachers' own constructions of meaning (D. Hargreaves, 1978; Hammersley, 1977a).

An ingenious attempt to marry ethnography and Marxism was made by Willis (1977). He portrayed the atmosphere and cultural detail of a group of twelve working-class 'lads' in an urban secondary school. Why, he wondered, do they think and behave as they do? And why do they and other working-class boys choose working-class jobs? The answer, he argued, lies in their social-class culture. Cultural forces operate as an external influence, often through families, but are actually recreated and substantially transformed by the boys themselves in response to a school situation which has structural similarities to the world of work. This is no pale acquiescence to economic determinism on the part of teenage males, as implied by Bowles and Gintis (1976). These boys, Willis maintained, actively created their own culture in a way that met the requirements of the capitalist system.

While this is generally regarded as one of the more promising attempts to link the micro and macro levels of analysis, it still leaves several teasing questions. For example, no explanation is offered for why *these* twelve boys adopted the attitudes they did, when many students of similar backgrounds chose other paths. We might note, too, that Marxism is not the only macro alternative, though it is the one that has received most attention hitherto.

No doubt the problem of linking micro and macro levels of analysis, society and the individual, structure and process will continue to exercise the minds of sociologists for some time. But as Willis's work has shown, such a linkage enriches ethnographic description and enlivens sociological theory.

## Teacher Practice

Ethnography can also lessen the distance between theory and practice in education. Sociology for many teachers is a rather abstruse, jargon-laden, theory-heavy, debunking discipline that offers little to professional educators. Some sociologists are not too concerned with such criticism and argue that the sociological task is solely to contribute knowledge at a theoretical level. They are satisfied if others apply or choose to ignore that knowledge. But other sociologists, especially those interested in changing schools, are anxious to disseminate their findings to school personnel. Ethnography could help them do this, and thus contribute to teacher professionalism because it: (a) is concerned with substantive issues that teachers recognize as their own; (b) deals with *their* problems; (c) attaches importance to their views, values, and motives; (d) takes the implications of their actions in different situations into account; and (e) even employs the concepts and language of school culture in drawing descriptions and spelling out theories. Thus, ethnography can help educators glean new insights, expand their views of reality, and balance their perspectives. Most importantly, through the emphasis on the self in the approach, as well as through any increased understanding, it can provide teachers with greater control over everyday events and hence increase their capacity to alter their own practice and instigate educational change if they wish to do so.

The practicality of ethnography for teachers is perhaps best illustrated by studies of pupil deviance. Three basic questions have been illuminated by this research. Who defines pupil behavior as deviant? Who does the deviating? And from what do they deviate (Woods 1984d)?

Insights into the first question are found in studies that focus on teacher definitions of reality. This research has found teacher differences of opinion on such matters as the nature of childhood and what constitutes 'good' and 'bad' pupils, warranted knowledge, and acceptable teaching. Teacher views on these matters has implications for their perceptions of deviance. Esland (1971), for example, draws a distinction between 'psychometric' and 'phenomenological' views of deviance. The former are underwritten by social Darwinist conceptions of childhood and learning, which define disruption as a natural evil that must be contained by rules and punishments. According to this view good pupils are docile and deferential. The phenomenological approach, by contrast, sees the child as 'a candle to be lit' rather than 'a vessel to be filled'. Here, students are expected to be active, and passive pupils are defined as deviant. Hammersley (1977a) presented a considerably extended typology.

For the purposes of some research, it is useful to define pupil deviance merely as non-compliance with teacher expectations. Several studies have shown that teachers with certain views are more likely to encounter pupil non-compliance than teachers with other views. D. Hargreaves *et al.* (1975), for example, identified two categories of teachers: 'deviance-provocative' and 'deviance-insulative'. The former group held social Darwinistic visions of childhood and pessimistic views of human nature. Such teachers issued ultimatums, took 'provocative' actions, caused classroom confrontations and punished students inconsistently. The latter group, by contrast, believed that conditions produced deviance, and when deviance occurred they attempted to change the conditions under which students worked but did not try to change the students themselves. A similar dichotomy at the school level has been noticed by Reynolds and Sullivan (1979) in two broad areas they label 'coercion' and 'incorporation'. Reynolds (1976a, 1976b) argues that school ethos (the predominant teacher group perspective) is more responsible for deviance and compliance than any other external force (see also Rutter *et al.*, 1979). Perhaps it is here where the use of dichotomies is best justified — where constellations of teachers' viewpoints come to form a school ethos.

On the question of which pupils deviate and why, we have seen the kinds of individual perspectives pupils hold regarding teachers, and the kinds of student cultures induced by school organization. A feature of such cultures is 'group perspectives', the common views or modes of interpreting the world that group members come to hold as they face common problems (Becker *et al.*, 1961). Several studies have found that group perspectives influence student choices at crucial periods in their careers, for example, in their choice of subjects and occupations. The research suggests that the group perspectives that influence these choices are linked to students' social class backgrounds (Ashton, 1973; Woods, 1979; Ball, 1981; Taylor, 1980). Such studies lend support to those of Sharp and Green (1975), Willis (1977), Anyon (1981a, 1981b), and Connell *et al.* (1982), which are more pointedly concerned with social class and its effects.

More recently, attention has turned to gender differences, and it has been discovered that, contrary to expected beliefs, girls deviate from school norms just as often as boys, though not so ostentatiously. The research also shows that the demands of a feminine gender code influence girls' academic performance. For example, girls are socialized toward certain subjects (the arts, home economics, needle crafts, typing and commerce) and away from others (the sciences, other than biology; woodwork and metal work; see Kelly, 1981). And in general, girls are encouraged to underachieve because academic success does not accord with the popular image of femininity (Sharpe, 1976; Deem, 1978; Byrne, 1978; Measor and Woods, 1984). These values are promulgated by family, media, pop culture (McRobbie and Garber 1976; McRobbie, 1980; Ball, 1981), peer group (Meyenn, 1980; Llewellyn, 1980), and teachers (Llewellyn, 1980; Spender and Sarah, 1980; Stanworth, 1983).

What is it that disruptive students disrupt? More than official codes or rules imposed from above, they appear to disrupt the peaceful equilibrium that students and teachers mutually define and maintain. This equilibrium has been variously represented as 'truce' (Reynolds, 1976a), 'aided colonization' (Woods, 1979), 'negotiation' (Delamont, 1976; Martin, 1976; Woods, 1978; Ball, 1980; Turner, 1982), 'working consensus' (D. Hargreaves, 1972; Pollard, 1979), 'bargaining' (Werthman, 1963), 'avoidance of provocation' (Stebbins, 1970) and 'confrontation avoidance' (A. Hargreaves, 1979). The last two labels are of a different order from the others because they are associated with teacher control techniques that can lead to deviance amplification (Lemert, 1967; J. Young, 1971; Cohen, 1972; Bird *et al.*, 1981). Negotiative equilibrium is about the construction of order in which both sides participate, though they may do so subconsciously. It will be seen that if teachers deviate from this delicately balanced, jointly accepted, heavily implicit structure of social relations which has been worked out over time through practice, it will in itself invite pupil retaliation (Werthman, 1963; Marsh *et al.*, 1978; Tattum, 1982).

Equilibrium might have been negotiated after a considerable period of disorder. For example, pupils may systematically 'test out' new or inexperienced teachers to gain leverage in the negotiation process (Ball, 1980; Beynon, 1984; Measor and Woods, 1984). A negotiated equilibrium is continually threatened by external cultural forces operating on pupils and situational constraints pressing on teachers. With regard to the latter, Chessum (1980), for example, has shown how teachers can take a reflective stance regarding student disruption, but in particular instances may resort to a 'personal and family pathology of disaffection' or a 'hard core' theory of deviance, both of which deny any rationality or legitimacy to pupil deviance (see also Keddie, 1971).

Bringing these underlying realities to the surface is potentially of great assistance to teacher practice, since it aids diagnosis. And, as with medicine, with the correct diagnosis, one is half way toward a cure.


## Reflectivity


Ethnography can also contribute to educational practice and teacher satisfaction through its reflective possibilities. Interactionists employ Mead's (1934) conception of selfhood that emphasizes the importance of a continual dialogue between the 'I' and the 'me' and between the 'self' and the 'other'. So as well as improved purchase on one's own views, interactionism carries considerable democratic advantage through its enhanced appreciation of others' points of view. For example, pupils' perceptions of being 'shown up' or 'picked on', 'having a laugh', 'dossing', 'blagging and wagging', 'bunking off' and even 'doing nothing', are presented in ethnography not as examples of anarchism, but as having priority, deep meaning, and rationality in the lives of pupils (Willis, 1977; Furlong, 1976; Woods, 1979; Corrigan, 1976; Turner, 1982).

With regard to the teacher self, recent ethnography has emphasized the 'making' rather than 'taking' of roles (Turner, 1962; Woods, 1981). This recognition of an element of volition is both optimistic and realistic. It recognizes the difficulties confronting teachers but holds out the prospect of their negotiating their way through their difficulties, though, admittedly, the passage may be tortuous. In consequence, ethnographers have become much interested in teacher interests, and their strategies for furthering them. Pollard (1980), for example, discussed the importance of self-image (maintaining a desired image of self as one pragmatically adapts to situational necessities); work load (monitoring one's effort and the need to conserve energy); health and stress (job hazards to be avoided); enjoyment (teachers also appreciate 'a laugh'); autonomy, order and instruction (maintaining personal independence, order and the freedom to teach). Pollard argues that teacher survival depends on achieving a balance of interest satisfaction and that they will 'juggle' their interests in order to maintain such an equilibrium. This strategy is similar to the 'trade-off' decisions teachers make when confronted by situational dilemmas (Berlak and Berlak, 1981). Elsewhere, ethnographers have become greatly interested in 'coping strategies' (Lacey, 1977; A. Hargreaves, 1978; Woods, 1979, 1981; Pollard, 1982), for they allow a consideration of the constraints operating on teachers, the teacher's own biography, interests and personal resources, and how teachers go about constructing action.

There are inevitably varieties of adaptation to the teacher role and different forms and levels of commitment to the job. Three main types of commitment have been noted in the research: vocational (involving a set of ideals about education and society that have little to do with teaching as such), professional (involving a career in a school and subject-based teaching), and career-continuance (a more utilitarian stance that seeks money, prestige or fringe benefits). The exposition of these types might encourage teachers to examine their own motives for teaching (Lacey, 1977; Woods, 1979, 1981; Nias, 1981). Life history research (Woods, 1984a) might encourage teachers to consider the bearing their own biographies have had on their teaching practices and career choices.

Ethnographers are more interested in subjective than in objective careers (Hughes, 1937; Becker, 1976). Again, teachers can identify personally with such investigations. They will certainly recall the trauma of initial socialization into the teacher role (Fuchs, 1969; Hannam *et al.*, 1971; Hanson and Herrington, 1976), the pressure to keep down classroom 'noise' regardless of its relationship to learning if they wished to be regarded as 'proper teachers' (Denscombe, 1980a), and the need to take on extra activities to facilitate advancement (Lacey, 1970). They will recognize the 'career maps', 'time tables', 'bench marks' and 'gatekeepers' of careers identified in the traditional interactionist literature (Lyons, 1981). But they will also feel the upheaval in these areas caused by the reorganization of the secondary school system, falling student enrollments, and the economic crisis.

While the first of these may have enhanced some teachers' careers, offering opportunities that were not there formerly, for others it has spoiled careers (Goffman, 1961). Riseborough (1981) gives the example of a group of ex-secondary modern school teachers who were demoted in status in a new comprehensive school in favor of younger teachers who were much less experienced but more highly qualified. These displaced teachers now gained little satisfaction from their work and formed an isolated clique that gained its psychological rewards by opposing the head master at every opportunity.

The general contraction of the education system is beginning to squeeze teachers' careers in other ways. Some face redundancy (lay-offs) or forced early retirement. Some, who saw far horizons when they joined the profession in the 1960s, now find their careers stuck at a particular point. Current work employing life history techniques is mapping out teachers' responses to this situation (Sikes, 1984a, 1984b; Measor, 1984a; Measor *et al.* 1984). One might argue that this kind of ethnography has a therapeutic value (indeed, many teachers say they enjoy talking freely and frankly to researchers). Life history research certainly has a broadcasting function, disseminating news about other individuals and the profession in general, in terms that teachers can understand and identify with personally. Perhaps it may also reveal some solutions.

## Some Problems in Ethnography

I have concentrated on the strengths and achievements of ethnographic work in Britain as I see them, but the ethnographic approach is not without its problems. I have touched on one or two of these, such as the micro–macro problem (a common issue in sociology) and the over, though not inevitable, concern with empiricism. One aspect of the latter is its alleged exclusive concentration on the present, or at least on the period covering the ethnographer's study, so that one might argue that the report is not a life-like image at all, but a snapshot frozen in time. Again, this is not inevitable. Indeed, some studies, though they are all too few, have shown the benefits of a wider contextualization (Lacey, 1970).

The snapshot problem arises from the nature of the method, with its traditional approach of one researcher doing one case study at a time. There are limits to what one person can achieve. As it is, most case study ethnographies seem marked, not by relaxed and systematic data gatherings, but by a muddling through and a frustrating sense that the really important action is happening elsewhere. One solution to this problem is some form of coordinated team work (Hammersley, 1980; Woods, 1984b). Not only would team work enable a division of labor, it would also allow many-sided issues to be put in better perspective and thus improve validity. For though ethnographic methodology has undoubtedly been made more rigorous (see Hammersley and Atkinson, 1983), it is very difficult for researchers not to indulge in selective perception. If two or more ethnographers are at work in the same area, they can check and balance one another's research (Measor, 1984a). However, while this may sound fine in theory, it militates against the highly personalized nature of ethnography.

Another recent development, in part inspired by the ahistorical nature of most ethnographies, is the use of life histories (Goodson, 1980; Woods, 1984e). Goodson argues that these 'set against the background of evolutionary patterns of schooling and teaching should provide an antidote to the depersonalized, ahistorical accounts of schooling to which we have become accustomed' (p. 74). Woods (1984e) argues that life histories are at their strongest when combined with ethnography or when they develop out of it. There are, after all, so many similarities between the two methods (for example, their forms of validation, use of key informants, and methods of analysis) that they might be considered as one. They then begin from strength, from a grounding in the present, whereas a constant danger in these follow-your-nose techniques is a continual attenuation of data. Life histories offer the added advantage of deep teacher involvement, thus increasing the potential for teacher reflection, and offering opportunities for closing the traditional gap teachers perceive between theory and practice. At a time when 'action research' (research which teachers themselves do within their own schools in response to their own problems) is becoming more and more popular (perhaps not only through a desire for increased professionalism but also as a kind of alternative career in view of the growing blockage discussed above), the increased use of life histories could contain many benefits for teachers and an improved methodology for ethnographers. The growing popularity of life history research was made evident when a recent conference at St Hilda's College, Oxford, was devoted to its consideration (Ball and Goodson, 1984).

An abiding problem in the ethnographic 'movement' is the coordination of studies. Again, the nature of the approach, with its emphasis in the individual case study, militates against coordination of findings. But there is little point in continually discovering the same thing or adding endlessly to the long line of examples of a well grounded concept. I have distinguished here between Stage 1 and Stage 2 studies (Woods, 1984b). The former are empirical studies, which do not usually proceed beyond the substantive theory. The latter are coordinating and analytical studies which examine a range of ethnographies on similar substantive issues, aim to produce a formal theory, and thus establish a firm theoretical base for a new wave of ethnographies. As we showed earlier, Stage 2 studies are under way, but more work in this area needs to be done.

Like their theoretical forebears in the Chicago school, current ethnographers in Britain have been accused of concentrating almost exclusively upon people in low power positions and of championing and sometimes romanticizing the underdog. Ethnographers seemed preoccupied for a long time with groups of deviant pupils, ignoring large masses of presumably 'conformist' students (Turner, 1982). Nor are there any ethnographies, for example, of head teachers and their deputies, or of administrators' offices, or of governing bodies; yet these are areas where many important decisions are made and upon which the whole fate of the school depends. This neglect is partly due, no doubt, to the ease of researcher access to people in low-power situations, and the comparative difficulty they have gaining access to the more powerful, and perhaps also due to an inbuilt sympathy for and identification with the underdog. However, even if researchers choose to take the underdog's side, perhaps more especially if they do, they must work to penetrate the corridors of power.

Ethnographers have also been accused of neglecting the power variable. The charge is not entirely true. As we have seen, some researchers are at pains to link their work to a wider systems perspective which embraces the impact of broad social forces. And at the situational level, much negotiation in interpersonal relationships is about the exercise of power. Ethnography is not necessarily a bland, apolitical study, or one which implicitly supports the status quo. This will be more evident, however, as ethnographers address their work more directly to formal theory, macro events and the political powerful.

Much remains to be done, therefore. Ethnography in itself is not a complete program, nor is it a perfect one. Further ethnographers will continue to refine methodology, map out hidden areas, work at developing theory, examine the micro–macro interface, and seek alliance with other related methodologies. However, I believe we can justly claim that a start has been made.

## References

ANYON, J. (1981a). 'Elementary schooling and distinctions of social class'. *Interchange*, *12* (1–3), 118–132.

ANYON, J. (1981b). 'Social class and school knowledge'. *Curriculum Inquiry, 11* (1), 3–42.

ASHTON, D. N. (1973). 'The transition from school to work'. In G. Esland, G. Salaman and M. Speakman (Eds), *People and Work*. Edinburgh: Holmes McDougall.

ATKINSON, P. A. and DELAMONT, S. (1977). 'Mock-ups and cock-ups: The stage-management of guided discovery instruction'. In P. Woods and M. Hammersley (Eds), *School Experience*. London: Croom Helm.

BALL, S. (1980). 'Initial encounters in the classroom and the process of establishment'. In P. Woods, (Ed.), *Pupil Strategies*. London: Croom Helm.

BALL, S. (1981). *Beachside Comprehensive*. Cambridge: Cambridge University Press.

BALL, S. and GOODSON, I. (1984). *Teacher Careers and Life Histories*. Lewes: Falmer Press.

BARNES, D. (1976). *From Communication to Curriculum*. Harmondsworth: Penguin.

BECKER, H. S. (1976). 'The career of the Chicago public schoolteacher'. In M. Hammersley and P. Woods (Eds.), *The Process of Schooling*. London: Routledge and Kegan Paul.

BECKER, H. S. (1977). 'Personal change in adult life'. In B. Cosin *et al.* (Eds.), *Schooling and Society* (2nd ed.). London: Routledge and Kegan Paul.

BECKER, H. S., GEER, B., HUGHES, E. C. and STRAUSS, A. L. (1961). *Boys in White*. Chicago: University of Chicago Press.

BERLACK, A. and BERLACK, H. (1981). *The Dilemmas of Schooling*. London: Methuen.

BEYNON, J (1984). ' "Sussing-out" teachers: Pupils as data gatherers'. In M. Hammersley and P. Woods (Eds), *Life in School: The Sociology of Pupil Culture*. Milton Keynes: Open University Press.

BIRD, C., CHESSUM, R., FURLONG, J. and JOHNSON, D. (1981). *Disaffected Pupils*. Educational Studies Unit. Department of Government, Brunel University, UK.

BIRKSTED, I. K. (1976a). 'School performance seen from the boys'. *Sociological Review*. *24* (1) (N.S.), 63–77.

BIRKSTED, I. K. (1976b). 'School versus pop culture? A case study of adolescent adaptation'. *Research in Education, 16* (November).

BOWLES, S. and GINTIS, H. (1976). *Schooling in Capitalist America: Educational Review and the Contradictions of Economic Life*. London: Routledge and Kegan Paul.

BRYAN, K. (1980). 'Pupil perceptions of transfer between middle and high schools'. In A. Hargreaves and L. Tickle (Eds), *Middle Schools: Origins, Ideology and Practice*. London: Harper and Row.

BRUYN, S. T. (1966). *The Human Perspectives in Sociology: The Methodology of Participant Observation*. Englewood Cliffs, NJ: Prentice Hall.

BYRNE, E. M. (1978). *Women and Education*. London: Tavistock.

CHESSUM, R. (1980). 'Teacher ideologies and pupil disaffection'. In L. Barton, R. Meighan and S. Walker (Eds), *Schooling, Ideology and the Curriculum*. Lewes: Falmer Press.

COHEN, S. (1972). *Folk Devils and Moral Panics*. London: Paladin.

CONNELL, R. W., ASHENDEN, D. J., KESSLER, S. and DOWSETT, G. W. (1982). *Making the Difference: Schools, Families and Social Division*. Sydney: George Allen and Unwin.

CORBISHLEY, P., EVANS, J., KENRICK, C. and DAVIES, B. (1981). 'Teacher strategies and pupil identities in mixed ability curricula: A note on concepts and some examples from maths'. In L. Barton and S. Walker (Eds), *Schools, Teachers and Teaching*. Lewes: Falmer Press.

CORRIGAN, P. (1976). 'Doing nothing'. In S. Hall and T. Jefferson (Eds.), *Resistance through Ritual*. London: Hutchinson.

DAVIES, S. (1982). *Life in the Classroom and Playground*. London: Routledge and Kegan Paul.

DEEM, R. (1978). *Women and Schooling*. London: Routledge and Kegan Paul.

DELAMONT, S. (1976). *Interaction in the Classrooms*. London: Methuen.

DELAMONT, S. (1981). 'All too familiar? A decade of classroom research'. *Educational Analysis*, *3* (1), 69–83.

DENSCOMBE, M. (1980a). ' "Keeping 'em quiet": The significance of noise for the practical activity of teaching'. In P. Woods (Ed.), *Teacher Strategies*. London: Croom Helm.

DENSCOMBE, M. (1980b). 'Pupil strategies and the open classroom'. In P. Woods (Ed.), *Pupil Strategies*. London: Croom Helm.

DENZIN, N. (1978). *The Research Act in Sociology: A Theoretical Introduction to Sociological Methods*. London: Butterworths.

EDWARDS, A. D. and FURLONG, V. J. (1978). *The Language of Teaching*. London: Heinemann.

ELDRIDGE, J. (1981). *Recent British Sociology*. London: Macmillan.

ESLAND, G. M. (1971). 'Teaching and learning as the organization of knowledge'. In M. F. D. Young (Ed.), *Knowledge and Control*. London: Collier-Macmillan.

FUCHS, E. (1969). *Teachers Talk*. New York: Anchor.

FURLONG, J. (1976). 'Interaction sets in the classroom'. In M. Hammersley and P. Woods (Eds), *The Process of Schooling*. London: Routledge and Kegan Paul.

FURLONG, J. (1977). 'Anancy goes to school: A case study of pupils' knowledge of their teachers'. In P. Woods and M. Hammersley (Eds.), *School Experience*. London: Croom Helm.

GALTON, M. and DELAMONT, S. (1980). 'The first weeks of middle school'. In A. Hargreaves and L. Tickle (Eds), *Middle Schools: Origins, Ideology and Practice*. London: Harper and Row.

GLASER, B. G. and STRAUSS, A. L. (1967). *The Discovery of Grounded Theory*. London: Weidenfelt and Nicolson.

GOFFMAN, E. (1961). *Asylums*. Garden City, N.Y.: Doubleday; and Harmondsworth: Penguin (1968).

GOODSON, I. (1975). 'The teachers' curriculum and the new reformation'. *Journal of Curriculum Studies*, *7* (2) 160–169.

GOODSON, I. (1980). 'Life histories and the study of schooling'. *Interchange*, *2* (4), 62–76.

GRUNDSELL, R. (1980). *Beyond Control: Schools and Suspension*. London: Writers and Readers.

HAMMERSLEY, M. (1974). 'The organization of pupil participation'. *Sociological Review*, *22* (3) 355–368.

HAMMERSLEY, M. (1976). 'The mobilization of pupil attention'. In M. Hammersley and P. Woods (Eds), *The Process of Schooling*. London: Routledge and Kegan Paul.

HAMMERSLEY, M. (1977a). *Teacher Perspectives*, Unit 9 of Course *E202*, 'Schooling and Society'. Milton Keynes: Open University Press.

HAMMERSLEY, M. (1977b). 'School learning: The cultural resources required by pupils to answer a teacher's question'. In P. Woods and M. Hammersley (Eds), *School Experience*. London: Croom Helm.

HAMMERSLEY, M. (1980). 'On interactionist empiricism'. in P. Woods (Ed.), *Pupil Strategies*. London: Croom Helm.

HAMMERSLEY, M. and ATKINSON, P. (1983). *Ethnography: Principles into Practice*. London: Tavistock.

HAMMERSLEY, M. and TURNER, G. (1980). 'Conformist pupils?' In P. Woods (Ed.), *Pupil Strategies*. London: Croom Helm.

HANNAM, C., SMYTH, P. and STEPHENSON, N. (1971). *Young Teachers and Reluctant Learners*. Harmondsworth: Penguin.

HANSON, D. and HERRINGTON, M. (1976). *From College to Classroom: The Probationary Year*. London: Routledge and Kegan Paul.

HARGREAVES, A. (1977). 'Progressivism and pupil autonomy'. *Sociological Review*, (August).

HARGREAVES, A. (1978). 'Towards a theory of classroom coping strategies'. In L. Barton and R. Meighan (Eds), *Sociological Interpretations of Schooling and Classrooms*. Driffield: Nafferton.

HARGREAVES, A. (1979). 'Strategies, decisions and control: Interaction in a middle school classroom'. In J. Eggleston (Ed.), *Teacher Decision-Making in the Classroom*. London: Routledge and Kegan Paul.

HARGREAVES, A. (1980). 'Synthesis and the study of strategies: A project for the sociological imagination'. In P. Woods (Ed.), *Pupil Strategies*. London: Croom Helm.

HARGREAVES, D. H. (1967). *Social Relations in a Secondary School*. London: Routledge and Kegan Paul.

HARGREAVES, D. H. (1972). *Interpersonal Relations and Education*. London: Routledge and Kegan Paul.

HARGREAVES, D. H. (1978). 'Whatever happened to symbolic interactionism?' In L. Barton and R. Meighan (Eds), *Sociological Interpretations of Schooling and Classrooms: A Reappraisal*. Driffield: Nafferton.

HARGREAVES, D. H. (1980). 'The occupational culture of teachers'. In P. Woods (Ed.), *Teacher Strategies*. London: Croom Helm.

HARGREAVES, D. H. (1981). 'Schooling for delinquency'. In L. Barton and S. Walker (Eds), *Schools, Teachers and Teaching*. Lewes: Falmer Press.

HARGREAVES, D. H., HESTER, S. K. and MELLOR, F. J. (1975). *Deviance in Classrooms*. London: Routledge and Kegan Paul.

HUGHES, E. C. (1937). 'Institutional office and the person'. In E. C. Hughes, *Men and their Work*. New York: Free Press.

KEDDIE, N. (1971). 'Classroom knowledge'. In M. F. D. Young (Ed.), *Knowledge and Control*. London: Collier-Macmillan.

KELLY, A. (Ed.). (1981). *Missing Half: Girls and Science Education*. Manchester: University Press.

LACEY, C. (1970). *Hightown Grammar*. Manchester: University Press.

LACEY, C. (1977). *The Socialization of Teachers*. London: Methuen.

LEMERT, E. (1967). *Human Deviance: Social Problems and Social Control*. Englewood Cliffs, NJ: Prentice Hall.

LLEWELLYN, M. (1980). 'Studying girls at school: The implications of confusion'. In R. Deem (Ed.), *Schooling for Women's Work*. London: Routledge and Kegan Paul.

LYONS, G. (1981). *Teacher Careers and Career Perceptions*. Slough: National Foundation for Educational Research.

MARSH, P., ROSSER, E. and HARRÉ, R. (1978). *The Rules of Disorder*. London: Routledge and Kegan Paul.

MARTIN, W. B. W. (1976). *The Negotiated Order of the School*. Toronto: Macmillan.

McROBBIE, A. (1980). 'Settling accounts with sub-cultures: A feminist critique'. *Screen Education, 34* (Spring).

McROBBIE, A. and GARBER, J. (1976). 'Girls and subcultures'. In S. Hall and T. Jefferson (Eds), *Resistance through Rituals*. London: Hutchinson.

MEAD, G. H. (1934). *Mind, Self and Society*. Chicago: University of Chicago Press.

MEASOR, L. (1984a). 'Interviewing in ethnographic research'. In R. Burgess (Ed.), *Qualitative Methodology and the Study of Education*. Lewes: Falmer Press.

MEASOR, L. (1984b). 'Critical periods'. In S. Ball and I. Goodson, (Eds), *Life Histories and Teacher Careers*. Lewes: Falmer Press.

MEASOR, L., SIKES, P. and WOODS, P. (1984). *Careers in Crisis*. Lewes: Falmer Press.

MEASOR, L. and WOODS, P. (1983). 'The interpretation of pupil myths'. In M. Hammersley (Ed.), *The Ethnography of Schooling*. Driffield: Nafferton.

MEASOR, L. and WOODS, P. (1984). *The Sociology of Pupil Transfer*. Milton Keynes: Open University Press.

MERTON, R. (1957). *Social Theory and Social Structure*. Glencoe, IL: Free Press.

MEYENN, R. (1980). 'School girls' peer groups'. In P. Woods (Ed.), *Pupil Strategies*. London: Croom Helm.

NIAS, J. (1981). 'Commitment and motivation in primary school teachers'. *Educational Review, 33* (3), 181–190.

POLLARD, A. (1979). 'Negotiating deviance and "getting done" in primary school classrooms'. In L. Barton and R. Meighan, (Eds), *Schools, Pupils and Deviance*. Driffield: Nafferton.

POLLARD, A. (1980). 'Teacher interests and changing situations of survival threat in primary school classrooms'. In P. Woods (Ed.), *Teacher Strategies*. London: Croom Helm.

POLLARD, A. (1982). 'A model of coping strategies'. *British Journal of Sociology of Education, 3* (1), 19–37.

REYNOLDS, D. (1967a). 'When teachers and pupils refuse a truce'. In G. Mungham and G. Pearson (Eds), *Working Class Youth Culture*. London: Routledge and Kegan Paul.

REYNOLDS, D. (1967b). 'The delinquent school'. In M. Hammersley and P. Woods (Eds), *The Process of Schooling*. London: Routledge and Kegan Paul.

REYNOLDS, D. and SULLIVAN, M. (1979). 'Bringing schools back'. In L. Barton and R. Meighan (Eds), *Schools, Pupils and Deviance*. Driffield: Nafferton.

RISEBOROUGH, G. F. (1981). 'Teacher careers and comprehensive schooling: An empirical study'. *Sociology, 15* (3), 352–381.

RUTTER, M., MAUGHAM, B., MORTIMORE, P. and OUSTON, J. (1979). *Fifteen Thousand Hours*. London: Open Books.

SCHUTZ, A. (1967). *The Phenomenology of the Social World* (G. Walsh and F. Lehnert, Trans.). New York: Northwestern University Press.

Sharp, R. and Green, A. (1975). *Education and Social Control*. London: Routledge and Kegan Paul.

Sharpe, S. (1976). *Just Like a Girl*. Harmondsworth: Penguin.

Sikes, P. (1984a). 'Teacher careers in the comprehensive school'. In S. Ball (Ed.), *Comprehensive Schooling: A Reader*. Lewes: Falmer Press.

Sikes, P. (1984b). 'The life cycle of the teacher'. In S. Ball and I. Goodson (Eds), *Life Histories and Teacher Careers*. Lewes: Falmer Press.

Spender, D. and Sarah, E. (Eds). (1980). *Learning to Lose: Sexism and Education*. London: The Women's Press.

Stanworth, M. (1983). *Gender and Schooling*. London: Hutchinson.

Stebbins, R. A. (1970). 'The meaning of disorderly behaviour: Teacher definitions of a classroom situation'. *Sociology of Education, 44*, 217–236.

Stebbins, R. A. (1980). 'The role of humour in teaching'. In P. Woods (Ed.), *Teacher Strategies*. London: Croom Helm.

Stone, G. (1962). 'Appearance and the self'. In A. M. Rose (Ed.), *Human Behaviour and Social Processes*. Boston: Houghton Mifflin.

Stubbs, M. (1976). *Language, Schools and Classrooms*. London: Wiley.

Tattum, D. P. (1982). *Disruptive Pupils in Schools and Units*. London: Wiley.

Taylor, S. (1980). 'School experience and student perspectives: A study of some effects of secondary school organization'. *Educational Review, 32* (1), 37–52.

Tuckwell, P. (1982). Pleasing Teacher. In T. Booth and J. Stathan (Eds), *The Nature of Special Education*. London: Croom Helm.

Turner, G. (1982). *Social Life in a Comprehensive School*. London: Croom Helm.

Turner, R. H. (1962). 'Role-taking: Process versus conformity'. In A. M. Rose (Ed.), *Human Behaviour and Social Processes*. London: Routledge and Kegan Paul.

Wakeford, J. (1969). *The Cloistered Elite: A Sociological Analysis of the English Public Boarding School*. London: Macmillan.

Walker, R. and Adelman, C. (1976). 'Strawberries'. In M. Stubbs and S. Delamont (Eds), *Explorations in Classroom Observation*. Chichester: Wiley.

Walker, R. and Goodson, I. (1977). 'Humour in the Classroom'. In P. E. Woods and M. Hammersley (Eds), *School Experience*. London: Croom Helm.

Werthman, C. (1963). 'Delinquents in schools: A test for the legitimacy of authority'. *Berkeley Journal of Sociology, 8* (1), 39–60.

Willis, P. (1977). *Learning to Labour*. Farnborough: Saxon House.

Woods, P. (1978). 'Negotiating the demands of schoolwork'. *Journal of Curriculum Studies, 10* (4), 309–327.

Woods, P. (1979). *The Divided School*. London: Routledge and Kegan Paul.

Woods, P. (1981). 'Strategies, commitment and identity: Making and breaking the teacher role'. In L. Barton and S. Walker (Eds), *Schools, Teachers and Teaching*. Lewes: Falmer Press.

Woods, P. (1984a). 'Teacher self and curriculum'. In S. Ball and I. Goodson (Eds), *Defining the Curriculum: Histories and Ethnographies of School Subjects*. Lewes: Falmer Press.

Woods, P. (1984b). 'Ethnography and theory construction in educational research'. In R. Burgess (Ed.), *Field Methods in the Study of Education*. Lewes: Falmer Press.

Woods, P. (1984c). 'New songs played skillfully: Creativity and technique in writing-up'. In R. Burgess (Ed.), *Qualitative Methodology and the Study of Education*. Lewes: Falmer Press.

WOODS, P. (1984d). 'A sociology of disruptive incidents'. In N. Frude and H. Gault (Eds), *Children's Aggression at School*. London: Wiley.

WOODS, P. (1984e). 'Conversations with teachers: Aspects of the life history method'. *British Educational Research Journal, 10* (2).

YOUNG, J. (1971). 'The role of the police as amplifiers of deviancy, negotiators of reality, and translators of fantasy'. In S. Cohen (Ed.), *Images of Deviance*. Harmondsworth: Penguin.

YOUNG, M. F. D. (Ed.). (1971). *Knowledge and Control*. London: Collier-Macmillan.

*Chapter 8*

# Putting Life into Educational Research

*Ivor Goodson*
*University of Western Ontario*
*London, Ontario N6A 3K7*
*Canada*

*Rob Walker*
*Deakin University*
*Belmont, Victoria 3217*
*Australia*

I experience the world within my actual reach as an element or phase of my unique biographical situation, and this involves a transcending of the Here and Now to which it belongs. (Schutz, 1962, p. 308).

In Britain, beginning in the early 1970s, there has been a considerable and growing interest within educational research and evaluation in the development of an ethnographic tradition. In part stimulated by changes in emphasis within sociology, and also spurred by the curriculum reform movement, a number of books, papers, and reports have advocated or practised such work. A survey of the field would include the work of Stubbs and Delamont (1976), Delamont and Chanan (1975), Hamilton *et al.* (1977), MacDonald and Walker (1974), Woods (1979), Pollard (1985), Hargreaves (1967), Willis (1977), and Sharp and Green (1975). While each of these studies have their distinctive styles and address particular audiences and concerns, it remains the case that they can be identified broadly as part of a 'qualitative' or 'naturalistic' research tradition.

In the United States the emphasis has tended to be on the classroom rather than the school, but there also has been a move to self-styled 'ethnographic' research. The work of Jackson (1968), Smith and Geoffrey (1968), Smith and Keith (1971), Henry (1963), Spindler (1982), Wolcott (1967), Rist (1978), and Stake and Easley (1977) is representative. As this work has accumulated, we have felt a growing sense of unease about the emergence of an abstracted, often ahistoric, and a depersonalized perspective, not always in the original studies, but often in attempts to generalize from them.

By chance we became interested in the work of Bob Pegg, who has been studying folk music at the Institute of Dialect and Folk Music at Leeds

University. By quoting from outside education, we hope to underline the fact that the pervasive difficulties encountered in educational studies are part of a much broader problem in the way that research is undertaken in this society. Pegg says:

> The right to select lies not with the folklorist ('Sorry old chap, can't have that — it's not a folk song'), but with the singer. Today's collector must have no preconceptions. His job is to record a people's music, whether it is a traditional ballad or a hymn or a musical song or last week's pop hit!

With this basic attitude comes another revelation:

> I began to realise that, for me, the people who sang the songs were more important than the songs themselves. The song is only a small part of the singer's life and the life was usually very fascinating. There was no way I felt I could understand the songs without knowing something about the life of the singer, which does not seem to apply in the case of most folklorists. They are quite happy to find material which fits into a preconceived cannon and leave it at that. I had to know what people thought about the songs, what part they played in their lives and in the lives of the community.

A similar point is made by the folksong collector Robin Morton (quoted in Madaus and McDonagh, 1982):

> The opinion grew in me that it was *in* the singer that the song becomes relevant. Analyzing it in terms of motif, or rhyming structure, or minute variation becomes, in my view, sterile if the one who carries the particular song is forgotten. We have all met the scholar who can talk for hours in a very learned fashion about folksongs and folklore in general, without once mentioning the singer. Bad enough to forget the social context, but to ignore the individual context castrates the song. As I got to know the singers, so I got to know and understand their songs more fully.

The preoccupation with 'the singer, not the song' needs to be seriously tested in ethnographic studies. This paper thus will argue that biographical material on teachers should be an integral part of accounts of classroom life.

## A Comment on Research

What Pegg and Morton say about folklorists and implicitly about the way their research is received by those they research, we feel could also be said about most educational research that goes on in Britain. That research tends to be highly esoteric and its findings inaccessible, except to those with specialized knowledge; inaccessible, that is, particularly to those researched. The major reason for this inaccessibility is that the research deals with the preconceptions of the researcher, not the researched. This happens because the context in which the research is planned is largely the research community itself and not the world of educational practitioners who are being researched. The reputation that practitioners ascribe to educational research — irrelevance, secrecy, and egocentricity among researchers — stems from the establishment of an impersonal relationship with the researched. The impersonal relationship is maintained in part to insure 'objectivity', but objectivity has become a distorted concept. Originally it was thought to be necessary in order to reduce the impact of the researcher's bias, but now it has come also to imply the alienation of the 'subject' from the process of the study.

Because of the researcher's strong commitment to a particular view of objectivity, as well as a sense of purpose to which the subject is generally denied access, minimal contact between the researcher and the researched is likely. The traditional research model defines the interaction of researched and researcher in a rather formal act of role-playing. This formal interaction severely constrains not only what the researcher can see but what can be effected. Without the understanding that can be developed only by a close personal relationship between researcher and researched, the researcher will inevitably miss important parts of the puzzle. Anthropologists recognize this in the distinction they make between 'emic' and 'etic' accounts, a distinction first noted by Kenneth Pike (1954–60) from reflection on his work as *both* an ethnolinguist *and* as a missionary (for a discussion of Pike's work, see Harris, 1964).

We suspect that what the impersonal researcher largely gets hold of is the subject's chosen presentation of self to an idea of the 'stereotype-researcher'. But Pegg's views take us further than these criticisms, which have been voiced before. Pegg says that it is not simply the researcher's procedure that gets in the way of the pursuit of data; the kind of data pursued also gets in the way. We are dealing with an overall conception as well as specific preconceptions. If we accept Pegg's contention that 'the people who sing the songs are more important than the songs themselves' and that 'there [is] no way [to] understand the songs without knowing about the life of the singer', and we believe we must accept it, then the objective, impersonal idea of traditional research itself is a major part of the problem. The shift from 'etic' to 'emic' accounts is not simply a methodological shift; it has ethical consequences.

Like Pegg, we suggest that to a great degree the right to introduce and define issues should lie with those being researched (i.e., 'not with the folklorist, but with the singer'). Further, we contend that the people who are researched are more important than any detached analysis of their actions ('The people who sing the songs are more important than the songs themselves'). The result of these beliefs would be a more collaborative, personalized (some might even say fraternized) vision of research. The focus moves away from psychometric pursuit of numbers and categories, away too from compartmentalized interaction studies, and toward a deeper engagement with the teacher's (or the child's) biography and lifestyle. Without movement into these areas (and the intrusive nature of the methods must be faced squarely), research will remain firmly locked into tacit 'no trespassing' arrangements which will preserve the phenomenon of the 'two worlds'.

## School Ethnographies

Having rid ourselves of this broad polemical comment on educational research in general, let us focus now on the ethnography of schooling. In many ethnographic studies of schools, classroom interaction, or in Pegg's terms 'the song', is placed firmly at the centre of both data collection and final reportage. While some studies of pupils' experience of school do show some concern with alternative definitions which underlie the formal definition of the situation (Armstrong, 1980; Rowland, 1983), few accounts of the teachers' role in the classroom show any concern with their alternative views. Hence the singer is viewed simply in terms of his or her songs, not in terms of his or her *life* or possible alternative definitions of the situation.

In one sense this myopia is justifiable, for the common elements of classroom interaction over time are indeed worthy of considerable comment and study. However, the basic assumption of timelessness which pervades many ethnographic accounts is misleading, for it suggests a simplification of the possibilities that underlie apparent formal similarity. The assumption of timelessness characterizes many classroom accounts. For instance, it is a pervasive factor in Philip Jackson's (1968) work on life in classrooms. Jackson says:

> . . . not only is the classroom a relatively stable physical environment, it also provides a fairly constant social context. Behind the same old desks sit the same old students; in front of the familiar blackboard stands the familiar teacher.

It is equally an assumption in the very different studies reported in *Mirrors for Behaviour* (Simon and Boyer, 1970).

We do not deny the significance of history, but it is important not to let historical determinism replace behaviorist assumptions in the way we think about schools and classrooms.

George Payne (1976) follows a similar line in his article, 'Making a Lesson Happen: An Ethnomethodological Analysis'. Payne asserts that:

> . . . a fundamental assumption of the ethnomethodological approach is that the social world is essentially an ongoing achieved world. The everyday world of social events, settings and relationships is all the time created and achieved by the members of society, and these events, settings and relationships are assumed to have no existence independent of the occasions of their productivity.

While at one level we would agree with this assertion, it is quite clear that the actors creating the social events which Payne describes do indeed have an existence which is independent and previous to the social events with which they are involved. Because Payne specifically precludes consideration of the personal histories of the participants of the social events which he is describing (if only for methodological reasons), many difficulties stand in the way of the construction of general categories with which to understand the specific social events he is describing. Hence, it would be possible for a variety of social events to be portrayed and for their internal logic to be laid bare without getting at a general understanding of why certain events are different from others and why what is common to certain events, in this case school lessons, recurs over time.

Our contention is that such timeless versions of ethnomethodology need to broaden their scope, away from merely explaining specific social events within the internal logic of those events, and toward developing general categories with which to understand the events. It is at this point, we believe, that some knowledge of the personal histories of the participants can add breadth and depth to the studies and fulfill the aspiration, and we think the obligation, to develop more generalizable categories of understanding.

Our argument has two parts. One is that the roles of teachers and researchers need to be re-thought on the basis of Lawrence Stenhouse's (1975) idea of 'teachers-as-researchers'. This has been developed particularly in the area of action research, notably by Carr and Kemmis (1986), who make a distinction between 'interpretive' research (including ethnography) and 'critical' research in the action research tradition.

But we also want to develop another idea. Bringing a 'life history' perspective to ethnographic/interpretive research provides an alternative way of building practitioners' concerns into the educational research enterprise. It presents a view that is less radical than action research and one that lacks philosophical elegance. But while logically weak, it may overcome pragmatically some problems encountered in action research (sustaining projects, for example), and thus secure a base for action research programs which reduces personal risks. What is at stake is the role definitions of 'researchers' and 'practitioners'. Action research defines these roles in such a way as to dissolve the distinction. In the approach we suggest, a greater degree of role specialization is retained for both teachers and researchers. We do not suggest that research is possible only into one's own practice; we are attempting instead to devise forms of research that are closer to the vernacular culture of schooling.

## Back to Tradition

In arguing for more extended use of personal histories, we should make it clear that we are not pushing a new approach — not at all; rather, we ask for a reaffirmation of a continuing tradition. Writing about this tradition,

Atkinson and Hammersley (1979) have asserted that 'the life history interview is one of the central research methods employed by ethnographers'. By life history they mean 'the elicitation of structured autobiographies', and, incidentally, they note that the first life histories were completed by anthropologists and generally took American Indian chiefs as their subjects.

In the 1920s and 1930s a large number of anthropological life histories were published, but from the 1940s until the present day life history has been somewhat unfashionable. A parallel trend occurred in sociology. There, the heyday of the life history was in the 1930s, when, for example, Sutherland's (1937) life history of Chic Conwell, a professional thief, and Clifford Shaw's (1930) *The Jack Roller* (a mugger, in more recent terminology) were published. However, there has been a revival recently, with studies appearing of, for example, a 'fence' (Klockars, 1977) and a transsexual (Bogdan, 1974).

The major work we want to redirect attention to is John Dollard's (1949) *Criteria for the Life History*, written in 1935. Dollard argued that 'the elements for which we are perennially seeking is a significant concept of the person to set off against our valuable formal descriptions of social life.' For him:

> . . . in the life history view the individual remains organically present as an object of study, he must be accounted for in his full, immediate personal reality. . . . The culture forms a continuous and connected wrap for the organic life. From the standpoint of the life history the person is viewed as an organic centre of feeling moving through a culture and drawing magnetically to him the main strands of the culture. In the end the individual appears as a person, as a microcosm of the group features of the culture. (Dollard, 1949)

This leads to the assertion that it is possible that 'detailed studies of the lives of individuals will reveal new perspectives on the culture as a whole which are not accessible when one remains on the formal cross-sectional plane of observation' (Dollard, 1949).

(The collection of oral history has also been increasingly recognized as an invaluable source of data by social historians. An impressive recent example is the collaboration of Joan Smith and Harry McShane, which provides a detailed account of McShane's long career in the Glasgow labour movement (McShane, 1978). In a similar tradition is the American work by Sennett and Cobb (1977).)

Much of Dollard's critique has been taken up by others, so that by now some of his polemical introduction to the work has a familiar ring. Dollard (1949) writes that:

> . . . as soon as we take the post of observer on the cultural level the individual is lost in the crowd and our concepts never lead us back to him. After we have 'gone cultural' we experience the person as a fragment of a (derived) culture pattern, as a marionette dancing on the strings of (reified) culture forms.

In contrast to this, the life historian:

> . . . can see his life history subject as a link in a chain of social transmission. There were links before him from which he acquired his present culture; other links will follow him to which he will pass on the current of tradition. The life history attempts to describe a unit in that process: it is a study of one of the strands of a complicated collective life which has historical continuity.

Dollard's work is particularly useful, we think, in discussing the tension between what might be called the 'cultural legacy', the weight of collective tradition and expectation, and the individual's unique history and capacity for interpretations and action. By focusing on this tension and by offering a possible solution, we believe the life history offers ethnographers significant possibilities. Thus Dollard believed that in the adequate life history, 'we must constantly keep in mind the situation both as defined by others and by the subject; such a history will not only define both versions but let us see clearly the pressure of the formal situation'. This resolution or attempt to address a common tension is of great value, for 'whenever we encounter difference between our official or average or cultural expectation of action in a "situation" and the actual conduct of the person, this indicates the presence of a private interpretation'.

Once alerted, we note that the approaches Dollard is concerned with have made recurrent appearances throughout the history of sociology. But significantly, those of us who look to the Chicago sociology of the 1920s tend to emphasize the structural or strategic nature of interaction developed in that tradition and to neglect its stress on biography and documentary history. Even Willard Waller (1977), generally considered one of the leading educational sociologists of the Chicago school, presents his data in a way that disguises how much of it is autobiographical, drawing on his own somewhat disasterous experiences as a teacher and his knowledge of his father's life as a school superintendent (see Faris, 1967).

Howard Becker (1962) and Erving Goffman (1964), both highly influential in recent research, have similarly merged biographical and situational descriptions to produce accounts that look respectable by suggesting time-free theories rather than first-hand biographical or journalistic accounts. (Becker's Chicago school teachers and Goffman's interaction strategies are typical.) Yet, while these theories tend to play down the significance of time, either in the historical sense or in the personal domain, the use of concepts such as 'career' constantly alert us to its presence.

Of course, a number of studies have focused on the teacher's life history previous to his appearance in the classroom. But most notably, these studies have looked at the more formal aspects of teachers' socialization during the training years; only in more autobiographical work such as Otty's (1972) *Learner Teacher* is any, albeit implicit, data given on life history and previous lifestyles. But following Dollard, we argue that the mainstream studies of teacher socialization and training only make sense as part of the life history. Certainly teacher socialization and classroom experience are potent agencies in the reproduction of certain forms of behaviour. But these experiences happen to widely differing human beings with sharply differentiated generational and class backgrounds, and as a result they help produce the range of teacher styles and performance with which we are all familiar. By failing to examine the varying life histories of the teachers, we ignore a major variable. Clearly, in classroom accounts we cannot assume this variable can be kept constant.

Richard Brown (1967) has suggested that biographical data might be located as a distinct category of research. He draws out two dimensions for categorizing ethnographic research. One relates to the distance or 'level of authority' that the author assumes towards the subject. How far, in other words, does the author frame and control the use of subjects' reported speech, in contrast to letting them 'speak for themselves'? The second dimension rather more subtly relates not so much to the strength of the authority, but to the 'relative' firmness of the boundaries between the word and meanings of the subject and those of the author. To illustrate this dimension, Brown examines passages from Nils Anderson (1923), Oscar Lewis (1959) and other authors, in which he claims it is difficult to detect which words, statements, and meanings belong to the author and which to the subject. On the basis of these distinctions, Brown (1967) sets out four types of research, illustrated in the Figure 8.1.

*Figure 8.1:  Boundaries Between Author's Context and Reported Speech (Brown, 1967, p. 8)*

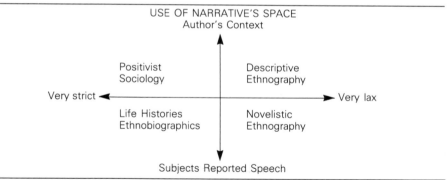

For present purposes Figure 8.1 is of interest because it separates life histories and ethnobiography from descriptive ethnography on two grounds. First, it claims that life histories tend to be true to the perceived realities of subjects' lives rather than be dominated by the concerns of the author's context. Secondly, life histories are more strict in maintaining a procedural boundary between the meanings of the author/researcher and the subject.

## Collecting Life History Data

The importance of life history data to ethnographers is best confirmed by the fact that teachers continually, most often unsolicited, import life history data into their accounts of classroom events. David Hargreaves (1975) has noted that a considerable amount of such data was generated in the research for *Deviance in Classrooms*. Inevitably, since teaching is such a personal matter, our ethnographic focus must ultimately acknowledge personal data as a central element in the construction of accounts.

Interestingly, one of the better known classroom ethnographers, Louis Smith, has come around to this point of view when seeking to follow up his original research, *Anatomy of Educational Innovation* (Smith and Keith, 1971). His new research, on the 'Kensington School' (Smith, 1987), attempts to answer two questions: first, what is the current structure of Kensington as an educational organization, and has the school reverted to its pre-innovational pattern? Secondly, what interpretation/explanation can be made of the presumed changes between 1964 and 1979? Smith notes in his research proposal that 'Methodologically this will involve a special kind of case study, a mix of ethnography and recent history.' Participant observation, interviews/ oral history, and primary documents, e.g., local newspapers, school records, and bulletins, are viewed as sources of data.

Central to Smith's research follow-up are two questions: 'What has happened to the original staff?' and 'How do they perceive the impact of the Kensington experience on their professional lives?'

> In answering these questions, the hope would be to capture each part of the school and its original faculty at a second period in time, to make comparisons, and to draw in differences about innovation and its effects on the lives of a small group of people. (Smith, 1987)

Smith asserts that the major concern is 'to place the issues of educational innovation into the broader context of the individual's *life*'.

In 1974, as part of a study of the effects of curriculum innovation projects in education, the SAFARI Project (MacDonald and Walker, 1974) attempted to collect a series of what the project called 'professional life histories' from a group of twenty science and mathematics teachers. All these teachers were in the first six years of teaching, and they had received considerable instruction from the Nuffield Science and Nuffield Maths Projects during their initial training. The aim of the study was to find out how the curriculum innovations looked to a 'second generation' of teachers who had gone into teaching heavily influenced by innovating projects.

Data was mainly collected intensively at a specially planned weekend conference. The conference had two tasks; one was for the participants to write their own professional life histories around certain predetermined themes, 'Why did you choose science?', 'How did you get to be a teacher?', 'How do you see yourself now?' The other task was for groups of the teachers to pursue a particular and related line of enquiry by collecting tape recorded interviews with other members of the conference. For instance, one group attempted to elicit accounts of successful teaching by asking, 'Tell me about a time when you really felt you had been successful in teaching something.' Another group asked, 'Is the teacher you are, the person you are?' Incidentally, this strategy of using two related tasks, one active, the other reflective, proved to be highly successful in generating enthusiasm. At the end of the weekend the project had twenty life histories, varying from brief to extensive, and a quantity of audio tape which later was transcribed. Contacts were kept with the teachers by mail, but a second meeting a year later did not materialize, perhaps because we doubted our ability to repeat the success of the first conference. Nevertheless, two filing-cabinet drawers of material were accumulated, much of it of great interest.

This material was used extensively in writing an Open University course unit (Unit 27, Course E203) and particularly a related radio programme. The programme was written by a BBC script writer, who took the data and assembled a twenty minute radio play using the words of the teachers but set in the context of an account of one day which had been sent to us by one of the teachers after the conference. There were a number of technical difficulties, especially one which asked the actors to speak the 'real' words of others out of context. In the final version, the script does not sound right. Perhaps it would have been better to work from the original recordings and to have edited them into what Charles Parker has called a 'radio ballad'. But this would have required recordings of much better quality than the ones we had and would have been very time-consuming to produce. Despite the problems, the radio script is the best use we have made of the material so far.

We tell this story to indicate that there are problems in using life history data, quite apart from the problems involved in collecting it. A series of tape recordings of lessons seems easier to analyze than recordings of people talking about themselves. Contemporary symbolic interactionist studies, and ethno-methodological studies more so, tend to put their emphasis on interaction in the here and now. Perhaps this is because the availability of audio- and videotape recorders gives us access to data that was previously unobtainable, allowing us to pin down ten minutes of events with great effect.

Part of what we have lost is the 'eye for documents' which Dollard stressed so strongly. In an attempt to write a 'social history of a school subject' (Goodson, 1980), we sought to amplify and extend the use of documentary material by personal interviews. The result was a view of a curriculum inno-vation which was grounded in both the historical evidence and the personal opinions of the major participants. The story which emerged was of an innovation whose motive force could only be understood through the life histories of the main participants and through close scrutiny of the evol-utionary traditions and subgroups which made up the subject community.

Mary Waring's (1979) work on Nuffield Science developed from a similar perspective. She wrote:

If we are to understand events, whether of thought or of action, knowledge of the background is essential. Knowledge of events is merely the raw material of history: to be intelligible reconstruction of the past, events must be related to other events, and to the assumptions and practices of the milieu. Hence they must be made the subject of inquiry, their origins as products of particular social and historical circumstances, the manner in which individuals and groups must be identified and explanations for their actions sought.

Our point is that in constructing the historical background to events, the focus on individual life histories should be given a focal position. Accounts of life histories could provide windows on the culture in which interaction, biography, social context, and history are intermingled and clash or fuse.

## Conclusion

We believe that many ethnographies of schooling have been characterized by an assumption of timelessness, by sole concern with the here and now of classroom events. The focus on classroom events together with the impersonal research procedures used, often leave the subject of the research with no opportunity to reflect — he is simply recorded in his reaction to the contexts defined by the classroom and the researcher. Following Dollard (1949), we believe we must 'constantly keep in mind the situation as defined by others *and* by the subject.' Using life histories will not only highlight both of these versions, but will 'let us see clearly the pressure of the formal situation and the force of the inner private definition of the situation.'

On the other hand, studies that have looked at history have tended to become trapped by it, seeing 'everything as the past'. By pursuing life history data, we believe there is a greater possibility of setting the research subject free; a greater opportunity for reflexivity is offered, and 'inner private definitions' can be presented. As Brown (1967) asserts, this has the dual advantage of being closer to the perceived reality of the subject's life and of making clear his 'ownership' of this whole range of data. It is thereby both conceptually broader and procedurally clearer.

Statements elicited through the pursuit of life histories can thereby add new dimensions to our interpretations of classroom events and may well set us off on new directions of investigation. The life history puts the classroom event into the perspective of the teacher's life span.

For example, when we asked one of the science teachers, 'How do you see yourself now?', he wrote:

> . . . as a teacher who forgets all the splendid lessons he has taught. A worried teacher who is beginning to question his relationship with kids (am I becoming a little sour and uninspired?). A teacher still full of good ideas but less and less putting them into practice. A teacher

at the crossroads. Has he got the ability to organise things so that his aims are fulfilled? He knows what to do — but finds it difficult getting it done. A teacher who *needs* six weeks holiday a year. A teacher who needs exciting colleagues around him, who is depressed by most of the young teachers he meets. A teacher who is beginning to think he might be failing after initial genuine success.

We believe that by writing this, the teacher created the basis for moving beyond his own definition of the situation.

## References

ANDERSON, N. (1923). *The Hobo*. Chicago: University of Chicago Press.
ARMSTRONG, M. (1980). *Closely Observed Children*. Readers and Writers Cooperative.
ATKINSON, P. and HAMMERSLEY, M. (1979). *Ethnography Project Guide*. London: Open University, Unit DE304.
BECKER, H. S. (1960). 'Notes on the concept of commitment'. *American Journal of Sociology, 66* (July), 32–40.
BECKER, H. S. (1962). 'The career of the Chicago public schoolteacher'. *American Journal of Sociology, 57* (March), 470–477.
BECKER, H. S., and STRAUSS, A. S. (1956). 'Career, personality and adult socialisation'. *American Journal of Sociology, 62* (November), 253–263.
BOGDAN, R. C. (Ed.). (1974). *Being Different: The Autobiography of Jane Fry*. New York: Wiley.
BROWN, R. H. (1967). *A Poetic for Sociology*. Cambridge: Cambridge University Press.
CARR, W. and KEMMIS, S. (1986). *Becoming Critical: Education, Knowledge and Action Research*. Lewes: Falmer Press.
DELAMONT, S. and CHANAN, G. (1937). *Caste and Class in a Southern Town*. New Haven, CT: Yale University Press.
DOLLARD, J. (1949). *Criteria for the Life History*. New Haven, CT: Yale University Press. (First published in 1935.)
FARIS, R. E. L. (1967). *Chicago Sociology, 1920–1932*. Chicago: University of Chicago Press.
GOFFMAN, E. (1964). 'The neglected situation'. In J. T. Gumperz and D. Hymes, (Eds), *The Ethnography of Communication*. Washington: American Anthropological Association, Special Publication 66, part 2.
GOODSON, I. F. (1980). *Curriculum Conflict, 1895–1975*. Unpublished doctoral dissertation, Sussex University.
HAMILTON, D., JENKINS, D., KING, C., MacDONALD, B. and PARLETT, M. (Eds.). (1977). *Beyond the Numbers Game*. New York: Macmillan.
HARGREAVES, D. (1967). *Social Relations in a Secondary School*. London: Routledge and Kegan Paul.
HARGREAVES, D. (1975). *Deviance in Classrooms*. London: Routledge and Kegan Paul.
HARRIS, M. (1964). *The Nature of Cultural Things*. New York: Random House.
HENRY, J. (1963). *Culture Against Man*. New York: Random House.
JACKSON, P. W. (1968). *Life in Classrooms*. New York: Holt.
KLOCKARS, C. B. (1977). 'Field ethics for the life history'. In R. S. Weppner (Ed.), *Street Ethnography*. Beverly Hills, CA: Sage.

LEWIS, O. (1959). *Five Families: Mexican Case Studies in the Culture of Poverty*. New York: Basic Books.

MACDONALD, B. and WALKER, R. (Eds). (1974). *SAFARI Working Papers*. East Anglia: University of East Anglia, CARE.

MADAUS, G. and McDONAGH, J. (1982). 'As I roved out: Folksong collecting as a metaphor for evaluation'. In N. L. Smith (Ed.), *Communication Strategies in Evaluation*. Beverly Hills, CA: Sage.

MCSHANE, H. (1978). *No Mean Fighter*. London: Pluto Press.

McTAGGART, R. and SINGH, M. (1986). *Fourth Generation Action Research*. A Conference Report. Belmont, Victoria, Australia: Deakin University.

OTTY, N. (1972). *Learner Teacher*, New York: Penguin.

PAYNE, G. (1976). 'Making a lesson happen: An ethnomethodological analysis'. In M. Hammersley and P. Woods (Eds), *The Process of Schooling*. London: Routledge and Kegan Paul.

PIKE, K. (1954–60). *Language in Relation to a Unified Theory of the Structure of Human Behavior* (Vols 1–3). Glendale, CA: Summer Institute of Linguistics.

POLLARD, A. (1985). *The Social World of the Primary School*. New York: Holt.

RIST, R. (1978). *The Invisible Children: Social Integration in American Schooling*. Cambridge, MA: Harvard University Press.

ROWLAND, S. (1983). *The Enquiring Classroom*. Lewes: Falmer Press.

SCHUTZ, A. (1962). 'Symbol, reality, and society'. In M. Nathanson, (Ed.), *Collected Papers, Vol. I: The Problem of Social Reality* (3rd ed.). The Hague: Martin Nijhoff.

SENNETT, R. and COBB, J. (1977). *The Hidden Injuries of Class*. New York: Vintage.

SHARP, R. and GREEN, A. (1975). *Education and Social Control*. London: Routledge and Kegan Paul.

SHAW, C. R. (Ed.). (1930). *The Jack Roller*. Chicago: University of Chicago Press.

SIMON, A. and BOYER, G. (Eds). (1970). *Mirrors for Behavior*. Philadelphia, PA: Research for Better Schools.

SMITH, L. M. (1987). *Kensington Revisited*. Lewes: Falmer Press.

SMITH, L. M. and GEOFFREY, W. (1968). *Complexities of an Urban Classroom*, New York: Holt.

SMITH, L. M. and KEITH, P. M. (1971). *Anatomy of Educational Innovation*. New York: Wiley.

SPINDLER, G. (Ed.). (1982). *Doing the Ethnography of Schooling*. New York: Holt.

STAKE, R. and EASLEY, J. (1977). *Case Studies in Science Education*. Urban, IL: University of Illinois Press.

STENHOUSE, L. (1975). *An Introduction to Curriculum Research and Development*. London: Heinemann.

STUBBS, M. and DELAMONT, S. (Eds). (1976). *Explorations in Classroom Observation*, New York: Wiley.

SUTHERLAND, E. (1937). *The Professional Thief*. Chicago: University of Chicago Press.

WALLER, W. W. (1977). *The Sociology of Teaching*. New York: Wiley. (First published in 1932.)

WARING, M. (1979). *Social Pressures and Curriculum Innovation*. London: Methuen.

WEPPNER, R. S. (Ed.). (1977). *Street Ethnography*. Beverly Hills, CA: Sage.

WILLIS, P. (1977). *Learning to Labour*. Farnborough: Saxon House.

WOLCOTT, H. (1967). *A Kwakiutl Village and School*. New York: Holt.

WOODS, P. (1979). *The Divided School*. London: Routledge and Kegan Paul.

*Chapter 9*

# Education and Grounded Theory[1]

*Sally A. Hutchinson*
*College of Nursing*
*University of Florida*
*Jacksonville Satellite Campus*
*Jacksonville, Fl 32209*

We should set aside all previous habits of thought, see through and break down the mental barriers which these habits have set along the horizons of our thinking and in full . . . freedom proceed and lay hold of those genuine problems still awaiting fresh formulation which the liberated horizons on all sides disclose to us. . . . These are hard demands, yet nothing less is required. (Husserl, 1960, p. 34)

## Introduction

Thomas Kuhn (1970), in *The Structure of Scientific Revolutions*, differentiates between paradigmatic research and paradigm transcending research. Paradigmatic research uses existing models or theories (paradigms) and obeys the laws that are inherent in the models. Examples in education include research that tests hypotheses derived from operant-conditioning theory or learning theory. In contrast, grounded theory research strives to be paradigm transcending. Heretical and iconoclastic, such research goes beyond existent theories and preconceived conceptual frameworks in search of new understandings of social processes in natural settings (Stern *et al.*, 1982).

In the early 1960s, sociologists Barney Glaser from Columbia University and Anselm Strauss from the University of Chicago serendipitously became colleagues at the University of California, San Francisco, where they were hired to teach graduate research courses. Their relationship was to become long and fruitful. Educated in Merton's middle range theory and Lazerfeld's quantitative analysis, Glaser was an interesting contrast to Strauss, who had studied with George Herbert Mead and was educated in the rather amorphous research methodology of 'The Chicago tradition'. The Glaser and Strauss (1967) combination of rigor and flexibility resulted in the development of a new qualitative methodology called 'grounded theory'.

The impetus for the new method grew from a dissatisfaction with existing sociological theories and research. Glaser and Strauss believed grand theories were generated from idle speculation rather than from data and those who generated grand theories were not interested enough in research to test them out. Grand theories employ global concepts that are often poorly defined and ambiguously related to one another and everyday life. Too often they purport to explain everything, while in fact they explain very little. Existing sociological research focused on testing and retesting these theories. Of more use, Glaser and Strauss believed, would be middle range or substantive theories that explained a specific area of empirical inquiry, e.g., an educational program for gifted children or magnet schools. The grounded theory method offered a systematic approach for generating substantive theories that were born in and helped explain the real world.

Grounded theory finds its philosophical foundation in the work of George Herbert Mead and American pragmaticism, and its sociological roots are in the work of Herbert Blumer and symbolic interactionism (Lewis and Smith, 1980). Symbolic interactionists believe that people interact with each other through meaningful symbols. Meanings evolve over time from social interactions. These beliefs are contrary to the positivist or traditionally 'scientific' understanding of the world. Positivists view the world as being 'out there', and available for study in a more or less static form. For symbolic interactionists, the human reality is not simply 'out there' awaiting scientific study. Instead it is socially and symbolically constructed, always emerging and relative to other facts of social life. Such a philosophy is reflected in each step of grounded theory research, but especially in its data collection strategies, participant observation and interviewing. In both strategies, researchers go to the 'participants' (called 'subjects' in experimental research) in an attempt at understanding their perspective within a given situation. The notion of discovery, so fundamental to grounded theory, includes discovering first the world as seen through the eyes of the participants and then the basic social processes or structures that organize that world.

The generation of grounded theory relies on the inquiring, analytical mind of the researcher/theorist. The task is to discover and conceptualize the essence of specific interactional processes. The resulting theory provides a new way of understanding the social situations from which the theory was generated.

Denzin (1970) makes the point that all data, qualitative or quantitative, serve four basic functions for theory: they *initiate* new theory or *reformulate, refocus,* and *clarify* existing theory (p. 120). Grounded theory serves each of these functions well. If little is known about a topic and few adequate theories exist to explain or predict a group's behavior, grounded theory is especially useful. Grounded theory can also offer an exciting new approach to an old problem. Interventions suggested from grounded theory may result in administrative, curricular, or programmatic changes. Because of its practical implications, grounded theory research can be classified as applied research.

## Grounded Theory As Qualitative Research

In what respects and manner is grounded theory qualitative? In their essay, 'Qualitative Inquiry: An Introduction', Sherman *et al.* (1984) discuss criteria essential to qualitative research. These include a focus on context, 'lived' experience, patterns of experience, and finally, judging or appraising.

Grounded theory studies grow out of questions researchers ask about people in specific contexts. In education, for example, researchers might ask, 'How do teachers work with mentally retarded, gifted, or deaf children? How do administrators interact with teachers? Pupils? Parents?' The data gathered and analyzed are contextual because participants are studied in naturalistic settings by means of participant observation. Because researchers alter the context in undetermined ways, they collect and analyze data about how people react to them and how they themselves react to the people and the setting.

In order to understand patterns of experience, grounded theory researchers gather data about the 'lived' experience of participants. Researchers immerse themselves in the social environment. Initial observations are used to understand and describe the social structure and patterns of behavior. As Herbert Blumer (1962) explained, participant observation allows the researcher to take the role of the people being studied, or what he awkwardly called 'the acting unit':

> Since the interpretation is being made by the acting unit in terms of objects designated and appraised, meanings acquired, and decisions made, the process has to be seen from the standpoint of the acting unit. . . . To try to catch the interpretive process by remaining aloof as a so-called 'objective' observer and refusing to take the role of the acting unit is to risk the worst kind of subjectivism — the objective observer is likely to fill in the process of interpretation with his own surmises in place of catching the process as it occurs in the experience of the acting unit which uses it. (p. 188)

In-depth interviews of the participants lend meaning to their observed experiences. Observing, by itself, is never enough because it begs misinterpretation. Interviews permit researchers to verify, clarify, or alter what they thought happened, to achieve a full understanding of an incident, and to take into account the 'lived' experience of participants.

Grounded theories are guided by the assumption that people do, in fact, have patterns of experience. They order and make sense of their environment, although their world may appear disordered or nonsensical to the observer. The order or pattern derives from their shared social and symbolic interactions. Reality is a social construct, or as Berger and Luckman (1966) describe it:

> The world of everyday life is not only taken for granted as reality by the ordinary members of society in the subjectively meaningful

conduct of their lives. It is a world that originates in their thoughts and actions, and is maintained as real by these. (pp. 19–20)

People sharing common circumstances, such as teachers in a middle school, share patterns of meanings and behavior as well. These patterns are the stuff and substance of grounded theory research.

Grounded theory is a form of social criticism; it does make judgements about identified patterns of social interaction. The mere documentation of social phenomena evokes an awareness that social reality is communally contracted and is thus subject to change. Newcomb and Conrad's (1981) study about mandated reform in higher education presents stages of change and the variables that effect the rate and degree of change. Recognizing the value of their theory, the authors offer clear and practical guidelines for the 'effective' implementation of mandated change.

Grounded theory is qualitative in its philosophy of science, its data collection, its methods of analysis, and its final product offers a rich and complex explanatory schema of social phenomena.


## Grounded Theory and Educational Research

From its inception, educational research has focused on theory testing, i.e., verificational studies. This research has been hampered by the fact that educational theory is anemic and has seldom led researchers to interesting questions or verifiable findings. Indeed, in recent years, the most prominent researchers in education, those in the process–product area, have prided themselves on the atheoretical nature of their work. Clearly, there is a need for middle-range, data-based theory in education that explains the everyday world of teachers, students, administrators, and the school bureaucracy.

In his paper, 'School Effects: The Case for Grounded Theory', Richer (1975) critiques contemporary educational research and argues for the use of grounded theory as a method for studying the effects of schooling. Charging that much of the existing research is an example of abstract empiricism, he presents his major theme: that the lack of relevant conceptual frameworks to guide and focus the research is directly related to the frequency of null findings and inconsistent results. Relevant frameworks, he proposes, cannot come from existing theories that are only marginally useful, but must come from inductive, concept generating research conducted in such naturalistic school settings as teachers' lounges, lunch rooms, and playgrounds. Martin (1978), in 'Neglected Aspects in the Sociology of Education in Canada', also advocates grounded theory research. He argues that research that reveals the complexities of the real world must derive from theory generated from that world; 'the relative merits of a theory for predicting, explaining, and being relevant cannot be separated from the way it is generated' (p. 17). He laments that few publications have used the grounded theory approach.

Educators need the freedom offered by grounded theory to intelligently and imaginatively explore the social psychological consequences of school life. Social psychological factors are perhaps the most relevant factors in human behavior. Grounded theory offers a systematic method by which to study the richness and diversity of human experience and to generate relevant, plausible theory which can be used to understand the contextual reality of social behavior. With such understanding, educators can assess what is happening in the groups studied and plan interventions to improve the quality of education.

## Some Grounded Theory Studies

In this section selected educational research using grounded theory is presented. In each study grounded theory was used with varying degrees of rigor and success. Additional unpublished studies can be found in ERIC (see also Askew, 1983; Gehrke and Parker, 1982; Rosner, 1983).

• Joseph Blase (1982) presents 'A Social-psychological Grounded Theory of Teacher Stress and Burnout', which he calls the Teacher-Performance Motivation Theory. In-depth interviews with forty-three high school teachers focused on the question, 'What does it mean to be a high school teacher?' Secondary questions examined how the meaning of high school teaching changed for respondents over time. Blase developed a thirty-eight-item questionnaire from interviews and observational data. The theory he finally developed was based on concepts corroborated by 90 per cent of teachers and confirmed by questionnaires and interview/observational data. Teacher burnout, according to Blase, occurs when: (1) teacher coping resources are inadequate; and (2) there are limited rewards in relation to work-related stressors. In such a situation, prolonged job strain inevitably leads to burnout. Blase presents a clear and logical conceptual map that explains the actions and beliefs of teachers and describes key concepts which are both analytic and sensitizing, a requirement for 'good' grounded theory.

• In a study entitled 'A Grounded Theory Study of Beginning Teachers' Role Personalizations Through Reference Group Relations,' Nathalie Gehrke (1981) interviewed eleven beginning high school teachers over a period of five years. She focused on patterns of teacher interaction with the potential reference groups in the school (p. 34). She discussed in her findings the teachers' early choice of a primary reference group. She categorized the six reference groups into three 'major orientation divisions' — a client, peer and authority orientation. Gehrke's research appears to be 'in process'. She proposes several useful hypotheses (p. 37):

1 (a) Teacher reference group foci show three orientations: *student, peer, and authority*.
  (b) Each orientation appears in both a focused and a general group.

2 (a) Teachers seek ties with groups that provide an optimum security level during their role transition.

(b) Anxious, self-doubting teachers choose to relate most intensely to the focused or specialized groups of the three prime orientations.

3 (a) As an individual's sense of teacher competence and self-esteem increases, the group focus of the individual changes to less supportive, higher risk groups.

(b) As a sense of competence increases, the teacher's focus will shift to the general focus groups of the prime orientations.

• Nathalie Gehrke (1982) reports on another part of her five-year study in 'Teachers' Role Conflicts: A Grounded Theory in Process'. Eleven beginning secondary teachers were interviewed and observed over a five-year period. Initial interview questions focused on teachers' expectations and perceptions of themselves, the schools, and their new roles (p. 41), and later were altered based on data analysis. Inter-role conflicts were discovered in the data and thus were more closely studied, eventually yielding four categories: perceptions of conflict, sources of conflict, conflict-arousing situations, and conflict-coping strategies. Gehrke then generated hypotheses from her categories (p. 45):

1 Perceptions of role conflict vary among teachers.
(a) Married teachers perceive greater inter-role conflict than unmarried teachers.
(b) Female teachers perceive greater inter-role conflict than male teachers.
(c) Teachers with children perceive greater inter-role conflict than teachers without children.
2 Fealty is a source of conflict between personal and professional roles. Allocation of resources is a demonstration of role fealty.
3 Teacher role conflicts change over time.
(a) The addition of new personal or professional roles produces conflict.
(b) Changes in any role produce conflict.
(c) Changes in individual needs of the role occupant cause conflict.
4 Teachers cope with role conflict in different ways to bring a sense of equilibrium.
(a) Teachers may cope by designating one role as primary.
(b) Teachers may cope by abandoning one role.
(c) Teachers may cope through role separation.

Gehrke clearly presents her work as 'theory in process', and she accurately describes as 'categories' her groupings of data. Her study is a good example of how useful 'theory in process' can be for practicing teachers and for direction for further research.

• Clifton Conrad (1978), in 'A Grounded Theory of Academic Change', criticizes the four principal models that have guided research on academic change. He believes the models have not been useful in explaining how change occurs or who and what are ultimately changed (p. 102). The dynamics and processes of change are not clear, nor are the relevant variables. Thus, Conrad's study questions were: 'What are the major sources of academic change? What are the major processes through which academic change occurs?' Conrad integrated data from interviews and documents at four universities and discovered a theory of academic change that he presents in a step-by-step set of theoretical statements. Essentially his theory 'identifies several major processes which link pressures for change and a policy decision to change: conflict and interest group pressures followed by power exertion, administrative intervention, faculty leadership exercised through interest group advocacy, and compromises which are negotiated through administrative leadership' (p. 101). Conrad weaves the grounded theory method in with the emerging theory so the reader sees how he arrived at his conclusion. He presents, elaborates on, and illustrates by example his collection, coding, and analysis of data. In the discussion section he compares and contrasts his theory with existing theories of academic change.

• In 'A Theory of Mandated Academic Change', Newcomb and Conrad (1981), state their purpose is to present a grounded theory that identifies conditions that facilitate effective implementation of federal mandates. The research question is, 'What are the key variables that influence an institution's ability to successfully adapt programs, policies, and practices in compliance with a federal mandate?' They look specifically at Title IX regulations and guidelines for elimination of sex discrimination in collegiate athletics. The authors collect extensive descriptive quantitative data that describe the athletic programs of eight four-year public colleges. Data analysis permitted the researchers to propose hypotheses concerning imposed or 'mandated' change. They then present four stages that colleges go through when implementing federal mandates (p. 559): (1) infusion; (2) preparation and policy formation; (3) trial and transition; and (4) policy execution. Four categories of variables that effect the rate and degree of the change include administrative leadership, the use of facilitative substructures, conditions in institutional subsystems; and governmental intervention. A discussion of the stages and categories is followed by the integrated theory. As they should be, the concepts in the theory are clearly defined and appear to 'fit' the data. Administrative leaders in higher education and government officials who must enforce implementation of mandates can learn much from the guidelines suggested by the study.

An examination of these studies supports the need for educational research using the grounded theory method. Although the studies are generally good, they are only a beginning and must be followed by studies that address crucial problems in education and adhere more closely to the grounded theory method.

## The Grounded Theory Method

Conrad (1978, 1982) contends that the method used in grounded theory research has not been presented clearly, a fact that may account for the dearth of grounded theory studies in education. A full account of the method cannot be set out here, but an introduction to the method will be presented. Anyone interested in doing grounded theory research should consult Glaser's (1978) book, *Theoretical Sensitivity*. Although tedious, difficult, and carelessly edited, it is the most comprehensive work on grounded theory available. It is best to read the book as you are doing your research; to read Glaser's work in isolation from empirical data is unproductive.

### Data Gathering

Data collection begins as soon as the researcher has identified a researchable problem and goes into the field. Once a setting has been chosen for study, the researcher immerses himself[2] in the social milieu. Initial observations allow the researcher to describe the social structure, observe patterns of behavior, and begin to understand the environment.

Since grounded research requires interpersonal interaction, the researcher must observe his own behavior as well as the behavior of his subjects. He must become aware of his own preconceptions, values, and beliefs. Only by being aware of his own 'mind-set' and 'bracketing' his own values can the researcher begin to search out and understand the world of others. 'Bracketing' refers to being aware of one's personal values and preconceptions and transcending them during the research in an effort to see a situation with a new perspective. Bracketing is vital to field research. Berger and Kellner (1981) explain:

> If such bracketing is not done, the scientific enterprise collapses, and what the sociologist then believes to perceive is nothing but a mirror image of his own hopes and fears, wishes, resentments or other psychic needs; what he will then not perceive is anything that can reasonably be called social reality. (p. 52)

Keeping a daily journal in which personal feelings and reflections are recorded can help the researcher become aware of and bracket his own values.

Interviews, generally informal in nature, augment formal observations and serve to clarify the meanings participants attribute to a given situation. Interviews help the researcher see situations through the eyes of the participants. The human touch, the capacity to empathize with others, is essential to successful interviewing.

Additional data might be gathered from student records, school policy documents, newspaper and television coverage, and fictional descriptions that expand and further clarify the data base. For example, Newcomb and Conrad

(1981) studied such documents as Title IX of the Higher Education Amendments of 1972 in order to understand the regulations their subjects were working under. Conrad (1978) examined: (1) membership lists and minutes from the appropriate committees, ad hoc groups, and faculty senates; (2) personal files of committee members; (3) campus newspaper articles; (4) published and unpublished reports; (5) personal letters; (6) speeches; (7) published articles; and (8) tapes of faculty meetings. These documents were extremely valuable in interpreting data gathered from interviewees and constituted an excellent check on the other data (p. 104). Such diverse 'slices of data' (Glaser and Strauss, 1967, p. 66), insure density and provide different perspectives for understanding social phenomena.

*Reliability and Validity*

Researchers ask the question, 'Does this array of data I have collected accurately reflect the milieu under study?' Richer (1975) contends that grounded theory research can produce theories that closely mirror the social reality of the school and are, therefore, more useful than speculative theories that are not data based (p. 395). Quantitative researchers frequently describe qualitative research as 'subjective' and therefore inherently unreliable and invalid. They regard the presence of the field researcher as an intrusive factor which inevitably influences the behavior of the participants. They also maintain that participants may lie, distort the truth, or withhold vital information, and that in such cases the researcher is misled by incomplete, inaccurate, or biased data (Becker, 1970).

A rebuttal to such assertions would propose that while a participant observer may initially influence the setting, social and organizational constraints usually neutralize this distorting effect. Participants will become more concerned with meeting the demands of their own situation than with paying attention to, pleasing, or playing games with the researcher (Becker, 1970, p. 43).

The temporal reality of field work provides an additional check on the data. Grounded research is conducted in the field over a protracted period of time. The researcher continually formulates hypotheses and discards them if they are not confirmed by further data. A grounded theorist looks for contradictory data by searching out and investigating unusual circumstances and negative cases. Data are compared and contrasted again and again, thus providing a check on validity. Distortions or lies will gradually be revealed. The multiple data collection methods used in grounded theory research — direct observation, interviews, and document analysis — diminish bias by increasing the wealth of information available to the researcher.

Richer (1975) suggests using several observers/data collectors so they can compare their findings. He cites Smith and Geoffrey's (1968) work in which a researcher and a teacher collaborated and states, 'these two perspectives provided a strong check against the possibility of observational bias and provided a meaningful interchange at the interpretive stage . . . high inter-observer reliability was consistently the case' (p. 396).

Can a theory generated in a specific context be generalized to a larger group? Can a theory of teaching conducted in one school be expected to be relevant to teaching in another school? A substantive theory can be said to be valid only for the studied population. A quality theory, however, will inevitably identify a basic social process relevant to people in similar situations. Of course, the generalizability of any theory can only be established through verificational studies.

Is grounded theory research replicable? 'Probably not.' Grounded theory depends on the interaction between the data and the creative processes of the researcher. It is highly unlikely that two people would come up with the exact same theory:

> The social location, the psychological constitution and the cognitive peculiarities of an interpreter are inevitably involved in the act of interpretation, and all of them will affect the interpretation (Berger and Kellner, 1981, p. 48).

The question of replicability is not especially relevant, since the point of theory generation is to offer a new perspective on a given situation that can then be tested by other research methods. Thus, qualitative research should not be viewed as antagonistic toward or incompatible with quantitative methodologies. Qualitative inquiry is a necessary and useful precursor to quantitative work.

*Data Recording*

The immediate recording of data is vital to the success of grounded theory generation. Researchers rely on taped interviews and/or hand-written field notes in order to construct accurate, typed protocols. However, the researcher must be sensitive to his environment in order to determine if using a tape recorder or taking notes in the presence of subjects will make them uncomfortable or disrupt their behavior.

The use of a tape recorder in a school that had recently experienced a grand jury investigation might inspire an understandable fear on the part of the interviewees. Even the unobtrusive use of pen and paper can be offensive to participants in highly stressful settings such as disciplinary hearings for teachers. In such cases, dictating notes after the proceedings is the more reliable method.

Field notes are typed double-spaced, with page numbers and appropriate headings such as place, date, time. Leaving a two-inch margin on the left hand side of the paper allows adequate room for coding. Numbering lines makes it easier to retrieve data and thus saves valuable research time.

## The Discovery of a Core Variable or Basic Social Psychological Process

Grounded theorists base their research on the assumption that all people who share common circumstances (e.g. middle school teachers, physically handicapped students) also share social psychological 'problems' that are not necessarily articulated or conscious but grow out of their shared life. This fundamental problem is resolved by means of social psychological processes, also called core variables.

The discovery of a core variable is the goal of the researcher and is essential to a quality grounded theory. Continuous reference to the data combined with rigorous analytic thinking will eventually yield such a variable. The core variable illuminates the 'main theme' of the actors' behavior and explicates 'what is going on in the data' (Glaser, 1978, p. 94). The core variable has three essential characteristics: it recurs frequently in the data; it links the data together; and it explains much of the variation in the data. This variable becomes the basis for the generation of the theory. The categories, properties, phases, and dimensions of the theory are inextricably related to the core variable.

Basic social psychological processes (BSPs) are a type of core variable that illustrate social processes as they are repeated over time (Glaser, 1978, p. 100). Once a BSP emerges and is verified, the researcher selectively codes only data that relate to it. Thus, the BSP becomes a guide for further data collection and analysis.

## Coding the Field Notes — Levels I, II, III

The grounded theory method requires that the researcher simultaneously collect, code, and analyze the data from the first day in the field. The method is circular, allowing the researcher to change focus and pursue leads revealed by the ongoing data analysis (see Figure 9.1).

Conrad (1978), in discussing his theory of academic change, does an excellent job of describing the circular process in action (pp. 105–107). He describes how he continually revised the emerging concepts as he interpreted new data. Some concepts that initially appeared valid were discarded or modified as data from different groups were obtained.

Level I coding begins with words that describe the action in the setting. Such codes are *in vivo* or substantive codes and may use the exact words that the actors use. Substantive codes tend to be catchy and meaningful. Examples of early substantive coding on teacher behaviors in research in process are 'favoring', 'punishing', 'begging', 'praising'. Substantive coding based only on the data prevents the researcher from the imposition of preconceived impressions.

Open coding refers to the coding of each sentence and each incident into as many codes as possible to insure full theoretical coverage. For example, an

Figure 9.1: *Temporality of Grounded Theory*

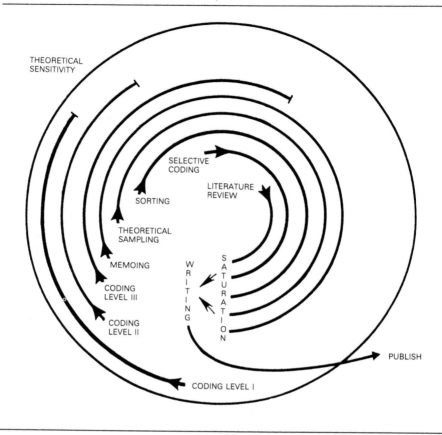

incident may be coded as both 'begging' and 'pleading'. All data must be coded, or the emerging theory will not fit the data and explain behavioral variations. If teachers spend much time complaining about their problems with the administration, for example, these data must be coded, along with data that indicate how the teachers work with the students.

Code words are written in the wide margins of the field notes. Level I codes break the data into small pieces; later, Level II and Level III codes elevate the data to more abstract levels. Level II codes can also be called categories and may result from the condensing of Level I codes. In the process, some data may be discarded if they prove to be irrelevant. Decisions about categories are made by asking certain questions of the data. For example, a researcher may ask, 'What does this incident indicate?', and then compare the incident with all others in the field notes. The researcher then asks, 'What category would similar incidents fall into?' Finally, the researcher compares each emerging category with all others to ensure that they are mutually exclusive and cover all behavioral variations.

Level III codes are theoretical constructs and are derived from a combination of academic and clinical knowledge. The constructs contribute theoretical meaning and scope to the theory (Glaser, 1978, p. 70). These theoretical codes may or may not be BSP, depending on the amount of behavioral variation they take into account. Theoretical constructs conceptualize the relationship among the three levels of codes, 'weaving the fractured data back together again' (Glaser, 1978, p. 116). This comprehensive pattern is, in fact, a grounded theory. The theoretical constructs are grounded in substantive or categorical codes, precluding the possibility of unfounded, abstract theorizing.

*Constant Comparative Method*

The constant comparative method is the fundamental method of data analysis in grounded theory generation. The aim of this method is the generation of theoretical constructs which, along with substantive codes and categories and their properties, form a theory that encompasses as much behavioral variation as possible. The proposed theory is molecular in structure rather than causal or linear.

While coding and analyzing the data, the researcher looks for patterns. He compares incident with incident, incident with category, and, finally, category with category or construct with construct. By this method the analyst distinguishes similarities and differences among incidents. By comparing similar incidents, the basic properties of a category or construct are defined. Differences between incidents establish coding boundaries, and relationships among categories are gradually clarified. Comparative analysis forces the researcher to expand or 'tease out' the emerging category by searching for its structure, temporality, cause, context, dimensions, consequences and its relationship to other categories. An in-depth examination of these properties is likely to yield a dense theory that also accounts for behavioral variation.

In addition to the comparison of incidents, the researcher compares the behavior patterns of different groups within the substantive area. Eventually, categories and their related properties emerge. In research on teachers, a researcher might compare behaviors of new and veteran teachers, black and white teachers, teachers with baccalaureate degrees and those with master's degrees, or teachers with a high sense of efficacy and those with a low sense of efficacy (Ashton and Webb, 1986). Such comparisons contribute substantially to the richness of the theory.

*Memoing*

In order to generate a quality theory, the descriptions of empirical events must be elevated to a theoretical level. 'Memoing' is a vital part of this process. The researcher quickly and spontaneously records his ideas in order to capture the initially elusive and shifting connections within the data. More and more memos accumulate. Memos may be long or short and are written without concern for style or formal punctuation. The emphasis is on conceptualization of ideas. One ends up with hundreds of memos documenting the researcher's thinking process. The ideas are retrievable because each memo is headed by the code or codes it describes. Memos can be shifted around to check the relationship with other codes. Irrelevant codes can be discarded and core codes retained. The emerging theory is, therefore, always modifiable.

While memoing, the researcher asks what relationship one code has to another. Are they separate codes? Is one code a property or a phase in another? Is one event the cause or consequence of another? What conditions influence the codes? The intent of this questioning is to develop codes that can be sorted and compared again and again. Through repetitive questioning, a grounded theory evolves. The basic social psychological process emerges and its properties become integrated. The generation of linkages occurs throughout the research process and is not complete until the final report is written.

*Theoretical Sampling*

Sampling decisions are made during the entire grounded theory research process. The researcher looks for relevant data to fill in the evolving categories and theoretical codes. Consequently, the researcher must engage in a constant dialogue with the data in order to establish direction for further sampling.

Diversity in sampling insures extensive data that covers the wide ranges of behavior in varied situations. For example, in Newcomb and Conrad's (1981) study on mandated academic change, the initial sample included thirteen four-year public colleges and universities. After a pilot study, the final sample was narrowed to include the two institutions that had the greatest degree of change and the two institutions that had made the least progress toward compliance (p. 558). The idea behind the sampling process was to maximize comparability.

*Sorting*

Sorting begins when the researcher first decides upon a core variable (BSP) which explains most of the behavioral variation in the data. This core variable offers focus and direction to the sorting process. The researcher then attempts to discover the relationship of the different levels of codes to the BSP. Gradually, an outline emerges from the sorted memos which is the basis for writing the theory. While sorting to produce an outline, one may draw and redraw schematic diagrams. These diagrams are very helpful in setting forth the developing theory.

### Saturation

Saturation refers to the completeness of all levels of codes when no new conceptual information is available to indicate new codes or the expansion of existing ones. While new descriptive data may be added, the information will not be useful unless the theoretical codes need to be altered. When all the data fit into the established categories, interactional and organizational patterns are visible, behavioral variation is described, and behavior can be predicted. The researcher, by repeatedly checking and asking questions of the data, ultimately achieves a sense of closure.

### Review of Literature

In verificational research, e.g., hypotheses testing studies, a literature review is completed prior to data collection and analysis. Existing theoretical and methodological literature is used to build a rationale for the proposed research. In contrast, grounded theorists generate a theory based on behavior patterns observed in the field and then turn to the literature to find support for the emergent theory. Literature that illuminates or extends the proposed theory is interwoven with the empirical data. Through its correspondence with 'the real world', literature establishes a vital connection between theory and reality. Gerke (1981) discusses how her grounded hypotheses are supported in the education literature, while Newcomb and Conrad (1981) clarify how their theory of change goes beyond the three existing models of institutional change.

### Writing the Theory

Really knowing not only means having [a pattern of meaning and behavior] conceptualized, but also being able to describe its day to day working as well as, if not better than, the man who is actually living and working in the setting. (Smith and Pohland, 1976, p. 269)

After theoretical sorting and saturation the researcher begins to write a substantive theory, with the BSP as its central focus. The phases of the BSP serve as subheadings for the elaboration of the categories. At this point, as Glaser (1978) explains, the theory 'freezes the on-going for the moment in a fixed conceptual description' (p. 129).

## The Evaluation of Grounded Theories

Since the methods and aims of grounded theory research are substantially different from those of verificational research, the criteria for evaluation differ as well. In *Discovery of Grounded Theory*, Glaser and Strauss (1967) list significant criteria for evaluation. A quality grounded theory has codes which *fit* the data and the area it is derived from. Data fall into place naturally, the researcher does not force them into codes. Readers of quality theories can see and understand this fit.

A quality theory *works*; that is, it explains major behavioral and interactional variations in the data. Such a theory can predict what will happen under certain conditions and with given variables. For example, Blase's (1982) teacher performance-motivation theory clearly describes how specific variables act and interact in what the author calls an 'ineffective (degenerative) performance cycle.' Thus, given specific conditions, teacher burnout can be predicted.

A quality theory must possess *relevance* which is related to the core variable and its ability to explain the ongoing social processes in the action scene. If the actors in the setting immediately recognize the researcher's constructs ('Wow, that's it!'), he can be confident that his theory has relevance. Relevance is dependent upon the researcher's theoretical sensitivity in enabling the BSP to emerge from the data without imposing his own preconceived notions or ideas.

Since social life is not static, a quality theory must be able to capture its constantly fluctuating nature. Thus, a good theory must be *modifiable*. For example, if values or related variables differ, a good theory can accommodate these changes. Flexibility is required for theoretical relevance.

*Density* and *integration* are additional criteria for assessing the quality of a theory. A theory is dense when it possesses a few key theoretical constructs and a substantial number of properties and categories. Good integration ensures that the propositions are systematically related and fit into a tight theoretical framework (Glaser and Strauss, 1968, p. 243).

### Summary

Figure 9.2 summarizes in schema form the method of grounded theory. Grounded theory offers a useful approach to research problems in education. Because the method forces researchers to focus on theory generation instead of verification, it can contribute substantive theories that explain and predict educational phenomena. Rich and complex data can be analyzed systematically, yielding a final product that is theoretically sound and can be put to practical use. Grounded theory permits structured entry to new, different, or unclear problems in education. A good theory proposes a new and relevant way of seeing. A combination of qualitative and quantitative methods can

*Figure 9.2: Grounded Theory*

T
H
E
O
R
E
T
I
C
A
L

S
E
N
S
I
T
I
V
I
T
Y

| PROCESS | PRODUCT |
|---|---|
| Constant comparative method | Level I codes — called *in vivo* or substantive |
| Constant comparative method | Level II codes — called categories |
| Constant comparative method | Level III codes — called theoretical constructs |
| Memoing | Theoretical ideas |
| Theoretical sampling | Dense data which leads to the illumination and expansion of theoretical constructs |
| Sorting | Basic social psychological process (BSP) — a central 'theme' |
| Selective coding based on BSP | Theory delimited to a few theoretical constructs, their categories and properties |
| Saturation of codes, categories and constructs | A dense, parsimonious theory covering behavioral variation; a sense of closure |
| Literature review | Discovering literature that supports, illuminates or extends proposed theory |
| Writing the theory | A piece of publishable research |

broaden a study's perspective. The method can also be used in the evaluation of educational programs and/or policies (see Patten, 1980). Education and educators can only benefit from such an approach.

## Notes

1   Parts of the method section and Figure 9.1 were published previously in a chapter entitled 'Grounded Theory' in P. Munhall and C. Oiler (Eds), *Nursing Research: A Qualitative Perspective*. New York: Appleton Century Crofts, 1986.
2   No distinction in respect to gender is made in this paper.

## References

ASHTON P. and WEBB, R. (1986). *Making a Difference: Teachers' Sense of Efficacy and Student Achievement*. New York: Longman.

ASKEW, J. (1983). 'Some thoughts on the value of grounded theory for the study and practice of higher education'. Paper presented at the Annual Meeting of The Association for the Study of Higher Education, Washington, DC, March 25–26.

BECKER, K. (1970). *Sociological Work*. Chicago: Aldine.

BERGER, P. and KELLNER, K. (1981). *Sociology Reinterpreted*. New York: Anchor.

BERGER P. and LUCKMANN, T. (1967). *The Social Construction of Reality*. New York: Anchor.

BLASE, J. (1982). 'A social-psychological grounded theory of teacher stress and burnout'. *Educational Administration Quarterly, 18*(4), 93–113.

BLUMER, H. (1962). 'Society as symbolic interaction'. In A. Rose (Ed.), *Human Behavior and Social Processes: An Interactionist Approach*. Boston, MA: Houghton Mifflin.

CONRAD, C. (1978). 'A grounded theory of academic change'. *Sociology of Education, 51* April, 101–112.

CONRAD, C. (1982). 'Grounded theory: An alternative approach to research in higher education'. *The Review of Higher Education, 5*(4), 259–269.

DENZIN, N. (1970). *The Research Act.* Chicago: Aldine.

GEHRKE, N. (1981). 'A grounded theory study of beginning teachers' role personalization through reference group relations'. *Journal of Teacher Education, 32*(6), 34–38.

GEHRKE, N. (1982). 'Teachers' role conflicts: A grounded theory-in-process'. *Journal of Teacher Education, 33*(1), 41–46.

GEHRKE, N. and PARKER, W. (1982). 'Generating curriculum theory through grounded theory research'. Paper presented at the Annual Meeting of the American Educational Research Association, New York, April.

GLASER, B. (1978). *Theoretical Sensitivity.* Mill Valley, CA: Sociology Press.

GLASER, B. and STRAUSS, A. (1967). *Discovery of Grounded Theory.* Chicago: Aldine.

GLASER, B. and STRAUSS, A. (1968). *Time for Dying.* Chicago: Aldine.

HUSSERL, E. (1960). *Ideas.* New York: Collier.

KUHN, T. (1970). *The Structure of Scientific Revolutions.* Chicago: University of Chicago Press.

LEWIS, D. and SMITH, R. (1980). *American Sociology and Pragmatism.* Chicago: University of Chicago Press.

MARTIN, W. (1978). 'Neglected aspects in the sociology of education in Canada'. *Canadian Journal of Education, 3*(4), 15–30.

NEWCOMB, J. and CONRAD, C. (1981). 'A theory of mandated academic change'. *Journal of Higher Education, 52*(6), 555–577.

PATTON, M. (1975). *Qualitative Evaluation Methods.* Beverly Hills, CA: Sage.

RICHER, S. (1975). 'School effects: The case for grounded theory'. *Sociology of Education, 48* (Fall), 383–399.

ROSNER, F. (1985). 'The future of teaching as a profession: Assessing classroom management and skills'. Paper presented at the Annual Meeting of the American Association of Colleges for Teacher Education, Detroit, February.

SHERMAN, R., WEBB, R. and ANDREWS, S. (1984). 'Qualitative inquiry: An introduction'. *Journal of Thought, 19*(2), 24–33.

SMITH, L. and GEOFFREY, W. (1968). *The Complexities of An Urban Classroom.* New York: Holt, Rinehart and Winston.

SMITH, L. and POHLAND, P. (1976). 'Grounded theory and educational ethnography: Methodological analysis and critique'. In J. Roberts and S. Akinsanya (Eds), *Educational Patterns and Cultural Configuration.* New York: McKay.

STERN, P., ALLEN, L. and MOXLEY, P. (1982). 'The nurse as grounded theorist: History, process and uses'. *The Review Journal of Philosophy and Social Science, 7*(2), 200–215.

*Chapter 10*

# Phenomenography: A Research Approach to Investigating Different Understandings of Reality

*Ference Marton*
*Department of Education*
*University of Göteborg*
*Box 1010*
*S-431 26 Mölndal, Sweden*

## Introduction

Phenomenography is a research approach designed to answer certain questions about thinking and learning. It was originally developed by a research group in the Department of Education, University of Gothenburg, Sweden. The word 'phenomenography' was coined in 1979 and appeared in print for the first time two years later (Marton, 1981).

Examples of phenomenography are presented in this paper, and general aspects of the method are made explicit. The evolution of the method is discussed, its similarities and differences with the phenomenological movement elaborated, and a brief account of phenomenography as a research method presented. Finally, the relevance of this method for research in education is clarified.

## What is Phenomenography?

In a recent phenomenographic study (Johansson *et al.*, 1985), researchers tried to determine what effect university courses in mechanics had on students' understanding of some rather basic physical phenomena. Consider one of the questions students were asked: 'A car is driven at a high and constant speed on a straight highway. What forces act on the car?' It was found that students answer this and similar questions in one of two distinctly different ways. They either think that the force in the direction of movement is exactly equal to the forces in the reverse direction, or they think that the forces in the direction of movement exceed the sum of the forces in the opposite direction.

The following excerpt from an interview gives an example of the first kind of conceptualization:

> *Researcher (R):* A car is driven at a high and constant speed on a straight highway. What forces act on the car?
>
> *Student (S):* Motor power from the engine, air resistance, frictional force on all the bearings and gravity and normal force.
>
> *R:* How are they related to each other?
>
> *S:* Gravity and normal force are equal, and the engine is used to counterbalance the sum of the air resistance and the frictional force.
>
> *R:* Is there anything left over?
>
> *S:* Well, nothing important.
>
> *R:* Why is that?
>
> *S: When he drives at a constant speed, all the forces counterbalance each other?*
>
> *R:* But isn't there any . . .?
>
> *S:* I suppose there is heat in the air, perhaps.
>
> *R:* Yes. Isn't [some force] used for [moving the car] forward . . .?
>
> *S:* Well, yes. When it accelerates more power is needed [in a] forward [direction] than when it is moving at a constant speed.

The alternative way of thinking is illustrated by the following excerpt from another interview:

> *R:* A car is driven at a constant speed straight forward on a highway. Can you draw the forces acting on the car?
>
> *S:* A car [the student is drawing on a piece of paper].
>
> *R:* Hmm.
>
> *S:* Viewed from above, then?
>
> *R:* Hmm.
>
> *S:* On a highway?
>
> *R:* Hmm. Ye-es.
>
> *S:* Well, we have gravity straight down there . . .
>
> *R:* OK.
>
> *S:* And then there is air resistance, right . . .
>
> *R:* Hmm.
>
> *S:* Then friction against the road surface where there is also some resistance. Then there's . . .
>
> *R:* Now let's see, I'll call the air resistance one and the friction against the road surface, you write that there, yes, an arrow which I shall call two. . . .
>
> *S:* I'll draw it like that too [the student adds an arrow to his drawing; see Figure 10.1].
>
> *R:* Yes.
>
> *S:* It'll be the same here against the wheels.

*Figure 10.1:* Students' Conceptualization of Forces Acting on a Car

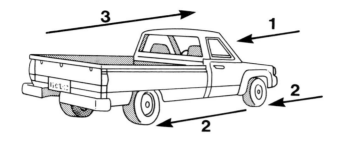

R: All of them are two, yes.
S: Hmm. Then the car is moved by the engine, then.
R: Hmm.
S: *And then a force which is directed forward which has to be greater than those there. Number three then has to be larger than number one and number two, otherwise it wouldn't move forward. . . .*
R: So that . . . the force that moves the car forward is larger than . . . the wheels . . . and this together. . . .

In the first case, the student focuses on the fact that the car is moving at .a *constant velocity*; in the second case, the student focuses on the fact that the car is *moving*. We may thus conclude that 'a body moving at an even speed' can be conceptualized in qualitatively different ways, either as:

(a) *Having a constant velocity, due to the equilibrium of forces,* or as
(b) *Moving, due to a 'motive inequilibrium' of forces.*

The two conceptions found among Swedish students can also be found in the history of physics. The first conception is Newtonian; it is the 'correct' way of thinking. The second was common during an earlier period in the history of science. In the present contexts, the fact that one conception is 'right' and another 'wrong' is of little interest. What I have tried to exemplify is the finding on which the whole 'phenomenographic enterprise' is based. When investigating people's understanding of various phenomena, concepts, and principles, we repeatedly found that *each phenomenon, concept or principle can be understood in a limited number of qualitatively different ways*. There were two ways of understanding in the example presented above; in other cases the variation may be larger. Let us consider another example, taken from research by Andersson and Karrqvist (1981). In this study, 13- to 16-year-old students from Swedish compulsory schools were asked to give a physical explanation of sight (i.e., the fact that we can see an object in front of us). Five qualitatively different ways of accounting for sight were discerned:

A  *The link between eyes and object is 'taken for granted'; it is not problematized; 'you simply see'.* (The necessity of light may be pointed out and an explanation for what happens inside the system may be given.)

B  *There is a picture going from the object to the eyes. When it reaches the eyes, we see.*

C  *There are beams coming from the eyes. When they hit the object, we see.*

D  *There are beams going back and forth between the eyes and the object. The eyes send out beams which hit the object, return and tell the eyes about it.*

E  *The object reflects light, and when it hits the eyes we can see the object.*

Again, there are some reasonably clearcut parallels between conceptions found among Swedish teenagers and those found in the history of science. For instance, while conception 'E' above corresponds to the main taken for granted assumptions of modern optics, conception 'B' resembles the ancient Greek atomists' concept of 'eidola' and conception 'C' comes close to Euclid's idea of the 'beam of sight'.

These two examples illustrate that phenomenography is a research method for mapping the qualitatively different ways in which people experience, conceptualize, perceive, and understand various aspects of, and phenomena in, the world around them.

### Man-world Relations as the Subject Matter of Phenomenography

As stated above, phenomenography investigates the qualitatively different ways in which people experience or think about various phenomena. This implies that phenomenography is not concerned solely with the phenomena that are experienced and thought about, or with the human beings who are experiencing or thinking about the phenomena. Nor is phenomenography concerned with perception and thought as abstract phenomena, wholly separate from the subject matter of thought and perception. Phenomenology is concerned with the *relations* that exist between human beings and the world around them.

Phenomenography is more interested in the *content* of thinking than is traditional psychology. Psychologists are interested in studying how people perceive and conceptualize the world. However, their focus is usually on the act of perception or conceptualization itself, and their aim is to characterize the process of perception and thought in general terms. Once this is accomplished, mainstream psychologists attempt to apply their conceptualizations to various content domains in order to clarify what it takes to perceive this or that phenomenon. They seek overarching laws of thought and perception that can be applied no matter what the situation or subject matter. Within phenomenography, thinking is described in terms of what is perceived and thought about; the research is never separated from the object of perception or the content of thought. (For instance, in the above examples, people's understandings of motion and vision were described in detail.) An effort is made to uncover all the understandings people have of specific phenomena and to sort them into conceptual categories. Because the objective of phenomenography differs from that of traditional psychology, its language must differ as well. Phenomenography does not use a psychological language that transcends subject matter. Neither does it use the language of physics.

Phenomenographers do not make statements about the world as such, but about people's conceptions of the world. Within each of the examples given above, one conception was presented that is currently considered to be 'true' and thus belongs in the domain of physics. However, phenomenography is also interested in mistaken conceptions of reality. Thus phenomenography occupies a space somewhere between natural science (disciplines that deal with what we hold to be true about the world) and traditional social sciences (which seek to discover laws of mental operations and social existence).

This is not to suggest that the subject matter of phenomenography has not been dealt with in established disciplines or by other research approaches. In fact, the contrary is true. There is an overwhelming amount of research that deals with what we call the 'phenomenographic knowledge interest'. The research of Piaget, for instance, especially in its earlier phases, clearly aims at providing a detailed description and analysis of the qualitatively different ways that children, in different stages of their development, view various aspects of the world.

Just as it has been shown in developmental psychology that many of the taken for granteds of adult thinking do not apply to the thinking of young children, in anthropology it has been shown that many of the taken for granteds of everyday life in one culture do not apply in another (see, for example, Mbiti's (1969) characterization of time in Africa). Similarly, differences can be observed between subcultures within the same society (see, for example, Schatzmann and Strauss's (1966) analysis of how socially stratified inhabitants of one American town had conceptually different accounts of the same event). Gestalt psychologists have studied how people perceive and understand phenomena. For example the founder of Gestalt psychology, Max Wertheimer (1945), provides a series of detailed accounts of people's thinking about specific problems, such as calculating the area of a parallelogram or finding the sum of the angles in a polygon.

From a phenomenographic perspective, these various schools of inquiry characterize how some particular phenomena are perceived by people of different ages, historical periods, cultures, or subcultures. The findings were not judged to be interesting in themselves, but generally served an instrumental function. They were thought to exemplify some more general phenomenon such as how the human mind develops. What has not been realized sufficiently is that the characterization of distinctively different ways that people understand various phenomena (for example, political power, the concept of number, or inflation) is of interest in itself.

I am arguing that the mapping of the hidden world of human conception should be a specialization in its own right. Of course, such a specialization is complementary to other disciplines. A careful account of the different ways people think about phenomena may help uncover conditions that facilitate the transition from one way of thinking to a qualitatively 'better' perception of reality. Such research would be of interest to those studying developmental psychology and the psychology of learning. Sociologists and anthropologists would be interested in learning why certain perceptions are more prevalent in one culture than in another.

The point of departure in phenomenography is always relational. We deal with the relation between the individual and some specified aspect of the world, or, to state it differently, we try to describe an aspect of the world as it appears to the individual. This means that we adopt an experiential, or what phenomenographers call a 'second-order' perspective (Marton, 1981). We do not try to describe things as they are, nor do we discuss whether or not things can be described 'as they are'; rather, we try to characterize how things appear to people. After all, human beings do not simply perceive and experience, they perceive and experience *things*. Therefore, descriptions of perception and experience have to be made in terms of their content. To characterize how something is apprehended, thought about, or perceived is, by definition, a qualitative question. Phenomenography provides descriptions that are relational, experiential, content-oriented, and qualitative.

*Categories of Description as Research Findings*

Phenomenographers categorize their subjects' descriptions, and these categorizations are the primary outcomes of phenomenographic research. Two issues are involved here. First, the results of phenomenographic research are the categorizations of descriptions; second, we contend that these categories are the most important result of the phenomenographic research enterprise. The first issue is dealt with first.

When we read and classify descriptions of a phenomenon, we are not merely sorting data; we are looking for the most distinctive characteristics that appear in those data; that is, we are looking for structurally significant differences that clarify how people define some specific portion of the world. In the above example of conceptions of the forces working on a car moving at a constant velocity, we focused on a single (and in our estimation crucial) factor: whether the forces in the direction of movement were seen as exceeding or equaling the sum of forces in the opposite direction. When we single out one factor, we obviously leave out others that are contained in the data. In this specific case, for example, we disregarded whether or not students mentioned vertical forces such as gravitation and normal force.

Furthermore, there may be other highly important factors upon which all subjects agree and thus are not focused upon by the researcher. For instance, Svensson (1984a) has pointed out that in the 'car on the highway' study all subjects adopted a holistic (as opposed to atomistic) approach to the problem. They reasoned within a cause–effect framework and considered velocity (the effect) to be related to the forces (the cause) acting on the automobile. However, in another investigation (Svensson, 1984b), where the problem again required cause and effect reasoning, it was found that participants often focused either on the cause or on the effect alone. Thus, researchers cannot take it for granted that subjects will always take a holistic rather than atomistic view of physical or mechanical events. Therefore, what is focused upon by the researcher must be a function both of the particular problem at hand and of the particular subjects participating in the study. Within this framework, we look for the most essential and distinctive structural aspects of the relation between the individual and the phenomenon. Leaving other aspects aside, we end up with categories of description which, though originating from a contextual understanding, are decontextualized and hence may prove useful in contexts other than the one being studied. Above all, each category is a potential part of a larger structure in which the category is related to other categories of description. It is a goal of phenomenography to discover the structural framework within which various categories of understanding exist. Such structures (a complex of categories of description) should prove useful in understanding other people's understandings.

Having discussed why phenomenographers try to communicate their conclusions as categories, I will now move to the second question: why we consider these categories to be the most significant outcome of our research.

In behavioural science research, we are usually supposed to know in advance the terms we will use to describe our observations. The categories are stated at the start, and we investigate the extent to which they are applicable in the cases we are investigating. For example, we may have a scale that measures the conceptual level of children. We may ascertain at what level our subjects are functioning and investigate how a child's conceptual level is related to some other, pre-specified area of educational experience. Compare this with a study of previously unknown flora and fauna on a remote island. In such a study, existing categories (species) are of limited usefulness. The botanist finds new species and, therefore, must construct new categories. Only then can the botanist determine how these new categories fit into the whole system of species classification. In this sense, the work of our fictitious botanist and the work of the phenomenographer are related. Just as the botanist finds and classifies previously undiscovered species of plants, the phenomenographer must discover and classify previously unspecified ways in which people think about certain aspects of reality. Because the different forms of thought are usually described in terms of categories, categories and organized systems of categories are the most important component of phenomenographic research.

When phenomenographers present their findings, someone usually asks: 'Would another researcher working independently arrive at the same set of categories if he or she were studying the same data?' On the surface, this appears to be a reasonable question. After all, research results are supposed to be replicable. However, two issues are buried in the question. One concerns the process of discovery: Would other researchers find the same conceptions or categories if they were doing the study for the first time? (Analogously, we might ask, 'Would two botanists discover the same plants and species if they independently explored the same island?') The other issue concerns whether a conception or category can be found or recognized by others once it has been described to them by the original researcher. The point I want to make is that replicability in the second sense is reasonable to expect, but in the first sense it is not. The original finding of the categories of description is a form of discovery, and discoveries do not have to be replicable. On the other hand, once the categories have been found, it must be possible to reach a high degree of intersubjective agreement concerning their presence or absence if other researchers are to be able to use them. Structurally, the distinction I draw here is similar to that between inventing an experiment and carrying it out. Nobody would require different researchers independently to invent the same experiment. Once it has been invented, however, it should be carried out with similar results even in different places by different researchers.

Having given an idea of what phenomenography is about, I now address the question of how the method evolved.

## The Evolution of a Research Specialization

To begin with, there was an interest among the first members of our research group in learning, or, more specifically, in learning that takes place in formal settings such as schools and universities. Initially, we followed the well-worn paths traveled by other researchers interested in the psychology of learning; we created more or less artificial situations hoping that we would arrive at some generalizable insight that could be applied across many situations. Gradually, however, we realized the limits of generalizations across content domains. For example, a description of the process of structuring in a free-recall situation does not have far-reaching relevance when describing the process of structuring when reading argumentative prose.

In the early 1970s we began to develop an alternative research approach. In one study, we asked students to read excerpts from their textbooks (or other material similar to their texts). We then asked them to tell us what they got from their reading and to describe how they went about reading the material. We transcribed the interviews. After reading and re-reading these transcripts, a striking fact appeared. Students understood the very same text materials in a number of qualitatively different ways. The fact that the same text, when considered as a whole, carried different meanings for different students was more interesting to us than the more usual finding that students retained different quantities of information. We need not relate the particulars of these studies here; they are available in the literature. Suffice it to say that in study after study students reported quite different understandings of the same material and that their understandings could be classified into a few, clearly definable categories. For example, in one study (Marton, 1975; Marton and Säljö, 1976) four kinds of understandings were discovered. The first accurately reflected the content of the article; the second was a less precise rewrite of the author's main point; the third contended that the author was arguing for something he was in fact arguing against; and the forth contended that the author was merely describing events, when in fact he was arguing for a specific point of view. Though different, all four conceptions were related to the main point of the article.

In other studies, however, descriptions of text material transcended the text itself. Though related to the text material, these descriptions were given from a perspective that was not present in the material being read. Occasionally, the descriptions clearly improved upon the text (see, for example, Säljö, 1975). The fact that we repeatedly found sets of qualitatively different conceptions of text material, and the realization that our outcome descriptions resembled the model of description employed in Piagetian studies[1] led our research in a new direction. We reasoned that if people had qualitatively different understandings of written material and if those understandings could be classified into a finite number of categories, then it was reasonable to expect that people in general hold qualitatively different conceptions of all kinds of phenomena. Indeed, such differences could be a potent source of explanation when investigating the question of how to account for qualitative differences in learning outcomes.[2] This is the basic idea of phenomenography, and it has been confirmed many times. When we ask people about their experiences of conceptions of various phenomena, again and again we find a limited number of qualitatively different ways in which the phenomena are comprehended.

During recent years, there have been three lines of development in our research group in Gothenburg.[3] First, though we focus on people's understandings of phenomena, there has been a continuing interest in the general aspects of learning. We have found that the qualitative difference in learning outcomes are consistently related to the qualitatively different approaches adopted by the learners. Säljö (1975) showed that differences in approach are also related to differences in how the situations are defined. Furthermore, differences in their definition of the situation are closely related to the learners' preconceptions of what learning is. Also, we have found (Pramling, 1983) that the origin of children's conception of learning is related to their discovery (or failure to discover) that there is a difference between 'wanting' to do something and actually 'being able' to do it. A healthy conception of learning is contingent upon the realization that the transition between 'want to' and 'able to' is related to experience (for example, practice and exercise).

A second line of research sprang from the content-oriented nature of our study of learning. Various research projects were started concerning the learning of basic concepts and principles in such areas as economics, physics, and mathematics. The research examples given at the start of this paper were drawn from this line of research. In these studies researchers have tried to map students' preconceived ideas about specific phenomena. Researchers are interested in finding out if students' preconceptions get modified through formal instruction and, if so, what changes occur and what are they like?

For instance, Lybeck (1981) studied secondary school students' understandings of tasks requiring propositional reasoning. Problems of this type were presented to students: 'If 4 cm$^3$ of a material weighs 6 g, how much would 6 cm$^3$ of the same material weigh?' There are at least two, equally correct ways of handling this problem. One might reason, 'As the weight of the material is 1.5 times greater than its volume (6/4); 6 cm$^3$ should weigh 1.5 times as much, i.e., 9 g'. Or one might reason, 'The volume is 1.5 times larger in the second case (6/4), the weight, therefore, should be 1.5 times larger in the second case as well (6 × 1.5 = 9 g).' The difference between these two approaches is that in the first, two different qualities (mass and volume) are related to each other, while according to the second, we carry out the arithmetic operation separately. The first approach represents the very idea of quantification, the most central aspect of modern physics. It is, for example, the only way of arriving at the concept of density. Though the distinction is of vital importance, it is seldom made explicit in textbooks or in classrooms. This research has prompted us to suggest that curriculum and textbooks should facilitate a development from one way of reasoning to another.

Another example of research into the understanding of specific subject matter is offered by Marton and Neuman's (1986) work on the role the number concept plays in the acquisition of skills in elementary arithmetic. They found that some preschool children and indeed some 7-year-olds use numbers simply as names. As they count they understand themselves to be calling things 'one', 'two', 'three', and so on. In addition they learn, thanks to the naive reinforcement of adults, that when counting a group of objects the name of the last object also serves as the name of the whole group. In the child's view, this is why the last 'name' has to be repeated when counting a group of objects:

*Teacher:* How many apples have we here? Can you count them?
*Pupil:* One, two, three, four . . . four.
*Teacher:* Yes, that's right, four.

One child who operated with the 'naming' conception of numbers was asked how many fingers she had on her right hand. She answered, 'Five.'

When she was then asked how many fingers she had on her left hand, she answered, 'Ten.' Of course, the 'names' of the fingers on the right hand are 'One', 'two', 'three', 'four', and 'five'. In the child's view, the last mentioned name (five) is also the name of the finger group. The names of the fingers on the left hand are 'six,' 'seven', 'eight', 'nine', and 'ten'. Therefore, this finger group is 'called' 'ten'. Once it was understood that the child conceived of numbers as names, it was possible to correct her misunderstanding and to avert other problems before they to developed.

The third line of research centers around the 'pure' phenomenographic interest in describing how people conceive of various aspects of their reality. In most cases, the concepts under study are phenomena confronted by subjects in everyday life rather than in course material studied in school. Investigations of this kind are usually conducted as formal interviews. Participants are asked about their understanding of such things as inflation, social security, taxes, or political power. In one such study, Theman (1983) investigated people's conceptions of political power. He began his study by asking residents of Gothenburg about a minor demonstration against the construction of a down-town garage. The building site had been occupied by protesters and their protest was one of the influences that finally convinced the city to halt construction.

Theman conducted his interviews during the period of the protest. An analysis of interview data revealed that four different definitions of power were held by the citizens of Gothenburg. The first two were born in the dualism between an absolute and a relative conception of power. The former refers to the belief that power comes in fixed quantities and that in order for one person to gain power it must be wrested away from someone else. The latter conception refers to the belief that power is not absolute but is created in certain situations where possibilities for action appear. Many citizens possessed one or another of these conceptions of power. Others contended that under different circumstances power can be of either the absolute or relative kind. A fourth group avoided the dualism altogether by adopting a magical conception of events that denied the existence of political power. Such people contended that our lives are ruled by unknown, alien forces and that the course of events is entirely beyond our control.[4]

In this section I have given examples of three lines of research followed by our research group in recent years. The first concerns content-related studies of the more general aspects of learning, the second concerns studies of learning and teaching in various content domains, and the third represents an interest in mapping conceptions of the world and relating categories of description to one another. The main difference between the first two orientations and the third is that in the former cases we focus on the relation between the conceptions and the conditions and processes from which they originate. In the third line of research we focus on the conceptions themselves as categories of description and on the relations among these categories. The term 'phenomenography' has been used to refer to all three orientations together. It has also been used more narrowly to describe the third orientation alone (Svensson, 1984a). Quite obviously the first and inclusive interpretation of phenomenography has been used in this paper. The second, more restrictive definition has been mentioned, and examples of that line of research have been given. However, the restrictive orientation has not been elaborated in detail.

## Phenomenography and Phenomenology

There are different ways in which one can try to discuss a research specializ-ation. In the first section, I presented some examples of our research and some general aspects of our approach. I briefly described the development of our approach and variations that have evolved within it. Another way of characterizing a research specialization is by making explicit its relation to other specializations, research traditions, or schools of thought. In the case of our research, there is a need to point out the similarities and differences between phenomenography and the phenomenological movement.

Phenomenography is not an offspring of phenomenology. The method, as we have seen, was developed out of some common sense considerations about learning and teaching. Our findings were presented to a wider audience and they attracted both interest and criticism. Our critics contended that ours was basically a descriptive enterprise and thus at odds with a research paradigm where prediction and control are the ultimate and only legitimate goals. Such criticism invited reflection.

We thought that phenomenology — based on the Husserlian imperative to return to 'the things themselves' — offered a philosophical explanation for what we were doing. For instance, we do not take for granted what 'being a good learner' means and then try to explain why some people are better learners than others. Instead, by carefully examining such specific things as the different accounts subjects have of the same text, we attempt to charac-terize the fundamental differences in the outcomes of learning. Our research focuses on the things people have learned, and by doing so we aim to clarify not what it means in general to 'be a good learner', but rather, what it means to learn specific content.

Phenomenology provides alternate epistemological assumptions to those adopted in 'mainstream' psychological research. (For examples of the main-stream paradigm, see Kerlinger, 1979, Bower and Hilgard, 1981.) Of course, the goals of phenomenology are other than those of normal science; phenom-enological work is propaedeutic to the normal science. According to the basic tenets of phenomenology, all knowledge (and hence all scientific knowledge) is rooted in our immediate experience of the world. It is the task of phenomen-ology to depict the basic structure of our experience of various aspects of reality and to make us conscious of what the world was like before we learned how to see it. Phenomenology is based on the German philosopher Franz

Brentano's (1973) concept of intentionality. All that is psychological includes consciousness but refers to something beyond consciousness itself. For example, we do not merely love, we love someone; we do not merely learn, we learn something; we do not merely think, we think about something. The relational point of view taken in our phenomenographic research can be seen as a special case of the principle of intentionality. All four features of phenomenography referred to earlier (the relational, experiential, contextual, and qualitative) are characteristic features of phenomenological research as well. In what way then does the phenomenographic approach differ from the phenomenological tradition? For the purposes of this paper, we will focus on only three areas of disagreement.

First, phenomenology, in the form Edmund Husserl advocated, is an alternative to empirical research and can be described as a first-person enter-prise. Researchers (philosophers) 'bracket' (hold in check) their preconceived notions and depict their immediate experience of the studied phenomenon through a reflective turn, bending consciousness back upon itself. All phen-omenologically inspired empirical research (which aims at studying other people's experience rather than one's own) has to transcend the original form of phenomenology in this respect. And indeed, this is exactly what has been done by Amedeo Giorgi and his colleagues at Duquesne University. Their attempt to base psychological research on a phenomenological epistemology comes closest to (but does not duplicate) the phenomenographic research approach. This group has developed a methodology for analyzing and describing the experiences of subjects by means of written and spoken inter-views (see Giorgi, 1975, or Alexandersson, 1981; Alexandersson makes a useful comparison between Giorgi's method and our own).

The second point of disagreement between phenomenology and phen-omenography concerns phenomenology's focus on the essence of experience. While phenomenographers try to characterize the variations of experience, for phenomenologists the essence of experience usually is interpreted as that which is common to different forms of experience. For example, contemplate the question: What is common to all different colors?, or, to put it another way: What is the essence of color? The only thing that is inevitable about colour is that it seen on the surface of objects. Thus, the essence of color is that it is an extension of a surface. The essence of objects and our experience of them is arrived at through what is called *imaginative variation*. What remains constant, in spite of the variation, is the essence. Ihde (1977, 1986) provides another interpretation of essence. He claims that the very structure of the variation itself is the essence of experience. Such a conceptualization is much closer to our thinking. In this sense, phenomenographic analysis, especially when we are carrying out an investigation of people's experiences of a single phenomenon, can be seen as the empirical equivalent of imaginative variation.

There is a third and perhaps the most fundamental difference between the cannons of phenomenology and our own empirical research approach. Edmund Husserl, the father of phenomenology, was anxious to find experience unaffected by scientific thinking. Therefore, he emphasized the distinction between immediate experience and conceptual thought. In a phenomenological investigation, we should 'bracket' the latter and search for the former. Phenomenographers do not make use of this distinction, at least not as a starting point in research. We try instead to describe relations between the individual and various aspects of the world around them, regardless of whether those relationships are manifested in the forms of immediate experience, conceptual thought, or physical behavior. Although it does make a difference on the psychological level in which form the relationship is manifested, our assumption is that there is a structural level which is not affected by these psychological differences (Marton, 1982).

## Some Methodoligical Aspects Of Phenomenography

I turn now to the question of what it is like to carry out phenomenographic research. Quite obviously there are different sources of information by means of which we may gain an understanding of how people conceive of various aspects of their world. Wenestam (1982), for instance, analyzed children's drawings in order to reveal their conceptions of death. We can also interpret how people conceptualize their world by studying their behavior under certain controlled conditions or in everyday life. The products of people's work can be studied as sedimentations of the ways they think about their world (cf., Marton, 1984). However, interviewing has been the primary method of phenomenographic data collection. What questions are asked and how we ask questions, of course, are highly important aspects of the method. For present purposes it will suffice to say that we use questions that are as open-ended as possible in order to let the subjects choose the dimensions of the question they want to answer. The dimensions they choose are an important source of data because they reveal an aspect of the individual's relevance structure. Furthermore, though we have a set of questions at the start of the interview, different interviews may follow somewhat different courses.

After the interviews have been completed they are transcribed and the transcripts are the data we analyze. As we pointed out above, we cannot specify exact techniques for phenomenographic research. It takes some discovery to find out the qualitatively different ways in which people experience or conceptualize specific phenomenon. There are no algorithms for such discoveries. However, there is a way of proceeding with the task which can be described, even if it cannot be specified in detail.

The first phase of the analysis is a kind of selection procedure based on criteria of relevance. Utterances found to be of interest for the question being investigated (for example, What are the different conceptions of political power?) are selected and marked. The meaning of an utterance occasionally lies in the utterance itself, but in general the interpretation must be made in relation to the context from which the utterance was taken. Svensson and

Theman (1983) have shown that the very same utterance takes on different meanings when it appears in different contexts. The phenomenon in question is narrowed down to and interpreted in terms of selected quotes from all the interviews. Of course, the quotes themselves are interpreted and classified in terms of the contexts from which they are taken.

The selected quotes make up the data pool which forms the basis for the next and crucial step in the analysis. The researcher's attention is now shifted from the individual subjects (i.e., from the interviews from which the quotes were abstracted) to the meaning embedded in the quotes themselves. The boundaries separating individuals are abandoned and interest is focused on the 'pool of meanings' discovered in the data. Thus, each quote has two contexts in relation to which it has been interpreted: first, the interview from which it was taken, and second, the 'pool of meanings' to which it belongs. The interpretation is an interactive procedure which reverberates between these two contexts. A step by step differentiation is made within the pool of meanings. As a result of the interpretive work, utterances are brought together into categories on the basis of their similarities. Categories are differentiated from one another in terms of their differences. In concrete terms, the process looks like this: quotes are sorted into piles, borderline cases are examined, and eventually the criterion attributes for each group are made explicit. In this way, the groups of quotes are arranged and rearranged, are narrowed into categories, and finally are defined in terms of core meanings, on the one hand, and borderline cases on the other. Each category is illustrated by quotes from the data.

An important difference between this way of proceeding and traditional content analysis is that, in the latter case, the categories into which the utterances are sorted are determined in advance. The former kind of analysis is dialectical in the sense that meanings are developed in the process of bringing quotes together and comparing them. As the meanings of categories begin to form, those meanings determine which quotes should be included and which should be excluded from specific categories. The process is tedious, time-consuming, labor intensive, and interactive. It entails the continual sorting and re-sorting of data. Definitions for categories are tested against the data, adjusted, retested, and adjusted again. There is, however, a decreasing rate of change and eventually the whole system of meanings is stabilized.

## Educational Applications of Phenomenography

We should keep in mind that phenomenography was developed within the framework of educational research. Mental models, which locate the objects of description in the minds of people, are in line with the 'knowledge interest' of psychology. However, psychological models are not particularly helpful in solving practical, pedagogical problems. Relational thinking, central to phenomenography, lends itself better to such purposes. Learning, thinking, and understanding are dealt with as relations between the individual and that which he or she learns, thinks about, and understands. If we understand the relationship that exists between an individual and what he or she is trying to learn, our pedagogical opportunities are greatly expanded. By changing that which has to be learned or understood, we change the relationship between the object of learning and the individual.

In a way, we cannot speak of the educational applications of phenomenography, because method was not developed separately from education and then applied to the field. Phenomenography was developed in response to educational questions. The 'purer', more abstract form of phenomenographic research (discussed earlier in this paper) was derived from the more pragmatic and educationally based research approach, not the other way around. All the research projects referred to under the headings of 'first and second research orientations' in the second part of this paper spring from our interest in education. As pointed out above, the first kind of research was devoted to describing the precise differences in what people learn in specific learning tasks and how those differences are related to the different approaches students adopt in learning those tasks. The second group of research projects concerned learning and teaching in various subject matter domains such as economics, physics, and mathematics. In this case, students' preconceived notions of phenomena were mapped and their connection with educational experiences were explored.

Quite obviously, the knowledge generated by these forms of phenomenographic research has direct educational relevance. In a more narrow sense, however, what is of immediate pedagogical interest is how students' conceptions can be changed by teachers and how better understandings can be arrived at by students. In fact, such aims are built right into these descriptive investigations. One function of mapping students' thinking at the start of a unit is that it focuses the teacher's attention on information that is not a part of the students' stock of knowledge. In this way, the research projects mentioned above have a clear-cut pedagogical orientation.

Our studies of students' ways of thinking have had some interesting by-products. We have found that when fundamental issues are discussed during interviews, the subjects may become conscious of contradictions in their own reasoning and attempt to rid themselves of such contradictions by considering alternative ideas. In the following excerpt from an interview (Johansson *et al.*, 1985), we observe a student shifting from an incorrect to an improved conception of reality. The particular question, already discussed above, was used to investigate students' understanding of the forces working on a car moving at a constant velocity down a straight road.

*Researcher (R):*  So a car is driven straight forward at a high constant speed and you are to draw or tell me what forces act on the car.
*Student (S):*  Well, it's wind resistance, then.
*R:*  Ye–es. What is that?

S:  It's the air's particles which . . .
R:  Yes.
S:  And it sort of stands still in relation to the car.
R:  What effect does it have, then?
S:  Against the direction of the car.
R:  I see.
S:  And the engine, or the motive force, then.
R:  Hmm.
S:  Due to the engine functioning in the car's direction. Then there are different sorts of friction in the car itself which act against, or it can look like it's sideways.
R:  Yes. How is the motive power? How great is it?
S:  Yes, it's much greater than the others.
R:  Ye-es. Individually or together?
S:  Together.
R:  If you have any more forces here, now you've said you can write it down, by the way, it would be interesting to see approximately how you . . .
S:  Yes. Then we can say that there's a car here, then . . . [see Figure 10.2].
R:  Yes.
S:  Exactly.
R:  Hmm.
S:  Then you say that one here is the motive force . . .?
R:  Hmm.
S:  Shall we draw them as vectors, then?
R:  Yes, it's alright if you draw an arrow.
S:  And so that the wind comes from in front.
R:  Yes.
S:  Then [the] wind [is] number two.
R:  Yes.

*Figure 10.2: Students' Conceptualization of Forces Acting on a Moving Car*

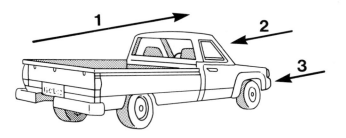

S:   And there we have number three when there's friction in the bearings and so on.

R:   Yes.

S:   Yes it will, and between the wheels and the road surface.

R:   Can it be moved like you did?

S:   Yes, one can add those two together.

R:   Yes. And how were numbers two and three in relation to number one?

S:   They were clearly smaller.

R:   And have you got any more forces that act on the car?

S:   We-ell, *I'm not sure about that, you know, maybe they're equally great, since the car is moving at a high [and] constant speed.* I'm not sure about that.

R:   How come you . . . how did you think when it was equally great . . . when it's greater.

S:   Since the car moves forward.

R:   Yes.

S:   But since it doesn't increase in speed perhaps it — they're equally great instead.

R:   Hmm.

S:   Probably, number one is greater only when it [the car] is accelerating.

As we have pointed out, the conception the student shows initially (the force in the direction of the movement exceeds the sum of the forces in the opposite direction) is always linked with focusing on the fact the body is *moving* (instead of being at rest). The other conception, the one he ends up with (the force in the direction of movement equals the sum of the forces in the opposite direction) is always linked with focusing on the fact that the body is moving at a *constant velocity* (instead of accelerating or decelerating). We can see that the student in this interview switches from one conception to another when he refocuses his attention from movement to velocity. Such a refocusing could probably be strategically triggered in students by a knowledgeable teacher.

Another by-product of students' participation in primarily descriptive research efforts is that in group discussions revolving around different ways of thinking, students may become conscious of the fact that there are different ways of thinking. This is a very fundamental insight, a step on the way to adopting a qualitatively better way of thinking. Lybeck (1981) gives an excellent example of how a group of students, by learning about others' ways of thinking, function together on a higher conceptual level than any of the single individuals and how, by setting 'the group mind' to work, they solve a problem in physics which none of them would have been able to solve on their own.

Encouraging teachers to pay attention to students' ways of thinking and to facilitate students' realization that there are different ways of thinking may be the most important pedagogical implications of phenomenographic view of learning. We can, nevertheless, go further than that and be more specific concerning how the conceptual structure underlying skills in various content domains can be built up in a systematic way. Marton and Neuman's (1986) work, quoted above, offers an example of this. They have carefully mapped the interrelated conceptual prerequisites underlying different levels of skills in elementary arithmetic and have developed methods for facilitating their acquisition. The preliminary results are extremely promising, but more definite answers are yet to come.

## Acknowledgment

The research reported here was supported financially by a grant from the Swedish Council for Research in the Humanities and Social Sciences.

## Notes

1  I would like to express my deep gratitude to Professor Erik Wallin of the University of Uppsala who first drew my attention to the parallelism between the Piagetian model of description and our own.
2  It may be noted in passing that in our first investigation, discussed above, we intended to rule out this source of explanation by means of the choice of the text and the selection of the participants. All the participants were supposed to have all the necessary conceptual prerequisites. Yet they nevertheless differed in their understanding of the text read. The variation in the outcome must have depended on a variation in what was taking place during the reading itself. Indeed, we found that the qualitative differences in outcome corresponded to qualitative differences in the approaches to the learning task adopted by the learners. Some focused on the text itself; they tried to memorize as much as possible; others focused beyond the text, on issues not directly discussed in the text. The former way of setting about the learning task was called the *surface approach*, and it always resulted in a less satisfactory learning outcome. The second way was called the *deep approach*, and it was — in most cases — associated with a good understanding of the main point in the text.
3  Due to limitations of space, I restrict myself to commenting on the work of 'the kernel group' in Gothenburg. Other research with a similar orientation carried out elsewhere is not dealt with here.
4  In actual fact, Theman distinguishes between the 'what' and 'how' of conceptions (i.e., *what* [kind of phenomena] is conceptualized and *how* it is conceptualized). The four conceptions accounted for here represent only the second aspect.

## References

ALEXANDERSSON, C. (1981). 'Amedeo Giorgi's empirical phenomenology'. *Reports from the Department of Education, University of Goteborg.*

ANDERSSON, B. and KARRQVIST, C. (1981). 'Ljuset och dess egenskaper' [The light and its qualities]. *EKNA-rapport nr 8, Institutionen for Praktisk Pedagogik, Goteborgs Universitet.*

BOWER, G. M. and HILGARD, E. R. (1981). *Theories of Learning* (5th ed.). Englewood Cliffs, NJ: Prentice Hall.

BRENTANO, F. (1973). *Psychology from an Empirical Standpoint.* New York: Humanities Press. (Published originally in German, 1874).

DAHLGREN, L. O. (1980). 'Children's conception of price as a function of questions asked'. *Reports from the Department of Education, University of Goteborg.*

GIORGI, A. (1975). 'An application of phenomenological method in psychology'. In A. Giorgi, C. Fisher and E. Murray (Eds), *Duquesne Studies in Phenomenological Psychology* (Vol. III). Pittsburgh, PA: Duquesne University Press.

IHDE, D. (1977). *Experimental Phenomenology.* New York: Putman.

IHDE, D. (1986). 'On non-foundational phenomenology'. *Publikationer from Institutioner for Pedagogik, Goteborgs Universitet, Fenomenografiska Netiser, nr 3.*

JOHANSSON, B., MARTON, F. and SVENSSON, L. (1985). 'An approach to describing learning as change between qualitatively different conceptions'. In A. L. Pines and L. H. T. West (Eds), *Cognitive Structure and Conceptual Change.* New York: Academic Press.

LYBECK, L. (1981). *Arkimedes i Klassen. En Amnenpedagogisk Berattelse [Archimedes in the Classroom. A Narrative on the Didactics of Subject Matter].* Goteborg: Acta Universitatis Gothoburgensis.

KERLINGER, F. N. (1979). *Behavioral Research: A Conceptual Approach.* New York: Holt, Rinehart and Winston.

MARTON, F. (1970). *Structural Dynamics of Learning.* Goteborg: Acta Universitatis Gothoburgensis.

MARTON, F. (1975). 'On non-verbatism learning: I. Level of processing and level of outcome'. *Scandinavian Journal of Psychology, 16,* 273–279.

MARTON, F. (1981). 'Phenomenography — Describing conceptions of the world around us'. *Instructional Science, 10,* 177–200.

MARTON, F. (1982). 'Towards a phenomenography of learning: III. Experience and conceptualization'. *Reports from the Department of Education, University of Goteborg.*

MARTON, F. (1984). 'Towards a psychology beyond the individual'. In K. M. J. Lagerspetz and P. Niemi (Eds), *Psychology in the 1900's.* Amsterdam: North Holland.

MARTON, F. and NEUMAN, D. (1986). 'Why some children fail to learn the four rules of arithmetic'. Paper presented at the Psychology of Mathematics Education Conference, London, July 20–25.

MARTON, F. and SÄLJÖ, R. (1976). 'On qualitative differences in learning: I. Outcome and process'. *British Journal of Educational Psychology, 46,* 4–11.

MARTON, F. and SÄLJÖ, R. (1984). 'Approaches to learning'. In F. Marton, D. Hounsell and N. J. Entwistle (Eds.), *The Experience of Learning.* Edinburgh: Scottish Academic Press.

MBITI, J. (1969). *African Religions and Philosophy.* London: Heinemann.

PRAMLING, I. (1983). *The Child's Conception of Learning*. Goteborg: Acta Universitatis Gothoburgensis.

SÄLJÖ, R. (1975). *Qualitative Differences in Learning as a Function of the Learner's Conception of the Task*. Goteborg: Acta Universitatis Gothoburgensis.

SCHATZMAN, L. and STRAUSS, A. (1966). 'Social class and modes of communication'. In A. G. Smith (Ed.), *Communication and Culture. Readings in the Codes of Human Interaction*. New York: Holt.

SVENSSON, L. (1984a). 'Kroppar i linjar rorelse. Teknologers tankande om nagra fenomen inom mekaniken' [Bodies in linear movement. Students' thinking about some phenomena within mechanics]. *Pedagogiska Institutionen, Goteborgs Universitet*.

SVENSSON, L. (1984b). 'Conceptions of statistical relations within the context of thinking about causal relations'. *Reports from the Department of Education, University of Goteborg*.

SVENSSON, L. (1984). 'Manniskobilden i INOM-gruppens forskning: Den larande manniskan' [The view of man in the research of the INOM-group: The learning man]. *Pedagogiska Institutionen Goteborgs Universitet*.

SVENSSOR, L. and THEMAN, J. (1983). 'The relationship between categories of description and an interview protocol in a case of phenomenographic research'. *Reports from the Department of Education, University of Goteborg*.

THEMAN, J. (1983). *Uppfattningar av Politisk Makt [Conceptions of Political Power]*. Goteborg: Acta Universitatis Gothoburgensis.

WENESTAM, C. G. (1982). 'Children's reactions to the word "death".' Paper presented at the American Educational Association Annual Meeting, New York.

WERTHEIMER, M. (1945). *Productive Thinking*. New York: Harper.

*Chapter 11*

---

# An Introduction to Curriculum Criticism

---

*Dorene Doerre Ross*
*College of Education*
*University of Florida*
*Gainesville, FL 32611*

Curriculum criticism is a multidisciplinary approach to the study of educational materials and settings. Criticism combines and adapts information collection and reporting techniques of social anthropology and aesthetic criticism in order to help others perceive and understand educational phenomena more fully. The function of the curriculum critic, like that of a literary or art critic, is to describe the essential qualities of phenomenon studied, to interpret the meanings of and relationships among those qualities, and to provide reasoned judgements about the significance and value of the phenomenon.

This article provides an overview of curriculum criticism focusing on its roots, the methodological processes and issues, and the potential contribution of the approach. While curriculum criticism has been used to study both educational materials and settings, the majority of the literature focuses on methods and examples of criticisms of educational settings perhaps because critics have assumed literary criticism can be adapted relatively easily to the criticism of published curriculum materials, and therefore have turned their attention to adapting criticism to the study of ongoing settings. Consequently, discussion of curriculum criticism in the article focuses mainly on its use in educational settings, although some mention is made of its use in the study of materials.

### Roots of Curriculum Criticism

Criticism has its roots in two qualitative areas of inquiry — aesthetic criticism and social anthropology. The use of aesthetic criticism as a tool for curriculum analysis was first suggested by Mann (1969), who proposed the curriculum be viewed as a literary object. He noted that the function of the literary critic is to disclose the choices made by the artist and the meaning of those choices. By examining curriculum in this way, Mann believed educators would gain insights not possible through the technical analysis of curriculum, which involves an evaluation of the match between intended outcomes and conditioned means for achieving outcomes.

Although Mann developed his ideas no further, others gradually began to explore them, with Eisner (1972; 1977; 1978; 1979, pp. 190–260; 1980) as the major spokesperson elaborating the purposes and processes of curriculum criticism. He stated that the principal aims of the critic are to look for patterns of key elements (or pervasive qualities) in educational settings, and to reveal and explain the meaning and complexity of the particular behaviors involved in teaching and learning in various contexts. In numerous publications, he stressed the importance of understanding the artistic elements of teaching. While educators have utilized traditional scientific methods to foster the growth of science in education, Eisner noted that the use of artistic traditions which might facilitate growth of the art of education has been neglected.

Curriculum critics have suggested the use of critical methods from a variety of different art forms — e.g., literary arts, dance, visual arts (Barone, 1980; Eisner, 1979; Kelly, 1975; Kyle, 1979; Mann, 1969; McCutcheon, 1979b). All stress three common critical traditions which provide a core of methods useful in analyzing curriculum. First, a critic discloses the meaning of an art object by revealing the key structural elements of the object and the choices made by the creator in designing the object. Second in criticism, the critic must translate a non-linguistic experience into verbal discourse. In most cases critics stress the use the evocative, descriptive language and the use of linguistic devices such as metaphor and characterization to accomplish this translation. Third, critics must make judgements about what is valuable in an art object. These judgements are based on the critic's knowledge of the art form (connoisseurship) and on publicly disclosed criteria or principles.

Curriculum criticism has also utilized methodological traditions from social anthropology. Criticism is an empirical effort that must be based on extensive observation. While aesthetic critics use observational methods when critiquing art forms such as theater and dance, the object of their observations is different in character from an educational setting. An artistic production lasts a short period of time, can usually be viewed repeatedly in its entirety and can be compared to other productions of the same dance or play. Educational settings are not similarly bounded in time. Experiences are not repetitive in the same sense, and comparison across settings is more complex.

Because criticism is a qualitative inquiry that focuses on context, meaning and the explanation of phenomena, critics logically drew on the disciplined methods of observation and interpretation associated with fieldwork in social anthropology. McCutcheon (1976), then a student working with Eisner, provided a thorough explanation of the synthesis of methods from anthropology and aesthetic criticism into a methodology for conducting curriculum criticism. Since that time methodological procedures and issues have been the focus of numerous authors (Barone, 1980; Eisner, 1979; Kelly, 1975; Kyle,

1982; McCutcheon, 1979b; Willis, 1978a). A brief discussion of methods and issues follows.

## Methods of Curriculum Criticism

Few differences exist among curriculum critics in describing the methods used or the products of the critical method. While criticisms may vary in emphasis, as will be discussed in the section on writing, no differing schools of thought or procedures exist. This apparent consensus may well be due to the newness of the field or to the relatively small number and similar educational background of the researchers writing about the approach.

Because this area of inquiry is so new, barely 14 years old, the methods are continually evolving. The following discussion of methods, therefore, cannot be considered exhaustive but rather suggestive of the ongoing work of curriculum critics as they attempt to establish this area of inquiry.

### *Data Gathering Methods*

Curriculum criticism is based upon the knowledge the researcher has gained about the phenomenon studied through the collection of a large quantity of empirical data. Critics have drawn on the various techniques associated with anthropological studies for disciplined and systematic methods of collecting data. These include observation, interviewing, and the collection of educational artifacts (e.g., tests, teachers' planbooks, children's books, memos, textbooks). The majority of the data collected is obtained through direct observation of ongoing events in the educational setting, and through interviews designed to gain information about the meaning of events to participants. As in ethnography, the data can be recorded in several ways (e.g., fieldnotes, on audio or video tape, in photographs or slides), however the predominant method is the use of field notes.

In discussing the collection of data, critics stress several procedural principles also stressed in other qualitative methodologies. First, observation must be non-interventionist (Eisner, 1980). That is, the presence of the observer should change the setting as little as possible. Second, the observer should record any and every observable event that might contribute to an understanding of the phenomenon. While critics do not limit their observation to recording those events which can be quantified or measured, they must also be careful to record specific observable events rather than conclusions of motive or intent. As Barone (1980) stated, the exact words, actions and products of the participants form the core of evidence upon which criticism is based. Such evidence must be accurate and complete to be of value. Third, although a critic might begin with a 'foreshadowed' question, the observed phenomenon, not pre-specified hypotheses, determines the focus of observations and of the resultant criticism (Mann, 1969; McCutcheon, 1979b). (A foreshadowed question is a pre-specified question which the researcher uses as a guide for observation, helping to focus the information collection process.) And last, the critic should remain aware of the possible perspectives of other critics. This awareness encourages the critic to look at the phenomenon from multiple perspectives and to collect more data (McCutcheon, 1979b). For example, Ross (1981) analyzed a kindergarten teacher's practices from a developmental perspective which did not support the teaching strategies used. In an attempt to understand the reasons behind the teacher's choices, she then analyzed the strategies using principles derived from a behaviorist perspective. By looking at the data from two differing educational perspectives, a broader understanding of the teacher's practices from a developmental perspective which did not support the teaching strategies used. In an attempt to understand the reasons behind the teacher's choices, she then analyzed the strategies using principles derived from a behaviorist perspective. By looking at the data from two differing educational perspectives, a broader understanding of the teacher's practices was obtained.

One feature that distinguishes criticism from other qualitative methodologies is the role of connoisseurship in observation. Connoisseurship is the act of appreciation of subtle qualities of a setting and of relationships among qualities that enables one to make comparisons to other settings (Eisner, 1975, 1977, 1979). Just as a wine connoisseur can distinguish subtle, yet important, characteristics of wine that most people cannot perceive, the educational connoisseur attends to the subtle particulars of classrooms. This ability to perceive differences forms the basis for critical judgements about wines and educational settings.

While many ethnographers argue that researchers should not study familiar settings, the aesthetic critic stresses that previous experience and expertise with the studied art form is essential if one is to understand the work. Similarly, the educational critic believes the researcher must draw on his or her background of educational knowledge and experience in order to make sense of what is happening, to determine what is unique about each setting, and to make valid critical judgements. As McCutcheon (1976) noted, familiarity with a wide range of education settings, rather than blinding one to the characteristics of a particular setting, provides the basis for noting subtle differences and characteristics which might otherwise pass unnoticed.

*Writing Criticisms: The Art of Disclosure*

The development of the empirical base is guided by connoisseurship, the art of appreciation. The complementary skill of the critic, the ability to share perceptions, is described as the art of disclosure. Although disclosure could occur orally or through a media presentation, critics most commonly share perceptions through written criticisms, which include description, interpretation, and appraisal or judgement of the educational phenomenon. The lines between data collection, analysis, and writing are blurred. Although interpretation and appraisal are discussed separately from data collection, the reader should understand that in reality the processes are not discrete. In a cyclical fashion the researcher observes, interprets, and appraises, with each possible interpretation or appraisal guiding subsequent observations. Similarly, the separation of the three processes of description, interpretation, and appraisal is not as precise as the following explanation makes it seem.

*Description.* Through description, the critic recreates the experience of an educational setting for those who were not there. As Eisner (1977) explained, 'The critic . . . aims at providing a rendering in linguistic terms of what it is that he or she has encountered so that others not possessing his level of connoisseurship can also enter into the work' (p. 347). Description should transport the reader to the scene, convey the pervasive qualities or characteristics of the phenomenon, and evoke the feeling and nature of the educational experience. To accomplish this, critics stress the use of linguistic devices such as metaphor, contrast, redundancy, and emphasis, frequently used in fiction and poetry but seldom used by educational researchers (Barone, 1980; Eisner, 1977; Kelly, 1975). The use of these devices should create a description so vivid the reader can almost see it and hear it. The following example is illustrative:

> The classroom is almost a caricature of the society.
> The curriculum is served up like Big Macs, reading, math, language, even physical and affective education are all precooked, prepackaged, artificially flavored. . . .
> Teaching is orderly; learning is ordered. Page 47 always follows p. 46. . . .
> Each day is remarkably like the day before and the day after. The school year seems to have been made with 174 pieces of carbon paper. The same things are done at the same times in the same ways in the same books. Only the pages change. (Donmoyer, 1979)

The description of the educational phenomenon serves as the basis for interpretation and appraisal. While not all critics believe descriptions should be written as evocatively as Donmoyer does (see Munby, 1979; Popkewitz, 1978; Rosario, 1978), they do agree that description must be complete enough to allow the reader to trace the line of reasoning used in forming interpretations and to identify possible mistakes in judgment. Thus, the description should be filled with concrete data from a variety of sources and yet must also be written in a style that captures and communicates the nature of the educational experience.

*Interpretation.* All phenomenological methodologies are concerned with understanding the meaning of events to those involved and to others. Interpretation is the explanation of such meanings. In curriculum criticism, interpretation involves the search for the meaning of educational activities and interactions to all participants and to the critic.

McCutcheon (1979b; 1981, pp. 5–10) described three types of interpretations used by curriculum critics: (1) the construction of patterns through the analysis and resynthesis of constituent parts; (2) the interpretation of the social meaning of events; and (3) the analysis of relationships between educational events and external factors. Briefly, each type of interpretation will be described.

All behavior is culturally patterned (Sapir, 1963). A pattern can be defined as a characteristic way of behaving which may be conscious or unconscious to the actor. Patterns reveal the relationships among discrete events and thus increase understanding of each event. For example, Kyle (1980) analyzed the curriculum of a fifth grade classroom to reveal patterns in administrative decisions which influenced the teacher's curriculum decisions. She reported that administrative decisions about such things as required and supplemental curriculum materials, requirements for student promotion, the adherence to a highly specified daily schedule, and the standardization of the rate of student progress limited the teacher's curriculum choices and her ability to adapt the curriculum to individual students. Thus, patterns of administrative decisions helped to explain or give meaning to the patterns of the teacher's curriculum decisions and the resultant learning opportunities for children. As Kyle's study demonstrates, identifying patterns within an educational setting and the interrelationships among those patterns can increase understanding of educational events.

The second type of interpretation involves developing an understanding of the social meaning of events or the meaning of behavior within the setting. Developing this understanding involves the presentation of a 'thick' description which reveals the underlying structure of a social event. Ryle (related in Geertz, 1973, pp. 6–7) differentiated between 'thick' and 'thin' descriptions of behavior. In his example, Ryle noted that that the 'thin' descriptions of the physical behavior of 'rapidly contracting the eyelids of [the] right eye' remained unchanged whether the act was a friendly wink, a twitch, a conspiratorial signal or a parody of a twitch. A 'thick' description would indicate the meaning of the behavior. It is this 'thick' description of a behavior, the clarification of meaning, which is sought in an interpretation of the social meaning of classroom events.

The final form of interpretation is the analysis of the relationship between educational events and external considerations. For example, theory from education and the social sciences, history, current social or political events, and established educational practices may provide a framework that promotes a better understanding of a particular educational setting (Eisner, 1979; McCutcheon, 1981). The texts chosen by a school system, theories about learning and socialization, legislative mandates, educational budgets and public opinions are all examples of external factors which influence a curriculum. McCutcheon's (1979a) criticism revealed a teacher who, because of parental pressure and administrative policies, incorporated experiences into his curriculum that he did not endorse. In this case understanding the role of external forces was important in explaining a curriculum which included conflicting elements that might otherwise have seemed incomprehensible.

*Appraisal.* Evaluation, generally avoided by the social anthropologist but considered essential by the aesthetic critic, is a judgement of significance or quality grounded in reason and based on knowledge of the pervasive characteristics of the educational phenomenon. Critics use two types of appraisal, one intrinsic, one extrinsic (Hirsch, 1967, pp. 153–160; McCutcheon, 1979b). In intrinsic appraisal the stated aims of the teacher (principal, textbook, author, etc.) are accepted as valid and the critic judges whether these aims were met. For example, Cornbleth (1978) assessed a variety of published social studies curricula to determine whether the aims of an inquiry approach were met. She found that each included some elements important to an inquiry approach but omitted others of considerable importance. Thus, her appraisal raised questions about whether social studies curricula achieve their stated aim of fostering inquiry skills.

Extrinsic appraisal is an evaluation of aims. Are the aims desirable or worthwhile? For example, McCutcheon (1978) appraised the educational significance of a science lesson:

> We might wonder about the academic content of the lesson (Is it worthwhile?). Isn't it likely that fourth graders know the relative size and position of planets already? Indeed, during the discussion preceeding the activity, it seemed they already had a great deal of sophisticated information about the solar system. Chris, for example, anticipated the rotation demonstration. A more complex assignment seems possible, one . . . [which] would expand their knowledge about the solar system. (pp. 199–200)

Extrinsic appraisal compares the aims of the teacher to some external criteria. The criteria used must be appropriate to the particular situation, and the critic must share the criteria with the reader (Eisner, 1977; Hirsch, 1967; Munby, 1979). In the above example, the criterion is the researcher's knowledge of the children and their abilities. Other possible criteria include educational, social, and political theory and researcher knowledge of classrooms and children in general. For example, Ross (1979) questioned the effectiveness of a teacher's practices, using Piaget's theory of learning as the criterion. Apple and King (1978) appraised a kindergarten curriculum through reference to social and economic theory. They described the features of the curriculum which provided social control and economic adjustment suitable for the purposes of the American political and economic system.

*Differing Points of Emphasis in Writing.* All criticism is based on the three processes of description, interpretation and appraisal. However, critics use different points of emphasis or methods of organization in order to communicate an understanding of the educational phenomenon they studied. Critics discuss three different categories of points of emphasis. One set of critics vary their emphasis by focusing primarily on one of the three writing processes. McCutcheon (1979b) provided examples from art criticism of critics who are known primarily for their description, interpretation or appraisal.

A second set of critics provide varying emphasis in their criticisms through the use of literary devices. For example, Barone (1980) and Kelly (1975) discussed the use of theme in criticism. Theme provides the central controlling idea for a piece of criticism. Barone (1980) noted that a theme may be grand (derived from a pervasive societal theme) or particularistic (derived from the pervasive qualities of the particular setting). The criticism by Apple and King (1978) is an example of a criticism with a grand theme. In this case, the critics appraised the features of a kindergarten curriculum by referring to theoretical principles inherent in the American social and economic system. Kyle's (1980) criticism which reported the relationship between administrative decisions and a teacher's curriculum decisions is an example of a criticism with a particularistic theme.

Point of view is another literary device which might be used in criticism. Point of view is the manner in which the criticism is communicated. The point of view one chooses influences what will and will not be revealed in a criticism. For example, the student perspective is a point of view that is frequently neglected in educational writings. Other literary devices which might be used include plot, characterization and landscape, i.e., the physical and human surroundings (Barone, 1980; Kelly, 1975).

Willis (1978b) discussed a third category of point of emphasis. He stated that criticism can have an aesthetic, personal or political dimension. The aesthetic dimension focuses on the integrity of the form of the pieces of the curriculum and the intended or possible functions of the curriculum. McCutcheon's criticism provides an example of a criticism which emphasizes the aesthetic dimension. In this criticism, McCutcheon (1978) focuses on communicating the general feeling of a fourth grade classroom, showing how the various aspects of classroom life contribute to the ambience.

The personal dimension focuses on individual insights and perceptions of meaning. For example, Milner (1978) wrote a criticism of a special education curriculum that centers primarily on the author's perspective. Apple. and King's (1978) criticism, cited above, is an example of a criticism focusing on the political dimension or the relationship between the encountered event and the collective socio-political meanings and action.

In their methodological writings, critics discuss these three differing categories of points of emphasis. In writing criticisms, however, the categories are not distinct. Many criticisms include all or most of the elements mentioned in each categorization system above. However, each has a different principal point of emphasis or combination of points of emphasis. Thus, these three categorizations do not indicate different schools of thought among critics but rather suggest the multiple considerations of critics in organizing and writing criticism to convey the meaning of educational phenomena.

## Evaluation: Judging the Quality of Criticism

As in other forms of qualitative inquiry, the issue of evaluation is frequently raised. Evaluation of criticism perhaps is a more plaguing concern than evaluation of other qualitative studies because critics not only interpret, they appraise. And critics use literary devices associated with fiction and poetry. How does the reader know that the critic has not just told a good story, created a pleasant piece of fiction?

Logically, critics view criteria common to the evaluation of other qualitative studies as also appropriate to the evaluation of criticism. (Readers interested in a thorough discussion of criteria for evaluating qualitative studies should see Becker, 1970; Dawson, 1979; McCutcheon, 1981; Ross and Kyle, 1982; Wilcox, 1982; and Wolcott, 1975.) Those criteria which are particularly stressed by critics will be discussed briefly.

First, description, interpretations, and appraisals should be supported by continued reference to pieces of evidence (Barone, 1980; McCutcheon, 1979b; Pepper, 1945). This inclusion of facts enables the reader to evaluate interpretations and appraisals personally. In judging the adequacy of interpretations the quality of evidence presented is as important as the quantity (Hirsch, 1967). One method for evaluating the quality of each piece of evidence is to compare it with other evidence. For example, information obtained through interviews can be compared to observations to assess quality. Additionally, sufficient time must be spent in the field to determine the pervasive characteristics of the setting and to judge the adequacy of evidence used to determine those characteristics (Eisner, 1975, 1977).

Second, critics stress that alternative hypotheses should be explored and the line of reasoning used to reach conclusions revealed (McCutcheon, 1979b, 1981). The task of the researcher is to collect as much data as possible, from as many sources as possible. The researcher must then evaluate the quality of each piece of evidence, explore alternative interpretations, and then logically present a case to the reader exposing the line of reasoning at all decision points. The exploration of alternatives should include a search for negative evidence. In this way, the researcher exposes biases, and the reader may judge whether a slanted view has been given.

Through the process of structural corroboration the researcher develops and supports interpretations and appraisals (Eisner, 1979, pp. 215–216; McCutcheon, 1979b; Pepper, 1945, p. 7). As a lawyer presents a case to a jury, laying out all the assumptions, exposing the evidence, and developing a theory to explain the evidence, so too the critic presents a case. Each new fact must support the hypothesis, increasing the consistence and coherence of interpretations. The ability of an interpretation to explain all the facts strengthens the probability that it is true. Additionally, as the critic builds the case, the criteria used for appraisal must be specified and must be appropriate to the particular phenomenon studied (Hirsch, 1967, pp. 165–184).

A third criterion for judging quality is to compare the information presented in the criticism with other knowledge (Eisner, 1975; McCutcheon, 1981). Critics should discuss the relationship of their findings to appropriate theoretical constructs and the other quantitative and qualitative studies. Additionally, readers can compare the findings to their own practical knowledge about the nature of educational settings.

A final criterion is the significance and usefulness of the criticism. The criticism should increase the reader's understanding of the phenomenon studied (Eisner, 1979; Willis, 1975). Essentially, this means the criticism must have sufficient depth to reveal subtle qualities and reveal the underlying complexity of the phenomenon studied. Use of the third criterion, comparison of the information presented to other knowledge, provides clues about the significance and usefulness of the criticism. If the criticism broadens, or makes more apparent, the practical significance of theory, the criticism has met the criterion of significance.

## The Educational Uses of Curriculum Criticism

Criticism can be used as a research or an evaluation method, though the inclusion of appraisal means that it is more frequently used in evaluation. Whether used for research or evaluation, the findings are useful to educators in several ways.

Criticism, like other qualitative methodologies, allows educators to consider and develop understandings about the educational process rather than focusing solely on educational outcomes as is characteristic of much research. As Barone (1980) wrote, criticism 'avoids the simplistic notion that test scores, or narrow slices of behavior, supply us with the only valid information about student progress or (even more simplistically) about the worth of a teacher or a program' (p. 30). Thus, criticism helps the reader view educational phenomena from a variety of perspectives and thus increases understanding of their complexity and richness. This increased understanding is important for several reasons. First, the revelation of different interpretations may spark much needed dialogue among educators (Eisner, 1979, pp. 210–211). For too long, educators have approached problems as if simple and universal solutions existed. Dialogue about the multiple possible meanings of any educational event would encourage educators to seek more diverse, particularistic solutions to educational problems.

Second, criticism provides examples of teaching which raise questions and issues which teachers might not otherwise consider (Eisner, 1979, pp. 210–211). Eisner stated that criticism helps teachers learn how to see the subtleties of an educational environment and thus raises issues for deliberation which may have an impact on practice. For example after reading a criticism about a teacher who allowed others to make many decisions for her, Andrini (1981), also a classroom teacher, reported increased deliberation about influences on her instructional decisions. Thus, criticism can enable practitioners to increase their consciousness about various educational phenomena.

Third, criticism may help researchers to identify new directions for research (Eisner, 1975). Like other qualitative methodologies, criticism can lead to the generation of hypotheses and the identification of variables which may indicate important directions for quantitative researchers. Additionally, criticism may help to clarify the meaning of variables and the ways in which variables interact, thereby complementing the findings of quantitative studies and perhaps suggesting new directions for research.

In summary, the principal value of curriculum criticism is similar to the value of many other qualitative methodologies. It increases understanding of particular social phenomena, disclosing a variety of possible meanings and increasing reader insight. Additionally criticism appraises educational phenomena. Education is a goal-oriented discipline. One's values guide the selection of goals and the means to achieve goals. Curriculum criticism opens the issue of values to discussion by including an appraisal of educational events. Such dialogue about values and about the reasons for value choices is essential to the improvement of educational decision-making and practice.

## The Broader Application of Criticism

The methods, issues, and application of curriculum criticism to education have been discussed. To date, curriculum critics are educators, yet the methodology seems equally applicable to other social scientists. Most social and behavioral sciences involve human interaction, decisions based on value choices, and a combination of theoretical and practical knowledge. A variety of disciplines might use critical methods in studying and appraising relevant phenomena. For example, attorneys might profit from criticism of their practices while presenting evidence and arguments to juries. Why are some attorneys more likely to be believed? What subtle factors influence the decisions of jurors? Or social workers might use criticism to study such issues as the best ways to approach hostile, cooperative or apprehensive clients or the factors that help make foster parents more effective. Other examples of areas which might profitably explore the use of criticism include medicine and health-related services, counseling, the ministry, and city planning. Certainly, particularistic problems in methods and issues will need to be explored within each field. However, the broader principles outlined in this article will be applicable across disciplines.

## References

ANDRINI, C. (1981). 'Reaction to a curriculum criticism: A teacher's view'. Paper presented at the Annual Meeting of the American Educational Research Association, Los Angeles.

APPLE, M. W. and KING, N. (1978). 'What do schools teach?' In G. Willis (Ed.), *Qualitative Evaluation: Concepts and Cases in Curriculum Criticism*. Berkeley, CA: McCutchan.

BARONE, T. E. (1980). 'Effectively critiquing the experienced curriculum: Clues from the new journalism'. *Curriculum Inquiry, 10* (Spring), 29–53.

BECKER, H. S. (1970). *Sociological Work*. Hawthorne, NY: Aldine.

CORNBLETH, C. (1978). 'Inquiry theory and social studies curricula: Problems in planning for thinking'. Paper presented at the Annual Meeting of the American Educational Research Association, Toronto.

DAWSON, J. A. (1979). 'Validity in qualitative inquiry'. Paper presented at the Annual Meeting of the American Educational Research Association, San Francisco.

DONMOYER, R. (1979). 'School and society revisited: An educational criticism of Miss Hill's fourth-grade classroom'. In E. W. Eisner (Ed.), *The Educational Imagination*. New York: Macmillan.

EISNER, E. W. (1972). 'Emerging models for educational evaluation'. *School Review, 80* (August), 573–590.

EISNER, E. W. (1975). 'The perceptive eye: Toward the reformation of educational evaluation'. Paper presented at the Annual Meeting of the American Educational Research Association, Washington, DC.

EISNER, E. W. (1977). 'On the uses of educational connoisseurship and criticism for evaluating classroom life'. *Teachers College Record, 78* (February), 345–358.

EISNER, E. W. (1978). 'Humanistic trends and the curriculum field'. *Journal of Curriculum Studies, 10* (September), 197–204.

EISNER, E. W. (1979). *The Educational Imagination*. New York: Macmillan.

EISNER, E. W. (1980). 'Toward a conceptual revolution in evaluation'. *Educational Forum, 44* (March), 373–374.

GEERTZ, C. (1973). *The Interpretation of Cultures*. New York: Basic Books.

HIRSCH, E. D. (1967). *Validity in Interpretation*. New Haven, CT: Yale University Press.

KELLY, E. F. (1975). 'Curriculum evaluation and literary criticism: Comments on the analogy'. *Curriculum Theory Network, 5*(2), 87–106.

KYLE, D. W. (1979). *Life as Teacher: The Disclosure of Teacher's Activities and Emergent Problems*. Unpublished doctoral dissertation, University of Virginia.

KYLE, D. W. (1980). 'Curriculum decisions: Who decides what'. *Elementary School Journal*, (November), 77–85.

KYLE, D. W. (1982). 'Using educational criticism for middle school evaluation'. *American Middle School Education, 5* (Spring), 10–15.

MANN, J. S. (1969). 'Curriculum criticism'. *Teachers College Record, 71* (September), 27–40.

McCUTCHEON, G. (1976). *The Disclosure of Classroom Life*. Unpublished doctoral dissertation, Stanford University.

McCUTCHEON, G. (1978). 'Of solar systems, responsibilities and basics: An educational criticism of Mr. Clement's fourth grade'. In G. Willis (Ed.), *Qualitative Evaluation: Concepts and Cases in Curriculum Criticism*. Berkeley, CA: McCutchan.

McCUTCHEON, G. W. (1979a). 'A conflict of interests: An educational criticism of Mr. William's fourth grade'. In E. W. Eisner (Ed.), *The Educational Imagination*. New York: Macmillan.

McCUTCHEON, G. (1979b). 'Educational criticism: Methods and application'. *Journal of Curriculum Theorizing, 1* (Summer), 5–31.

McCUTCHEON, G. (1981). 'On the interpretation of classroom observations'. *Educational Researcher, 10* (May), 5–10.

MILNER, E. W. (1978). 'The amphibious musician'. In G. Willis (Ed.), *Qualitative Evaluation: Concepts and Cases in Curriculum Criticism.* Berkeley, CA: McCutchan.

MUNBY, H. (1979). 'Example of curriculum review and criticism'. *Curriculum Inquiry, 9* (Fall), 229–249.

PEPPER, S. (1945). *The Bases of Criticism in the Arts.* Cambridge, MA: Harvard University Press.

POPKEWITZ, T. (1978). 'The social structure of school and reform: A case study of IGE/S'. In G. Willis (Ed.), *Qualitative Evaluation: Concepts and Cases in Curriculum Criticism.* Berkeley, CA: McCutchan.

ROSARIO, J. (1978). 'On the child's acquisition of aesthetic meaning: The contribution of schooling'. In G. Willis (Ed.), *Qualitative Evaluation: Concepts and Cases in Curriculum Criticism.* Berkeley, CA: McCutchan.

ROSS, D. D. (1979). 'Piaget: Practical applications in public school settings'. Paper presented at the Annual Meetings of the USC–UAP International Interdisciplinary Conference on Piaget and the Helping Professions, Los Angeles.

ROSS, D. D. (1981). 'Ms. Shore's classroom: A curriculum criticism'. Paper presented at the Annual Meeting of the American Educational Association, Los Angeles.

ROSS, D. D. and KYLE, D. W. (1982). 'Qualitative inquiry: A review and analysis'. Paper presented at the Annual Meeting of the American Educational Research Association, New York.

SAPIR, E. (1963). 'The unconscious patterning of behavior in society'. In D. Mandelbaum (Ed.), *Selected Writings of Edward Sapir.* Berkeley, CA: University of California Press.

WILCOX, K. (1982). 'Ethnography as a methodology and its application to schooling'. In G. Spindler (Ed.), *Doing the Ethnography of Schooling.* New York: Holt.

WILLIS, G. (1975). 'Curriculum criticism and literary criticism'. *Journal of Curriculum Studies, 7* (May), 3–17.

WILLIS, G. (Ed.). (1978a). *Qualitative Evaluation: Concepts and Cases in Curriculum Criticism.* Berkeley, CA: McCutchan.

WILLIS, G. (1987b). 'Qualitative evaluation as the aesthetic: Personal and political dimensions of curriculum criticism'. In G. Willis (Ed.), *Qualitative Evaluation: Concepts and Cases in Curriculum Criticism.* Berkeley, CA: McCutchan.

WOLCOTT, H. F. (1975). 'Criteria for an ethnographic approach to research in schools'. *Human Organization, 34* (Summer), 111–127.

*Chapter 12*

# Qualitative Research and the Uses of Literature

*Maxine Greene*
*Teachers College*
*Columbia University*
*New York, NY 10027*

Qualitative research is concerned with meanings as they appear to, or are achieved by, persons in lived social situations. Research of this kind cannot be carried out by people who see themselves as detached, neutral observers concerned with the kinds of observation, measurement, and prediction that are presumed to be unbiased, unaffected by the inquirer's vantage point or location in the world. For one thing, the life of meaning does not present itself for examination from without. It is not a function of behavior; it is attained in the course of action or conscious, reflected-on conduct. Since action involves choosing or the taking of initiatives, it always futures; it is anticipatory. The initiator of an action, as he/she is 'condemned to meaning' (Merleau-Ponty, 1962, p. xix), is always in process, in search of understanding. It is true that meanings already achieved become sedimented; they become ground or background for further experiencing. Dewey (1934) said that 'experience becomes conscious, a matter of perception, only when meanings enter it that are derived from prior experiences' (p. 272). When this happens, the funded meanings are reviewed, as experience is extended and expands.

Those of us in search of educational understanding are concerned, then, with interpretations of particular kinds of human action in an intersubjective world. Whether we are looking through the lenses of history, or sociology, or psychology, we are attending to beings who are forever incomplete, reaching out to make sense of the actualities of their lives. We can 'catch' some of that incompleteness through participant observation, or through certain modes of listening, or the reading of 'free writing', or by paying heed to the ways in which people move and create images and play. All these are ways of engaging in 'qualitative research'. They all involve interpretation by the researcher or student, from particular standpoints and against the background of accumulated meanings. There is, in other words, always a horizon of pre-understanding on the part of the researcher, even as there is a horizon of pre-understanding in the situation being studied. One question that arises has to do with how the two horizons are related. A merging of them, it has been said, 'must be considered a basic element in all explanatory interpretation' (Palmer, 1969, p. 25).

Because of this, it seems to me that there can be no greater 'purity' in the interpretations made of actual situations than in those made of the unreal situations created by imaginative literature. I use works of imaginative literature in teaching educational history and philosophy of education, and I do so because of the sense of intelligibility they provoke and because of the way they involve students personally and intersubjectively in conscious pursuits of meaning. I choose works I believe to be thematically relevant to what we are studying, not works that have to do specifically with teaching and learning in classrooms or with cultural reproduction in any general sense. I have found that informed encounters with literary texts permits students to confront their own lived realities in ways that have consequences for understanding what I hope to be their own projects — meaning their ways of gearing into and identifying themselves in the world. To be a teacher, I am convinced, is to be present in what one is doing, personally present. It is to perceive one's work as an aspect of one's own search for freedom and fulfillment, a response to what Schutz (1967, p. 247) called the 'fundamental anxiety', or the fear that one's existence makes no difference in the world.

Now, it is the case that not all theories of literature or approaches to literary criticism justify a focus on the reader and the reader's own quest for meanings. Indeed, literary criticism *per se* cannot be considered a qualitative study. We need only recall the so-called 'New Criticism', which treated literary texts as self-enclosed, internally coherent, separated off from ordinary experience and social life. Certain of the more contemporary structuralist approaches treat literary works as structures of signifiers and signified in complex interrelationship, in many ways detached from reality (Culler, 1975). At times, structuralism merges with semiotics or the systematic study of signs (Eco, 1984). It is true that, for structuralist and semiotic thinkers, engagements with texts focus attention on language, 'defamiliarize' what may have been taken for granted, and therefore effect some transformation of consciousness; but there is little concern in that approach for lived experience and diverse disclosures of meaning — the kind of disclosures that reach beyond the texts. The 'deconstructive' approach (Derrida, 1978) not only challenges traditional oppositions (true/false, rational/mad, central/marginal, black/white, male/female). It attempts to upset the whole notion that texts are logical systems. For Derrida, writing evades all essences and systems; meaning continually spills over. Writing always means more than it says; there can be no self-contained structures, no hierarchies, no solid foundations.

My own view is deeply affected by Dewey's (1934) conception of art as experience, by the phenomenological view of existence as a question of possibility and understanding as part of the structure of existence. It is affected as well by Sartre's (1965) notion of literature as an address to the reader's freedom and by what is called 'reader reception' theory. This puts great stress on the ways in which the reader constitutes texts as meaningful and the ways in which imaginative texts disconfirm habitual modes of perceiving, thus making the reader acknowledge what they are (Iser, 1978). Moreover, according to this view, certain works 'interrogate' their readers and require them to transform ordinary beliefs and expectations. What may follow is a heightened self-consciousness and a willingness to be changed.

It is with some of this in mind that I assign Nathaniel Hawthorne's (1969) *The Scarlet Letter* in a class in the history of American education. I cannot say that there is a particular meaning in the book that I expect students to find. I cannot say (in spite of all the detailed introduction called 'The Customs House') precisely what Hawthorne intended or what he achieved through the writing of the novel, in part because Hawthorne is no longer here to ask. Nor can I expect or guarantee that if my students read the novel well the problems presented by the book — of nature and culture, sin and guilt, the oppression of women, ostracism and acceptance, faith and speculation, puritanism, adultery, art — will finally be resolved. All I can do is offer possibility and do a bit of pointing so as to make the work accessible on more than the surface level. I choose to use this particular work because it is, in so many senses, a drama having to do with the tension between the natural and the cultural and because that tension seems to be of profound educational importance. But I have to create a situation in which my students come themselves upon this tension and interpret it against their own pre-understandings (which are, after all, the pre-understandings that define our culture). The book, in some way, must interrogate them and what they believe, if it is to 'work' at all.

*The Scarlet Letter* is, obviously, made out of language; it was created by a man who, like all other human beings, shared in a particular socially constructed reality at a specific moment in history. Transmuting aspects of his experience into words, provoked (as he said) by the appearance of a 'rag of scarlet cloth' discovered in a Custom-House, to create an 'as if', an imaginary world, he left us a text that can only present itself as possibility to the modern reader. The novel refers to no existing empirical reality; it cannot be grasped in an instant; it has to be constituted over time by diverse individuals who are willing to lend it to their own lives. Borrowing from Iser (1978, pp. 107–134), I ask students to take into account the multiple perspectives through which the novel can be viewed: the students' own perspectives as readers, aware of what it signifies to enter a fictional world; the perspective created by the narrative point of view (itself affected by the author's pre-understandings); the perspective of the Puritan society described in the text; the shifting and contesting and overlapping perspectives of the elders of that society, of Hester Prynne, the Reverend Dimmesdale, Roger Chillingworth, little Pearl. The town, the woods, the public square, the scaffold, the households: all signify differently, depending on the perspective. As the reader moves through the book over time, as he/she looks through the multiple perspectives, he/she is (as it were) variously ordering the materials of his/her own consciousness. The words, the levels of language, the symbols evoke memories, embedded images, perceptions, intuitions the reader attempts to order and synthesize under the guidance of the text. Inevitably, ordinary experience is defamiliarized. New modes of ordering, new vantage points may bring the unseen into visibility, may make the taken for granted palpable and strange.

I have space for only one example — that of Hester's assumption of 'a freedom of speculation' (Hawthorne, 1969, p. 183) during her ostracized life in a lonely cottage by the seashore, on the outskirts of the town. It is not only that she questions the tenets of puritanism. She looks from an 'estranged point of view at human institutions, and whatever priests or legislators had established; criticizing all with hardly more reverence than the Indian would feel for the clerical band, the judicial robe, the pillory, the gallows, the fireside, or the church' (p. 217). Taking a critical stance, affirming that nothing natural can be wrong, she gives every appearance of rejecting the culture and relying on her own untrammelled impulse and spontaneity. The difficulty is that she becomes chilled by her own alienation. She is a woman in need of connectedness, drawn to mutuality and concern. Also, for all the offense with which she has been charged, she remains a participant in her society; ostracized or not, critical or not, she requires rootedness in some common world. The fact that the existing society is theocratic, dominating, and cruel at first oversimplifies the question of whether or not socialization (and all that accompanies it) is justified; but it is not long before students confront the ambiguities, the impossibility of a perfect solution.

Students are likely to find, as their viewpoint wanders from perspective to perspective in the course of reading the novel, that the perspectives do not mesh and that everything is *not* explained. There are gaps, say, inexplicable gaps between Dimmesdale's refusal to accept Hester's proposal that they leave the community for Europe or the West and his final attempt at confession before he dies after the Coronation Sermon. There are gaps between Hester's determination to leave and her eventual return. These gaps can only be filled by interpretative acts on the part of the reader who recognizes that the novel is and will remain an open question, that there *is* no perfect answer or meaning buried in it like gold in the hills. The interpretative work on the part of readers who see that the book has a public existence and an intertextual significance is the work needed for the achievement of meaning, an approximate resolution of the 'problem' of the book.

It is just that work that can engage students with an important aspect of the educational undertaking — and their relation to that undertaking. Surely part of our teaching has to do with awakening them to all the problems of membership in a culture, even as it has to do with empowering them to initiate persons who can withstand submergence and learn how to see and speak for themselves. In the case of American education, there are a number of imaginative works that move students to probe problems they might never have posed without the confrontations made possible by such works. I think of what, for many, is the paradigmatic text: *The Adventures of Huckleberry Finn* (Twain, 1959). Here, too, and in the extreme is the matter of nature and culture, if we are willing to associate nature with the river and the fraternal life on the river and culture with the riverbanks with all their violence and greed and fraud. This novel, like so many others, speaks on many levels and in many voices, but it confronts readers (if they allow it to) with questions that ought to be inescapable for practicing teachers. There is the matter of the slave economy and the 'pieties' and shams associated with it, the world view that even the restless Huck has absorbed. If he had not, he would not feel such guilt, not feel that he was taking up 'wickedness again' when he decides 'to go to hell' and not turn Jim in (p. 210).

But there is also the matter of the skills and capacities Huck learns on the river through an education largely irrelevant in the world represented by the churning steamboat that cuts the raft in two. He is not prepared to deal with deceptions, feuds, and false gentility; he cannot fend off Tom Sawyer's heartless 'games'. How *are* teachers to foster values like candor, integrity, decency, and compassion in a technological, pecuniary society? How *are* they to empower the young to function effectively in such a society and remain reflective and humane? How *are* they to free persons to name the world in their own vernaculars and at once take part in the culture's dialogue? Encounters with literature, in part because they become encounters with other consciousnesses, are apt to provoke such questions. They are not the kinds of questions answerable from the standpoint of the system or the institution, because imaginative works cannot deal except with realities made and interpreted (adequately or inadequately) from actors' vantage points.

The idea of perspective or vantage point is important to me in the teaching of educational history or philosophy, largely because I am convinced that we cannot posit a 'normal' or 'normalized' reality that is the same for everyone. Whether the setting is in the distant past or in the contemporary world, its meanings are contingent on participants' ways of paying attention and making sense. I teach Herman Melville's (1967) short stories, 'Bartleby the Scrivener' and 'Benito Cereno', with some of this in mind. As may be well known, Melville was often preoccupied with what he thought of as 'bachelorism', signifying a partial or shallow vision due to innocence, or denial, or inexperience, or complacency, or what we would call false consciousness. In both stories the structuring consciousness is that of a 'bachelor': a Wall Street lawyer who formulates his reality in the light of efficiency and what is most of use to him, and a New England ship captain whose self-righteousness and stereotypes prevent him from seeing that a slave revolt has taken place on a ship. In the first story, the negations of Bartleby (who 'prefers not to') temporarily shake the narrator's prudent, self-imposed placidity and force him to make accommodations he would never ordinarily make and to say, at one point, 'Ah, Bartleby! Ah, humanity!' (Melville, 1967, p. 99). It is not just that he recognizes the image of a failure, 'alone in the universe. A bit of wreck in the mid Atlantic' (p. 83). He breaks through what he calls his own 'necessities' and recognizes (for a moment) another human being. In the case of 'Benito Cereno', racist prejudice so fixes the captain's vision that he never reaches that point where the 'other' is concerned. He cannot even acknowledge what the Spanish captain recognizes as the 'shadow' cast by slavery.

What finally is to blame — character or the environment; individual short-sightedness or an inequitable world? These, too, touch on questions fundamental for the teacher, whether that teacher deals with the oppressed, the very poor, the delinquent, the prejudiced, the hedonist, the self-involved. The issue comes up as well where women are concerned, particularly with our new understanding with respect to gender. Among the books I teach is Kate Chopin's (1972) *The Awakening*, a late nineteenth century 'woman's' novel. One of the reasons for its power, I believe, is that there is no single answer to the interrogation it sets up for the reader who journeys through the book in search of meaning. Yes, Edna Pontellier was born at a time when wives were infantilized, when the alternatives seemed to be either promiscuity or domestic slavery. Yes, she was oppressed by a stern Presbyterian father, installed in a doll's house by an indulgent Creole husband (who would not even trust her with their children's care). And, yes, she has her moment of 'awakening', conceived as an 'indescribable . . . oppression . . . strange and unfamiliar . . . a mood' (p. 14). Before long, she finds herself involved with Robert Lebrun, usually thought of as a lap-dog by the Creole 'mother-women' from whom she feels estranged. The point is that she has alternatives once she awakens, but she cannot name or act upon them, and so she destroys herself. Social pressure interacts with temperament, ignorance, fear, conventionality. She is both conditioned *and* responsible, the innocent victim *and* the ineffective author of her own life. We can grasp how the world means to her, and yet we wonder and we grope. How do we educate the Edna Pontelliers? How can we initiate them into forms of knowing and, at once, release them to be?

Somewhat the same issue arises with *The Great Gatsby* (Fitzgerald, 1953), what with the 'gorgeous' American dreamer, Jay Gatsby, brought to his undoing in the 'foul dust' of the eastern air. He believes firmly that he can go back and recapture what has been lost; he believes absurdly that the rich in their 'vast carelessness' will take him into their world (p. 180). What, indeed, happens when the American Dream sounds only 'like money', when the dreamer feels he 'must be about His Father's business, the service of a vast, vulgar, and meretricious beauty' (p. 99)? What is the end-in-view of our teaching? How do we educate an informed public? What, in the last analysis, is conscience to mean? And the American identity?

Equally troubling questions arise when we read another novel I often use: Ralph Ellison's (1952) *Invisible Man*. I try to offer it as possibility, not solely as a book that recapitulates Black history in America, not only as a rendering of the 'boomeranging' of Black expectations in this country. Clearly, it has to do with a condition in white people's heads that imposes invisibility upon other groups; and it has to do with wildly shifting perspectives, with inno-cence, with Emersonian hopes, with the sound of the blues, and with the underground. But it also engages readers with an existential quest for 'visi-bility', with an individual constantly labeled, made into an object or a manip-ulable 'thing'. It is up to him, in the end, to recover and then identify himself, to name himself, to create his own visibility, to use his mind. The narrator says at the beginning: 'I was looking for myself and asking everyone except myself questions which I, and only I, could answer' (Ellison, 1952, p. 17). And, finally, 'In going underground, I whipped it all except the mind, the *mind*. And the mind that has conceived a plan of living must never lose sight of the chaos against which that pattern was conceived' (p. 502). This may suggest another reason for the use of imaginative literature.

There are, it must be evident, innumerable texts that might be used in educational history or 'foundations' courses, texts ranging from early nine-teenth century ones to Don De Lillo's (1985) contemporary *White Noise* and John Irving's (1985) *The Cider House Rules*. De Lillo's has to do with a 'noxious cloud' escaping from a railroad car in an ordinary college community; Irving's with the problem of unwanted children in America, with the ambi-guities of abortion, with being 'of use' to others, with rules. Both books are also relevant in philosophy of education courses, particularly those emphas-izing social philosophy and education. If philosophy involves the posing of critical questions with regard to what is said, known, assumed, and valued, imaginative literature has the potential of stimulating and complicating the undertaking.

Again, it is of the first importance that imaginative texts be distinguished from documentary or discursive texts. Literature, as has been suggested, does not simply refer to or describe or explain or account for an existing state of things. It may be said to refer, as Sartre (1965, p. 67ff.) has pointed out, to reader subjectivity, or to consciousness, or to experience. This does not, of course, mean that it refers to disembodied spirit or to soul or to a self-enclosed interiority, anymore than it refers to a universal. Subjectivity or consciousness or experience, in this context, signifies the way persons grasp the appearances of things, transact what surrounds, thrust into the intersubjective world, pose their questions, look for meanings. The constitution of a text as meaningful, then, takes place within and by means of those processes and from the vantage point of the particular reader or actor or agent involved.

My concerns in social philosophy and education cluster around theory in its classic sense — having to do with the nature of the rational or humane society. Or I take Isaiah Berlin's (1962) view of political theory as 'thoroughly committed not only to the analysis of, but to conclusions about the validity of, ideas of the good and the bad, the permitted and the forbidden . . .' (p. 17). Not only am I interested in enabling students to understand something of the ways in which social realities are constructed, in which power is distributed, in which social institutions take shape and interact with one another. Against this background, I want to provoke questions about justice and equity and decency and fulfillment. I want to explore ways in which education can contribute to the formation of a public and the opening of a public space. In such a qualitative enterprise there must be a double consideration of perspective and the achievement of meaning: on the part of the student (inquirer, questioner, scholar, reader) and on the part of the actual and possible participants in whatever social or cultural scene is being studied.

This entails an effort to comprehend, not only the many modes of social grouping and arrangement in the culture, but also the ways in which all this is experienced by individuals. Because I choose to focus on contemporary predicaments, much stress is laid upon the technologized, bureaucratized, administered nature of modern society. The matter of ideology is inescapable, as is the matter of hegemony. We cannot but direct attention to the multiple forms of what some call oppression or the mystifications (by language, by media) that prevent people from giving their authentic energies full play and from speaking in their own voices, for themselves. Since I am particularly interested in John Dewey's (1954) and Hannah Arendt's (1958) conceptions of the public, there is no way of overlooking the individual sense of agency or his/her awareness of vantage point. With all this in mind, I do not necessarily look for works of literature that deal with social issues or educational issues *per se*. Nor do I seek out novels written from political positions that coincide with mine.

I might use *White Noise* (De Lillo, 1985) in the hope that students would, in taking the dissonant perspectives present in that novel, order some of their own feelings and attitudes with respect to the technical languages that obscure the dangers to human life characteristic of this moment of time. The frozen powerlessness, the persistent fear of death, the reliance on consumerist comforts: all these pose, or ought to pose, soul-shaking questions to the educator. How, in a world of technicist 'noise', can we achieve what Habermas (1979) calls 'communicative competence?' How can we empower the young to resist the seductions of popular culture? *White Noise* concludes with an alarming rendering of the 'language of waves and radiation', and of people waiting in a supermarket line, their carts stocked with goods: 'A slowly moving line, satisfying, giving us time to glance at the tabloids in the racks. Everything we need that is not food or love is here in the tabloid racks. The tales of the supernatural and the extraterrestrial. The miracle vitamins, the cures for cancer, the remedies for obesity. The cults of the famous and the dead' (De Lillo, 1985, p. 326). How does this connect with talk of subject matter, common learnings, the culture's conversation? There may be no single answer; but, somehow or other, the questions ought to be posed.

There are occasions (when there is time, as there usually is not) for using Melville's (1950) *Moby Dick* to highlight problems of isolation and alienation in the acquisitive society — a society driven by a manic need to master the White Whale and what is one-dimensionally defined as evil itself, what the 'dismasted' Captain Ahab conceives as the malign. Often, I assign Joseph Conrad's (1972) *Heart of Darkness*, in part because of the confrontation between the ship captain, Marlow, who has known the wilderness and the incomprehensible, and the Director of Companies, the Lawyer, and the Accountant to whom he tries to explain 'the darkness'. By that he means the hopelessly paradoxical, that which escapes logic and the hold of reason. 'You can't understand,' Marlow tells them. 'How could you? — with solid pavement under your feet, surrounded by kind neighbours ready to cheer you or to fall on you, stepping delicately between the butcher and the policeman, in the holy terror of scandal and gallows and lunatic asylums — how can you imagine what particular region of the first ages a man's untrammelled feet may take him into by the way of solitude — utter solitude without a policeman — by the way of silence — utter silence, where no warning voice of a kind neighbour can be heard whispering of public opinion' (p. 70)?

In a certain respect, this may be viewed as another version of the nature/culture dialectic mentioned above; but it may also summon up the predicament of the stranger, the one who does not posit a policeman or possess a 'kind neighbour' or hear 'the whispering of public opinion'. Surely, whoever is involved, it is important to recognize the existence of submerged forces when it comes to the pursuit of meaning, perhaps particularly in a world racked by violence and irrationality. They may be the forces of unconscious desire or repressed energy. They may have to do with intuitions of 'horror' (as in the case of Conrad's Mr Kurtz), or dread, or boredom, or despair. 'The truth is hidden — luckily,' says Marlow. And it may indeed be necessary for teachers to cope with the fact that their deepest existential questions are unanswerable, even as they recognize the need for sense-making and some degree of rational order in their worlds.

I am reminded again of the 'chaos', as Ellison's (1952) narrator called it, against which whatever patterns we create are conceived. In philosophy classes, it seems to me, there must be some consciousness of the dangers of meaninglessness and, yes, 'chaos'. What we have to be concerned with in our teaching is the dullness, the indifference that allows persons simply to accede. I think of Virginia Woolf (1976) in *Moments of Being*, making the point that much of life tends to be 'embedded in a kind of nondescript cotton wool' (p. 70). She meant that we tend to be shrouded in the habitual, in routines, in what she called 'non-being'. Then she talks about certain shocks she experienced, 'exceptional moments', certain ones ending in a despair that held her powerless. But when she was able to find a reason, she found that she could overcome powerlessness: 'I was not powerless, I was conscious — if only at a distance — that I should in time explain it' (p. 72). Later, she realized that such sudden shocks were welcome, and she supposed that 'the shock-receiving capacity is what makes me a writer'. It may well be that the same capacity is what makes people students and, in time, reflective practitioners.

It is not surprising that many works of literature begin in a kind of *stasis* or fixity and move on to moments of awareness and reflectiveness. One of the paradigm cases may be Thomas Mann's (1955) *The Magic Mountain*, which begins with Hans Castorp's inability to question the taken for granted or to take a critical attitude towards 'the deficiencies of his epoch' (p. 32). He lives on the 'flat-land'; he is unquestioningly devoted to his work, which wears him out; he is afflicted with 'mediocrity'. The novel tells, of course, of his ascent to the sanitarium on the mountain, his confrontations with rationalism and mysticism and hedonism. He experiences what Mann described as an 'alchemistic, hermetic pedagogy'; and he learns to look through a multiplicity of perspectives as he grows and is transformed. This, of course, is the classic *Bildungsroman*, the educational novel. It provides complex possibilities of meaning where change and transformation are concerned. To what end? The person 'doing' philosophy cannot but ask this question, even as he/she is preoccupied with the nature of the 'worthwhile'.

Albert Camus' (1948) *The Plague* may offer a humanistic and moral answer for some, for all the 'gaps' among the perspectives it opens, for all the 'voices' that are heard. This novel, too, begins with images of *stasis*, habit, boredom in a town 'without intimations' where the chief concern is with 'doing business'. When the plague abruptly afflicts the town, it is understood and responded to in diverse ways. For this reason alone, an encounter with the text relates very closely to the experience of qualitative research, since it makes so very clear that the meaning of any situation is always a meaning *for* particular human beings with different locations in the world. Here, of course, the movement away from mere brute habit occurs, not because of a 'hermetic pedagogy', but because of the sanitary squads formed by certain citizens of the town. 'These groups,' writes the narrator, 'enabled our townfolk to come to grips with the disease and convinced them that, now that plague was among us, it was up to them to do whatever could be done to fight it. Since plague became in this way some men's duty, it revealed itself as what it really was: that is the concern of all' (p. 111).

Here we have what might be called a public act that opens up something approximating a public space. Readers coming on this perspective find themselves moving beyond the predicament of the 'single one' to a predicament of human beings involved with one another, and the questions inevitably multiply. Dr Rieux, revealed as the compiler of the chronicle, thinks at the end that he has to bear witness to the suffering of the plague-striken 'so that some memorial of the injustice and outrage done them might endure; and to state quite simply what we learn in a time of pestilence: that there are more things to admire in men than to despise'. Still, he knows that his story is not one of a final victory. 'It could only be the record of what had had to be done, and what assuredly would have to be done again in the never ending fight against terror and its relentless onslaughts, despite their personal afflictions, by all who, while unable to be saints but refusing to bow down to pestilences, strive their utmost to be healers' (Camus, 1948, p. 278). There may be significance in the open-endedness of such a work (since the plague bacillus never dies). Enabling persons to envisage insufficiency and terror, it might move them to do further thinking, to transcend.

Thoughts of transcendence bring up the problems of freedom and fatality, freedom and determinism; and I think about the fruitfulness of using Sophocles' *Oedipus Rex* and *Antigone*, and Shakespeare's *Hamlet*, and other tragedies in the philosophy classroom. There have been times when I have used Sophocles' *Electra* and Jean-Paul Sartre's *The Flies* in order to involve students in thoughts about freedom and necessity. Recently, I have been using Paul Nizan's (1973) autobiographical novel, *Antoine Bloye*, because of its Marxist view of economic causation and its existential view of human possibility. It deals with a railroad worker earlier in this century who is reared to become a middle manager in the railroad system. As a boy in an Arts and Trades School, he learns how to play the 'wise monkey' and wins a prize when he graduates. The prize is a book; and Antoine reads, at random, that man is free and 'ever aware of his power not to do what he does do and to do what he does not do' (Nizan, 1973, p. 54). Antoine decides immediately that to be poor is not to be free, that only the rich enjoy any freedom, 'people with an income'. The misconception or the mystification affects the way in which he addresses his life — alienated from his fellow-workers, waiting for something to happen rather than acting to bring something about, acquiescing in a conventional *petit bourgeois* life.

Later, when he is grown, the point is made that the only motions he had time for were the motions of his work:

> There was no opportunity to think about himself, to meditate, to know himself and know the world. He did no reading, he did not keep himself *au courant* . . . He glanced at newspapers casually. The events they told of belonged to another planet and did not concern him. The only publications he took a vital interest in were the technical magazines with their descriptions of engines. For a space of fourteen or fifteen years, there was no man less conscious of himself and of his own life, less informed on the world than Antoine Bloye. He was alive, no doubt; who is not alive? To go through the motions of life all you need is a well-fed body. He, Antoine, moved and acted, but the springs of his life, and the drive of his actions were not within himself. Will man never be more than a fragment of a man, alienated, mutilated, a stranger to himself. (Nizan, 1973, p. 113)

It is necessary for the reader to realize that Antoine is being presented through his son's perspective, and that the son is indignant and at once despairing. Above all, he wants to understand his father's life so as not to repeat it. He is intent upon overcoming, on achieving his own freedom; and the narrative veers back and forth between a determinist view and a view focused on Antoine's responsibility for his own complicity and his own defeat. Again, the reader is obliged to fill in, to respond to the interrogation of the book. Because of the importance of viewing students as free moral agents, there is something centrally important in the confrontation here.

Something similar happens in readings of Toni Morrison's (1975) *Sula*, which deals also with the problem of freedom, even as it deals with the problem of adequate perception. Here, the scene is a black community on 'the Bottom' in an Ohio town, where males are continually weakened and humiliated, where some of the women are strong and daring enough to try to 'save' them. Sula (knowing no single perception can contain what happens) achieves a dangerous freedom. She wanders, takes risks, teases, seduces, offends. When she is dying of cancer, she tells her friend Nel (whose husband she once stole and therefore liberated) that she will not go down as other women do, like a stump: ' "Me, I'm going down like one of those redwoods. I sure did live in this world". Nel asks, "Really? What have you got to show for it?" "Show? To who? Girl, I got my mind. And what goes on in it. Which is to say, I got me." "Lonely, ain't it?" "Yes. But my lonely is *mine*." . . .' (p. 123).

If it is indeed the case that freedom is an achievement, to be won only in dialectical tension with the determinants all around, these renderings of freedom ought to evoke resonances, even as they feed into the philosophical question that must be asked. Freedom is so often conceived of as an endowment to be enjoyed in some domain of apartness, where there is no interference and no restraint. The works I have mentioned make insupportable and indefensible the notion of an either/or. Again, the texts solve nothing, and they mean more than they say. But students can be left — must be left — with unresolved questions having to do with membership and freedom, participation and freedom. The contradictions are manifold; what are crucial are the options among which people can choose. Charles Taylor (1977), in 'Interpretation and the Sciences of Man', makes this particularly clear when he writes about how important it often is for people to see that they have to change their orientations rather than sharpening their intuitions when it comes to understanding different points of view. This may mean, he says, 'if not in adopting another orientation, at least in living one's own in a way which allows for greater comprehension of others' (p. 127).

It seems clear enough, in qualitative inquiry, that exact translations and precise predictions can never be made, that many 'conceptual webs' are simply incommensurable — meaning (according to Taylor) that the terms 'can't be defined in relation to a common stratum of expressions'. We can see this in many of the novels available to us; and, again, it seems to me to be one of the arguments for the use of fiction in our teaching. We are brought in touch with what Mikhail Bakhtin (1981) called multiple languages or 'heteroglossia'. He wrote, 'The novel orchestrates all its themes, the totality of the world of objects and ideas depicted and expressed in it, by means of the social diversity of speech types and by the differing individual voices that flourish under such conditions' (p. 263). What may happen is an encounter with a great variety of social voices in a kind of dialogue; and the ability to perceive this, to engage with multiple points of view, may be to be empowered to think about a polis or a public space.

I have been using the novels of Milan Kundera, in part to open up the dialectic, in part to expose students to distinctively modern contradictions, those too often glossed over and ignored in teacher education. An especially potent text is Kundera's (1984) *The Unbearable Lightness of Being*. Here, the tension between 'lightness' (meaning rootlessness, impulsivity, a freedom of 'insignificance') and 'weight' (meaning embeddedness, acquiescence, a sense of fatality and pressure and the 'grand march' of history) is explored. 'Which then shall we choose? Weight or lightness?' (p. 5). It is another of the inescapable questions, entangled with questions of value and the very nature of human reality. Kundera is also interested in what he calls 'kitsch' in totalitarian and democratic settings: sentimental or doctrinal illusions, beautiful lies. He writes (with respect to his character Sabina):

> As soon as kitsch is recognized for the lie it is, it moves into the context of non-kitsch, thus losing its authoritarian power and becoming as touching as any other human weakness. For none among us is superman enough to escape kitsch completely. No matter how we scorn it, kitsch is an integral part of the human condition. (p. 256)

Also, he says in another place, kitsch is our means of denial, our way of building folding screens against death. In my view, one of the obligations of educational philosophy — apart from countering 'bewilderment' and clarifying language — is to move as many people as possible into the context of non-kitsch.

I am trying to suggest, of course, that informed confrontations with literary texts may (through the process of defamiliarization, perhaps) enable students to perceive their own illusions and stereotypes, even as they expose them to the multiple ways in which the world means to those inhabiting it. I am using texts like Alice Walker's (1982) *The Color Purple* to enable students to break with traditional 'literary' modes of discourse and to participate with a degree of passion in the transformation of a young woman from abjectness and victimization to imaginative, concerned involvement with the world. I use Ntozake Shange's (1977) *For Colored Girls Who Have Considered Suicide, When the Rainbow is Enuf* in part because of the moment of transcendence made possible by the Lady in Grown's story of when, as a child, she burst into the Adult Reading Room in the St Louis Public Library and there discovered her 'reality'. I use Umberto Eco's (1983) *The Name of the Rose* in part because of the semiotic adventure it allows, in part because of the way in which it makes the reader suffer the horror of knowledge hoarded (in a labyrinthine library) rather than disseminated. I say 'in part', because I do not want to presume totalities or whole coherent systems, and because what students find will be (I hope) unpredictable.

This, to me, is the mood of qualitative research, a mood created by the realization that human beings are self-defining, self-creating, 'condemned to meaning', and in search of possibility. Imaginative literature, again, resolves no educational questions with any finality. It refers to no empirical realities. The texts, cherished and granted their integrity, open perspectives, disclose worlds, as they appeal to their readers' freedom. And so I argue for their use and try to discover how to integrate them in my own teaching. It is a ceaseless, tonic effort; and it helps keep me alive.


## References

ARENDT, H. (1958). *The Human Condition*. Chicago: University of Chicago Press.

BAKHTIN, M. M. (1981). *The Dialogic Imagination* (C. Emerson and M. Holquist, Trans.). Austin, TX: University of Texas Press.

BERLIN, I. (1962). 'Does political theory still exist?'. In P. Laslett and W. G. Runciman (Eds.), *Philosophy, Politics, and Society*. Oxford: Blackwell.

CAMUS, A. (1948). *The Plague*, New York: Knopf.

CHOPIN, K. (1972). *The Awakening*. New York: Avon. (First published in 1899.)

CONRAD, J. (1972). *Heart of Darkness*. Baltimore: Penguin. (First published in 1902.)

CULLER, J. (1975). *Structuralist Poetics*. Ithaca, NY: Cornell University Press.

DE LILLO, D. (1985). *White Noise*. New York: Minton, Balch.

DERRIDA, J. (1978). *Writing and Difference*. Chicago: University of Chicago Press.

DEWEY, J. (1934). *Art as Experience*. New York: Minton, Balch.

DEWEY, J. (1954). *The Public and Its Problem*. Athens, OH: Compass Press. (First published in 1927.)

ECO, U. (1983). *The Name of the Rose* (William Weaver, Trans.). San Diego, CA: Harcourt Brace Jovanovich.

ECO, U. (1984). *The Role of the Reader*. Bloomington, IN: Indiana University Press.

ELLISON, R. (1952). *Invisible Man*. New York: Signet.

FITZGERALD, F. S. (1953). *The Great Gatsby*. New York: Scribner. (First published in 1925.)

HABERMAS, J. (1979). *Communication and the Evolution of Society* (T. McCarthy, Trans.) Boston, MA: Beacon Press.

HAWTHORNE, N. (1969). *The Scarlet Letter*. Baltimore: Penguin. (First published in 1850.)

IRVING, J. (1985). *The Cider House Rules*. New York: Morrow.

ISER, W. (1978). *The Act of Reading*. Baltimore: Johns Hopkins Press.

KUNDERA, M. (1984). *The Unbearable Lightness of Being*. New York: Harper and Row.

MANN, T. (1955). *The Magic Mountain*. New York: Knopf. (First published in 1927.)

MELVILLE, H. (1950). *Moby Dick*. New York: Modern Library. (First published in 1851.)

MELVILLE, H. (1967). 'Bartleby the Scrivener' [and] 'Benito Cereno'. In H. Melville, *Billy Buddy, Sailor and Other Stories*. Baltimore, MD: Penguin. (First published in 1853 and 1856.)

MERLEAU-PONTY, M. (1962). *Phenomenology of Perception* (C. Smith, Trans.). London: Routledge and Kegan Paul.

MORRISON, T. (1975). *Sula*. New York: Monthly Press.

NIZAN, P. (1973). *Antoine Bloye*. New York: Monthly Press.

PALMER, R. (1969). *Hermeneutics*. Evanston, IL: Northwestern University Press.

SARTRE, J. P. (1965). *Literature and Existentialism*. New York: Citadel Press. (First published in 1949).

SCHUTZ, A. (1962). 'On multiple realities'. In Maurice Natausson (Ed.), *The Problem of Social Reality*. The Hague: Martinus Nijhoff.

SHANGE, N. (1977). *For Colored Girls Who Have Considered Suicide, When The Rainbow is Enuf.* New York: Macmillan.

TAYLOR, C. (1977). 'Interpretation and the sciences of man'. In F. R. Dallmayr and T. A. McCarthy (Eds.), *Understanding and Social Inquiry.* Notre Dame, IN: University of Notre Dame Press.

TWAIN, M. (1959). *The Adventures of Huckleberry Finn.* New York: Signet. (First published in 1884.)

WALKER, A. (1982). *The Color Purple.* New York: Harcourt Brace Jovanovich.

WOOLF, V. (1976). *Moments of Being.* New York: Harcourt Brace Jovanovich. (Selected writings, 1907–36.)

*Chapter 13*

# Critical Theory and the Politics of Culture and Voice: Rethinking the Discourse of Educational Research

*Henry A. Giroux*
*Department of Education*
*Miami University*
*Miami, Ohio 45056*

Within the last few decades dominant approaches to schooling in Western societies have become more vulnerable to a variety of theoretical discourses and their attendant modes of criticism. One consequence has been the recognition that within the field of educational theory and practice there are a number of competing discourses informed by different interests and political projects regarding what the proper role of schooling, teaching, and educational research should be in the advanced capitalist countries of the West. The theoretical and ideological terrains of these positions have been mapped out quite well by others, and there is no need for me to repeat the more traditional and liberal forms of inquiry (Giroux *et al.*, 1981; Bredo and Feinberg, 1982; Feinberg, 1983; Livingstone, 1983).

But along with this recognition has emerged a theoretical perspective which argues that a major task for educational researchers is to form a community that tries to understand more clearly what each of the various traditions might be doing. At first glance, this appears to be a reputable guiding principle for educators. But I believe that beneath the call for harmony, understanding, and tolerance there is a recycling, albeit in different form, of an underlying tenet of dominant ideology characterized by the refusal to engage the primacy of the political in educational inquiry (Carr, 1985; Soltis, 1984). Similarly, this form of ideology also fails to engage the role that educational researchers might play as intellectuals engaged in a struggle to create, defend, and extend the discourse of freedom and democracy in private and public life.

I believe that there is a more productive starting point for constructing a model of educational research. It is a model that is part of a tradition of radical scholarship that has emerged in North America, England, Australia, Latin America, and France within the last two decades and has taken as one of its fundamental concerns the need to re-emphasize the centrality of politics and power in its approach to educational inquiry and research (see Giroux, 1983). I will argue that within the different approaches that characterize the discourse of radical pedagogy there are a number of valuable theoretical elements that reveal the shortcomings of traditional and liberal approaches to schooling. At the same time, I believe that radical pedagogy in its current state needs to be interrogated and recast in an effort to move beyond the limits of this work, while at the same time incorporating its most valuable insights into a more comprehensive and critical theory of schooling.

In developing this position, I will first analyze some of the strengths and weaknesses of the various traditions that have emerged within radical educational theory. I will then argue that educational research has to be grounded in a theoretical perspective in which schools are seen as oppositional public spheres that take seriously the need to educate students in the discourse of critique, possibility and democracy. Related to this issue, I will argue that there is a need to address the overburdening conditions of labor which generally prevent teachers from rightfully assuming their role as intellectuals performing a dignified public service.

## Radical Educational Theory and the Language of Critique

Radical pedagogy emerged in full strength as part of the new sociology of education in England and the United States over a decade ago as a critical response to what can be loosely termed the ideology of traditional educational theory and practice. (The most celebrated texts that emerged in the 1970s were: Young, 1971; Bernstein, 1977; Bowles and Gintis, 1976; and Apple, 1977.) Preoccupied with the imperative to challenge the dominant assumption that schools are the major mechanism for the development of a democratic and egalitarian social order, radical educational theory set itself the task of uncovering how the logic of domination and oppression was reproduced within the various mechanisms of schooling. In doing so, the major ideological and political task of radical critics has been one of trying to unravel how schools reproduce the logic of capital through the ideological and material forms of privilege and domination that structure the lives of students from various class, gender, and ethnic groupings.

Radical critics, for the most part, agreed that educational traditionalists generally refused to interrogate the political nature of public schooling. In fact, traditionalists eluded the issue through the paradoxical attempt of depoliticizing the language of schooling while reproducing and legitimating capitalist ideologies. The most obvious expression of this approach could be seen in a positivist discourse that took as its most important concerns the mastery of pedagogical techniques and the transmission of knowledge instrumental to the existing society (see Giroux, 1981). In the traditional world view, schools were seen as merely instructional sites. That schools are also cultural and political sites was ignored, as was the notion that they represent areas of contestation among differentially empowered cultural and economic groups.

In the discourse of the radical educational theorists, traditional educational theory suppressed important questions regarding the relations among knowledge, power, and domination. Furthermore, out of this criticism emerged a new theoretical language and mode of criticism which argued that schools did not provide opportunities in the broad Western humanist tradition for self and social empowerment in the society at large. In opposition to the traditionalist position, left critics provided theoretical arguments and empirical evidence to suggest that schools were, in fact, agencies of social, economic, and cultural reproduction (Bowles and Gintis, 1976; Giroux, 1983). At best, public schooling offered limited individual mobility to members of the working class and other oppressed groups, but, in the final analysis, they were powerful instruments for the reproduction of capitalist relations of production and the dominant legitimating ideologies of ruling groups.

Radical critics of education provided a variety of useful models of analysis and research to challenge traditional educational ideology. Against the conservative claim that schools transmitted objective knowledge, radical critics developed theories of the hidden curriculum as well as theories of ideology that identified the specific interests underlying different knowledge forms (Giroux and Purpel, 1983; Oakes, 1985). Rather than viewing knowledge as objective, as something to be merely transmitted to students, radical theorists argued that knowledge was a particular representation of the dominant culture, a privileged discourse that was constructed through a selective process of emphases and exclusions (Apple, 1982). Against the claim that schools were only instructional sites, radical critics pointed to the transmission and reproduction of a dominant culture in schools.

Far from being neutral, that is, the dominant culture of the school was characterized by a selective ordering and legitimating of privileged language forms, modes of reasoning, social relations, and lived experiences. In this view, culture was linked to power and to the imposition of a specific set of ruling class codes and experiences (Bourdieu and Passeron, 1977). But school culture, it was claimed, functioned not only to confirm and privilege students from the dominant classes, it also functioned through exclusion and insult to disconfirm the histories, experiences, and dreams of subordinate groups. Finally, against the claim by traditional educators that schools were apolitical institutions, radical educators illuminated the ways in which the State, through its selective grants, certification policies, and legal powers, influenced school practice in the interest of particular dominant ideologies. (For recent examples, see Wise, 1979; and Carnoy and Levin, 1985.)

But in spite of its insightful theoretical and political analyses of schooling, radical educational theory suffered from some serious flaws. The most serious was its failure to move beyond the language of critique and domination. That is, radical educators remained mired in a language that linked schools primarily to the ideologies and practices of domination. In this view, schools are seen almost exclusively as agencies of social reproduction, producing obedient workers for industrial capital; school knowledge is generally dismissed as a form of bourgeois ideology, and teachers are often portrayed as being trapped in an apparatus of domination that works with all the certainty of a Swiss watch. The agony of this position has been that it prevents left educators from developing a programmatic language in which they can theorize *for* schools. Instead, radical educators have theorized primarily *about* schools as agencies of domination, and, as such, seldom concern themselves with the possibility of constructing new, alternative approaches to school organization, curricula, and classroom social relations.

Put another way, radical educators have abandoned the language of possibility for the language of critique. By viewing schools as primarily reproductive sites, radical educators have not been able to develop a theory of schooling that offers the possibility for counter-hegemonic struggle and ideological contestation. Within this discourse, schools, teachers, and students have been written off as merely extensions of the logic of capital. Instead of viewing schools as sites of contestation and conflict, radical educators often provide an oversimplified version of domination that seems to suggest that the only political alternative to the current role that schools play in the wider society is to abandon them altogether. Since schools are often viewed in radical educational theories as ideologically and politically overburdened by the dominant society, the moral and political necessity for developing a programmatic discourse for working within schools is seen as unproblematic. Thus, the role that teachers, students, parents and community people might play in waging a political battle in the public schools is rarely explored as a possibility. One consequence is that the primacy of the political in this project turns in on itself and accepts the defeatist logic of capitalist domination as the basis for a 'radical' theory of schooling.

Furthermore, in their failure to develop a form of educational theory that posits real alternatives within schools, radical educators remain politically powerless to combat the degree to which conservative forces adroitly exploit and appropriate popular concerns over public education. In other words, the educational left not only misrepresents the nature of school life and the degree to which schools *do not* merely ape the logic of corporate interests, by their lack of programmatic alternatives they also unwittingly reinforce the conservative thrust to fashion schools in their own ideological image. In short, radical educators have failed to develop a language that engages schools as sites of possibility, that is, as places where particular forms of knowledge, social relations, and values can be taught in order to educate students to take a place in society from a position of empowerment rather than from a position of ideological and economic subordination.

The problem I want to discuss thus is one that is central to any legitimate notion of radical pedagogy. That is, how is it possible to develop a radical pedagogy located in a discourse that acknowledges the spaces, tensions, and possibilities for struggle within the day to day workings of schools? Underlying this problematic is the theoretical and political necessity to generate a set of categories that not only provide new modes of critical interrogation and educational research, but also point to alternative strategies and social relations around which educators at all levels of schooling can redefine the nature of intellectual work and inquiry.

## Schooling, the Public Sphere, and Transformative Intellectuals

Any attempt to reformulate the role of educators as intellectuals has to begin with the broader question of how to view the purpose of schooling. I believe that central to a realizable radical pedagogy is the need to view schools as oppositional democratic public spheres. This means regarding schools as democratic sites dedicated to forms of self and social empowerment. Understood in these terms, schools are viewed as public places where students learn the knowledge and skills necessary to live in an authentic democracy. Instead of defining schools as extensions of the workplace or as front line institutions in the battle for international markets and foreign competition, schools as democratic public spheres are constructed around forms of critical inquiry that dignify meaningful dialogue and human agency. Students are given the opportunity to learn the discourse of public association and social responsibility. Such a discourse seeks to recapture the idea of critical democracy as a social movement that supports a respect for individual freedom and social justice. Moreover, viewing schools as oppositional public spheres provides a rationale for defending them along with progressive forms of pedagogy and teacher work as essential institutions and practices in the performance of an important public service. Defined in these terms, schools are to be defended in a political language as institutions that provide the ideological and material conditions necessary to educate a citizenry in the dynamics of critical literacy and civic courage, both of which constitute the basis for functioning as active citizens in a democratic society. (The relationship between schooling and democracy is brilliantly explored in Dewey, 1916; see also Aronowitz and Giroux, 1985.)

There is another important and related issue at work in defining schools as democratic public spheres. By politicizing the notion of schooling, it becomes possible to illuminate the role that educators and educational researchers play as intellectuals who operate under specific conditions of work and who perform a particular social and political function. The category of intellectual is useful in a number of ways for describing the nature and practice of teacher work. First, it provides a theoretical basis for examining teacher work as a form of intellectual labor, in contrast to defining it in purely instrumental and technical terms. In other words, it points to the interrelation of conception and practice, thinking and doing, and producing and implementing as integrated activities that give teaching its dialectical meaning.

Within this perspective there is a critical foundation for rejecting those philosophies and management pedagogies that separate conceptualization, planning, and design from the nature of teacher work itself. The concept of teacher as intellectual carries with it the imperative to critique and reject those approaches to teacher work that reinforce a technical and social division of labor that disempowers teachers by deskilling them. This category also carries with it the need to make problematic the ideological and practical conditions that teachers need to function in their capacity as intellectuals.

As intellectuals, teachers need to redefine and change the fundamental nature of the conditions under which they work. That is, teachers must be able to shape the ways in which time, space, and knowledge organize everyday life in schools. More specifically, in order to function as intellectuals, teachers must struggle to create the ideology and structural conditions necessary for them to write, research, and work with each other in producing curricula and instructional power. In the final analysis, teachers need to develop a discourse and a set of assumptions that allow them to function more specifically as transformative intellectuals (Aronowitz and Giroux, 1985).

All of this is to say that as intellectuals who combine reflection and action in the interest of empowering students with the skills and knowledge, teachers will need to address injustices and to be critical actors commited to developing a world free of oppression and exploitation. Such intellectuals are not merely concerned with promoting individual achievement or advancing students along career ladders, they are concerned with empowering students so they can read the world critically in order to change it through the power of struggle and community. I will elaborate on some of the concerns that are central to assuming the role of a transformative intellectual before I address the specifics of what it means to define radical pedagogy as a form of cultural politics.

A number of important concepts have methodological implications for teachers and researchers who assume the role of a transformative intellectual. The most important referent for such a position is recognizing those historical and contemporary instances of suffering that need to be understood in terms of their causes and manifestations. The political project at work here is one that points to uncovering examples of suffering and resistance which can alert us to the historical conditions that promote such experiences. Historical memory points, as Sharon Welch (1985) argues, to the role that intellectuals must play as bearers of dangerous memory. This refers to intellectuals who keep alive the historical and existential fact of suffering by uncovering and analyzing forms of subjugated knowledge, or those forms of knowledge that have been suppressed or ignored and through which we can once again discover the ruptural effects of conflict and struggle (Foucault, 1981).

Dangerous memory does more than define historical inquiry as part of an emancipatory teaching and research project. It also represents a declaration, a hope, a discursive reminder that people do not only suffer under the mechanisms of domination; they also resist; and, moreover, such resistance is always linked to forms of knowledge and understanding that are the preconditions for saying both 'no' to repression and 'yes' to the dynamics of struggle and the practical possibilities to which it addresses itself — in short, to a better way of life.

It is also essential that transformative intellectuals redefine the concept of power regarding the issue of knowledge, particularly with respect to the construction of classroom pedagogy and student voice. For transformative intellectuals, power has to be understood as a concrete set of practices that produce social forms through which different types of knowledge, sets of experience, and modes of subjectivities are constructed. Power in this sense includes, but goes beyond the call for, institutional change or the distribution of political and economic resources; it also signifies a level of conflict and struggle that plays itself out around the exchange of knowledge and the lived experiences that such knowledge produces, mediates, and legitimates.

Furthermore, power needs to be studied from the perspective of how it invests itself in various forms of knowledge, how it is inscribed in the body, within particular social practices, in organizational forms, and how it produces specific material and lived effects. Put another way, transformative intellectuals need to understand how subjectivities are produced and regulated through historically produced social forms and how these forms carry and embody particular interests (Giroux and Simon, 1984). At the core of this position is the need to develop modes of inquiry that not only investigate how experience is shaped, lived, and endured within particular social forms such as schools, but also how certain apparatuses of power produce forms of knowledge that legitimate a particular kind of truth and way of life. Power in this sense has a broader meaning in its connection with knowledge than is generally recognized. Power in this instance, as Foucault (1981) points out, is something that not only produces knowledge that distorts reality but also knowledge that provides a particular version of the 'truth'. In other words, 'Power is not merely mystifying or distorting. Its most dangerous impact is its positive relation to truth, the effects of truth that it produces' (Welch, 1985, p. 63).

Another major issue that transformative intellectuals must understand is that discourse is both a medium and a product of power. In this sense, discourse is intimately connected with those ideological and material forces out of which individuals and groups fashion a voice. As Bakhtin (1981) puts it:

> Language is not a neutral medium that passes freely and easily into the private property of the speaker's intentions; it is populated — overpopulated — with the intentions of others. Expropriating it, forcing it to submit to one's own intentions and accents, is a difficult and complicated process. (p. 294)

If language is inseparable from lived experience and the development of how people create a distinctive voice, it is also strongly connected to an intense struggle among different groups over what counts as meaning and whose cultural capital will prevail in legitimating particular ways of life. That is, discourse functions, for example, within schools to produce and legitimate configurations of time, space, and narrative which position teachers and students so as to privilege particular renderings of ideology, behavior, and the representation of everyday life. As a 'technology of power', discourse is given concrete expression in forms of knowledge that constitute the formal curriculum as well as in the structuring of classroom social relations that constitute the hidden curriculum of schooling. Needless to say, these pedagogical practices and forms are 'read' in different ways by both teachers and students. Nonetheless, within these practices are forces that actively work to produce subjectivities that consciously and unconsciously display a particular 'sense' of the world.

The importance of the relationship between power and discourse for a radical pedagogy is that it provides a theoretical grounding from which to research and interrogate how ideology is inscribed in those forms of educational discourse through which school experiences and practices are ordered and constituted. Moreover, it points to the necessity to account theoretically for the ways in which language, ideology, history, and experience come together to produce, define, and constrain particular forms of teacher–student practice. The value of this analysis is that it refuses to remain trapped in a perspective that examines student voice and pedagogical experience through the limiting theoretical lens of the reproductive thesis. That is, power and discourse are now investigated not merely as the homogeneous echo of the logic of capital, but as a polyphony of voices mediated within different layers of reality shaped through an interaction of dominant and subordinate forms of power. By recognizing and interrogating the different layers of meaning and struggle that make up the terrain of schooling, transformative intellectuals can help to develop a mode of educational inquiry that integrates the language of critique with a language of possibility, and in doing so provides the theoretical basis for a radical pedagogy as a form of cultural politics.

## Radical Pedagogy as a Form of Cultural Politics

In this section, I will draw principally from the works of Paulo Freire and Mikhail Bakhtin and attempt to construct a theoretical model in which the notions of struggle, student voice, and critical dialogue are central to the goal of developing an emancipatory pedagogy and basis for a critical mode of educational research. (The works from which I draw are: Freire, 1970, 1973, 1985; Bakhtin, 1981, 1984a, 1984b; and Volosinov, 1973, 1976.) Bakhtin's work is important because it views language usage as an eminently social and political act linked to the ways individuals define meaning and author their relations to the world through an ongoing dialogue with others. As the theoretician of difference, dialogue, and polyphonic voice, Bakhtin rightly emphasizes the need to understand the ongoing struggle between various groups over language and meaning as a moral and epistemological imperative. Accordingly, Bakhtin deepens our understanding of the nature of authorship by providing illuminating analyses of how people give value to and operate out of different layers of discourse; he also points to the pedagogical significance of critical dialogue as a form of authorship that gives meaning to the multiple voices that constitute the 'texts' that are constitutive of everyday life.

Paulo Freire both extends and deepens Bakhtin's project. Like Bakhtin, Freire offers the possibility for organizing pedagogical experiences within social forms and practices that 'speak' to developing more critical, dialogical, explorative, and collective modes of learning and struggle. But Freire's theory of experience is rooted in a view of language and culture in which dialogue and meaning are more strongly linked to a social project that emphasizes the primacy of the political, in which case the notion of empowerment is defined as central to the collective struggle for a life without oppression and exploitation.

Both authors employ a view of language, dialogue, chronotype, and difference that rejects a totalizing view of history, and both argue that a critical pedagogy has to begin with a dialectical celebration of the languages of critique and possibility, which finds its most noble expression in a discourse that integrates critical analysis with socially transformative action. Similarly, both authors provide a pedagogical model that begins with problems rooted in the concrete experiences of everyday life. In effect, Bakhtin and Freire provide valuable theoretical models from which radical educators can draw selectively in order to develop a discourse to analyze schools as ideological and material embodiments of a complex web of relations of culture and power as well as socially constructed sites of contestation actively involved in the production of lived experiences. Inherent in these approaches is a problematic characterized by the need to define how pedagogical practice represents a particular politics of experience, or, in more exact terms, a cultural field where knowledge, discourse, and power intersect so as to produce historically specific practices of moral and social regulation.

This problematic points the need to interrogate how human experiences are produced, contested, and legitimated within the dynamics of everyday classroom life. The theoretical importance of this type of interrogation is linked directly to the need for radical educators to fashion a discourse in which a more comprehensive politics of culture, voice and experience can be developed. At issue here is the recognition that schools are historical and structural embodiments of forms of culture that are ideological in the sense that they signify reality in ways that are often actively contested and experienced differently by various individuals and groups. Schools in this sense are ideological and political terrains out of which the dominant culture manufactures its hegemonic 'certainties'; but they are also places where dominant and subordinate voices define and constrain each other through an ongoing battle and exchange in response to the socio-historical conditions 'carried' in the institutional, textual, and lived practices that define school culture and teacher/ student experience within a particular specificity of time, space and place.

In other words, schools are anything but ideologically innocent, nor are they simply reproductive of dominant social relations and interests. At the same time, as previously mentioned, schools do exercise forms of political and moral regulation intimately connected with technologies of power that 'produce asymmetries in the abilities of individuals and groups to define and realize their needs' (Johnson, 1983, p. 11). More specifically, schools establish the conditions under which some individuals and groups define the terms by which others live, resist, affirm, and participate in the construction of their own identities and subjectivities.

Simon (1986) illuminates quite well some of the important theoretical considerations that have to be addressed within a radical pedagogy. He is worth quoting at length on this issue:

> Our concern as educators is to develop a way of thinking about the construction and definition of subjectivity within the concrete social forms of our everyday existence in a way that grasps schooling as a cultural and political site that [embodies] a project of regulation and transformation. As educators we are required to take a position on the acceptability of such forms. We also recognize that while schooling is productive, it is not so in isolation, but in complex relations with other forms organized in other sites. . . . [Moreover,] in working to reconstruct aspects of schooling [educators should attempt] to understand how it becomes implicated in the production of subjec-tivities [and] recognize [how] existing social forms legitimate and produce real inequities which serve the interest of some over others and that a transformative pedagogy is oppositional in intent and is threatening to some in its practice. (p. 34)

Simon argues rightly that schools are sites of contest and struggle, and as sites of cultural production they embody representations and practices that construct as well as block the possibilities for human agency among students. This becomes more clear by recognizing that one of the most important elements at work in the construction of experience and subjectivity in schools is language. In this case, language intersects with power in the way a particular linguistic form is used in schools to legitimate and structure the ideologies and modes of life of specific groups. Language thus is intimately related to power and functions to both position and constitute the way that teachers and students define, mediate, and understand their relation to each other and the larger society.

As Bakhtin has pointed out, language is intimately related to the dynamics of authorship and voice (Shukman, 1983; Voloshinov, 1973). It is within and through language that individuals in particular contexts shape values into particular forms and practices. As part of the production of meaning, language represents a central force in the struggle for voice within public spheres such as schools. For schools are one of the primary public spheres where languages are bent through the influence of authority, resistance, and dialogue to fashion the response of different individuals and groups to the world. For Bakhtin, the issue of language is explored as part of a politics of struggle and representation, a politics forged in relations of power over who decides and legislates the territory on which discourse is defined and negotiated. The driving momentum of voice and authorship is inseparable from the relations between individuals and groups around which dialogue begins and ends. In Bakhtin's terms, 'the word is a two-sided act. It is determined . . . by those whose word it is and for whom it is meant. . . . A word is territory shared by both addresser and addressee, by the speaker and his interlocutor' (Voloshinov, 1973, pp. 85–86). At issue here is the critical insight that student subjectivities are developed across a range of discourses and can only be understood within a process of social interaction that 'pumps energy from a life situation into the verbal discourse, it endows everything linguistically stable with living historical momentum and uniqueness' (Voloshinov, 1976, p. 106).

## Tasks for Radical Educators

With the above theoretical assumptions in mind, I argue in this final section in more specific terms for the development of a radical pedagogy as a form of cultural politics. I present the case for constructing a pedagogy of cultural politics around a critically affirmative language that allows radical educators to understand how subjectivities are produced within those social forms in which people move, but which are often only partially understood. Such a pedagogy makes problematic how teachers and students sustain, resist, or accommodate those languages, ideologies, social processes, and myths that position them within existing relations of power and dependency. Moreover, it points to the need to develop a theory of politics and culture that analyzes discourse and voice as an active process, one that is produced as part of a continually shifting balance of resources and practices in the struggle for privileging specific ways of naming, organizing, and experiencing social reality.

Discourse, in this case, becomes a form of cultural production, linking agency and structure through the ways in which public and private representations are concretely organized and structured within schools. Furthermore, it is understood as an embodied and fractured set of experiences that are lived and suffered by individuals and groups within specific contexts and settings. Within this perspective, the concept of experience is linked to the broader issue of how subjectivities are inscribed within cultural processes that develop with regard to the dynamics of production, transformation, and struggle. Understood in these terms, a pedagogy of cultural politics presents a twofold set of tasks for radical educators. First, they need to analyze how cultural production is organized within asymmetrical relations of power in schools. Secondly, they need to construct political strategies for participating in social struggles designed to fight for schools as democratic public spheres.

In order to make these tasks realizable, it is necessary to assess the political limits and pedagogical potentialities of the different but related instances of cultural production that constitute the various processes of schooling. It is important to note that I am calling these social processes instances of cultural production rather than using the dominant left concept of reproduction. While the notion of reproduction points adequately to the various economic and political ideologies and interests that get reconstituted within the relations of schooling, it lacks a comprehensive, theoretical understanding of how such interests are mediated, worked on, and subjectively produced, regardless of the interests that finally emerge.

A radical pedagogy that assumes the form of a cultural politics must examine how cultural processes are produced and transformed within three particular, though related, fields of discourse: *the discourse of production, the discourse of text analysis,* and *the discourse of lived cultures*. Each of these discourses has a history of theoretical development in various models of left analysis, and each has been subjected to intense discussion and criticism, which need not be repeated here (an analysis can be found in Johnson, 1983). What I will do is look at these discourses in terms of the potentialities they exhibit in their interconnections, particularly as they point to a new set of categories for developing forms of educational practices that empower teachers and students around emancipatory interests.

### Educational Practice and the Discourse of Production

The discourse of production in educational theory has focused on the ways in which the structural forces outside the immediacy of school life construct the objective conditions within which schools function. This position provides illuminating analyses of the state, the workplace, foundations, publishing companies, and other political interests that directly or indirectly influence school policy (e.g., Carnoy and Levin, 1985). Moreover, schools are understood within a network of larger connections that allow analyses of them as historical and social constructions, embodiments of social forms that always bear a relationship to the wider society. At its best, the discourse of production alerts us to the need to understand the importance of ideological and material structures as particular sets of practices and interests that legitimate specific public representations and ways of life.

It is inconceivable to analyze the process of schooling without understanding how these wider forms of production are constructed, manifested, and contested both in and out of schools. An obvious example of this is to analyze the ways in which state policy embodies and promotes particular practices that legitimate and privilege some forms of knowledge over others, or some groups over others. Equally significant would be an analysis of how dominant educational theory and practice are constructed, sustained, and circulated outside of schools. For instance, radical educators need to do more than just identify the language and values of corporate ideologies as they are manifested in school curricula, they also need to deconstruct the processes through which they are produced and circulated.

Another important aspect of this approach is that it points to the way in which labor is objectively constructed; that is, it provides the basis for an analysis of the conditions under which educators work and the political importance of these conditions in either limiting or enabling pedagogical practice. This issue is especially important for analyzing the critical possibilities that exist for public school teachers and students within specific conditions of labor to act and to be treated as intellectuals, or, to put it in the words of C. W. Mills (1979, p. 370), as people who can generate, criticize, and get 'in touch with the realities of themselves and their world'.

What should be stressed, however, is that if teachers and students are subject to conditions of overcrowding, lack time to work collectively in a creative fashion, or are subject to rules and regulations that disempower them, the technical and social conditions of labor have to be understood and addressed as part of the dynamics of reform and struggle (Aronowitz and Giroux, 1985). The discourse of production represents an important starting point in a pedagogy of cultural politics for evaluating the relationship between schools and wider structural forces against the ways in which such a relation contributes to a politics of human dignity. More specifically, we seek a politics fashioned around the ways in which human dignity is realized in public spheres that provide the material conditions necessary for work, dialogue, and self and social realization, in the interest of developing democratic and emancipatory communities. Accordingly, these public spheres represent what Dewey (1984), Mills (1979), and others have called the conditions for freedom and praxis, political embodiments of a social project that takes liberation as its major goal.

*Radical Pedagogy and the Discourse of Textual Analysis.*

Another important element in the development of a radical pedagogy is a discourse of textual forms. In this case, it is necessary to enlist forms of analysis that can critically interrogate cultural forms as they are produced and used within specific classrooms. The significance of this approach is that it provides teachers and students with the critical tools necessary to analyze those socially constructed representations and interests that organize and emphasize particular readings of curricula materials.

A discourse of textual analysis not only draws attention to the ideologies out of which texts are produced, it also allows educators to distance themselves from the text so as to uncover the layers of meanings, contradictions, and differences inscribed in the form and content of classroom materials. The political and pedagogical importance of this form of analysis is that it opens the text to a form of deconstruction that interrogates it as part of a wider process of cultural production. In addition, by making the text an object of intellectual inquiry, such an analysis posits the reader to be, not a passive consumer, but an active producer of meanings. The text, in this view, is no longer endowed with an authorial essence waiting to be translated or discovered. On the contrary, it becomes an ensemble of discourses constituted by a play of contradictory meanings, some of which are visibly privileged and some of which, in Macherey's (1978, p. 6) terms, represents 'a new discourse, the articulation of a silence'. Critical to this perspective are the notions of critique, production and difference, all of which provide important elements for a counter-hegemonic pedagogical practice. Belsey (1980) weaves these elements together quite well in her critique of the classical realist text:

> As an alternative it was possible to recognize [the classical realist text] as a construct and so to treat it as available for deconstruction, that is, the analysis of the process and conditions of its construction out of the available discourses. Ideology, masquerading as coherence and plenitude, is in reality inconsistent, limited, contradictory, and the realist text as a crystallization of ideology, participates in this incompleteness even while it diverts attention from the fact in the apparent plenitude of narrative closure. The object of deconstructing the text is to examine the process of its production — not the private experience of the individual author, but the mode of production, the materials and their arrangement in the work. The aim is to locate the point of contradiction within the text, the point at which it transgresses the limits within which it is constructed, breaks free of the constraints imposed by its own realist form. Composed of contradictions, the text is no longer restricted to a single, harmonious and authoritative reading. Instead, it becomes plural, open to re-reading, no longer an object for passive consumption but an object of work by the reader to produce meaning. (p. 104)

Textual criticism is a particularly important mode of analysis for radical educators because it argues against the idea that the means of representation in texts are merely neutral conveyors of ideas. Furthermore, it points to the need for careful systematic analyses of the way in which material is used and ordered in school curricula and how its 'signifiers' register particular ideological pressures and tendencies. At its best, such an analysis allows teachers and students to deconstruct meanings that are silently built into the structuring principles of the various systems of meaning that organize everyday life in schools. In effect, it adds an important theoretical dimension to analyzing how the overt and hidden curricula work in schools.

At the day-to-day level of schooling, this type of textual criticism can be used to analyze how the technical conventions or images within various forms such as narrative, mode of address, and ideological reference attempt to construct a limited range of positions from which they are to be read. Richard Johnson (1983) is worth quoting on this point:

> The legitimate object of an identification of 'positions' is the pressures or tendencies on the reader, the theoretical problematic which produces subjective forms, the directions in which they move in their force — once inhabited. . . . If we add to this, the argument that certain kinds of text ('realism') naturalise the means by which positioning is achieved, we have a dual insight of great force. The particular promise is to render processes hitherto unconsciously suffered (and enjoyed) open to explicit analysis. (pp. 64–65)

Coupled with traditional forms of ideological critique of the subject content of school materials, the discourse of text analysis also provides valuable insight into how subjectivities and cultural forms work within schools. The value of this kind of work has been exhibited in analysis of the structured principles used in the construction of pre-packaged curriculum materials, where it has been argued that such principles utilize a mode of address that positions teachers merely as implementers of knowledge (Apple, 1982). Such a positioning clearly is at odds with treating both teachers and students as critical agents who play an active role in the pedagogical process. In a brilliant display of this approach, Judith Williamson (1978) has provided an extensive study of the way in which this type of critique can be applied to mass advertising. Similarly, Ariel Dorfman (1983) has applied this mode of analysis to various texts used in popular culture, including the portrayal of characters such as Donald Duck and Babar the Elephant. It is in his analysis of *Readers Digest* that Dorfman exhibits a dazzling display of the critical value of text analysis. In one example, for instance, he analyzes how *Readers Digest* uses a mode of representation that downplays the importance of viewing knowledge in its historical and dialectical connections. He writes:

> Just as with superheroes, knowledge does not transform the reader; on the contrary, the more he [sic] reads the *Digest*, the less he needs to change. Here is where all that fragmentation returns to play the role it was always meant to play. Prior knowledge is never assumed. From month to month, the reader must purify himself, suffer from amnesia, bottle the knowledge he's acquired and put it on some out-of-the-way shelf so it doesn't interfere with the innocent pleasure of consuming more all over again. What he learned about the Romans doesn't apply to the Etruscans. Hawaii has nothing to do with Polynesia. Knowledge is consumed for its calming effect, for 'information renewal', for the interchange of banalities. It is useful only insofar as it can be digested anecdotally, but its potential for original sin has been washed clean along with the temptation to generate truth or movement — in other words: change. (p. 149)

Inherent in all of these positions is a call for modes of criticism that promote dialogue as the condition for social action, a dialogue that is rooted in a pedagogy informed by a number of assumptions drawn from the works of Bakhtin and Freire. These include: treating the text as a social construct that is produced out of a number of available discourses; locating the contradictions and gaps within an educational text and situating them historically in terms of the interests they sustain and legitimate; recognizing in the text its internal politics of style and how this both opens up and constrains particular representations of the social world; recognizing how the text works to actively silence some voices; and, finally, discovering how it is possible to release from the text possibilities that provide new insights and critical readings regarding human understanding and relations.

In order to develop a critical pedagogy as a form of cultural politics, it is essential to develop a mode of analysis that does not assume that lived experiences can be inferred automatically from structural determinations. In other words, the complexity of human behavior cannot be reduced to merely identifying the determinants, whether they be economic modes of production or systems of textual signification, in which such behavior is shaped and against which it constitutes itself. The way in which individuals and groups both mediate and inhabit the cultural forms presented by such structural forces is in itself a form of production and needs to be analyzed through related but different modes of analyses. A discussion of the discourse of lived cultures will develop this point.

## *Radical Pedagogy and the Discourse of Lived Cultures*

Central to this view is the need to develop what can be loosely called a theory of self-production (Touraine, 1977). In the most general sense this would demand an understanding of how teachers and students give meaning to their lives through the complex historical, cultural, and political forms that they both embody and produce. (For an exceptional analysis of how feminist administrators and teachers mediate their work through a self-conscious and critical analysis of their ideologies, see Weiler, 1988; analyses of this issue are prominent also in the work of Greene, e.g., 1978.) A number of issues need to be developed within a critical pedagogy around this concern. First, it is necessary to acknowledge the subjective forms of political will and struggle that give meaning to the lives of the students. Specifically, the discourse of lived cultures need to interrogate how people create stories, memories, and narratives that posit a sense of determination and agency. This is the cultural 'stuff' of mediation, the conscious and unconscious material through which members of dominant and subordinate groups offer accounts of who they are and present different readings of the world. It is also part of those ideologies and practices that allow us to understand the particular social locations, histories, subjective interests, and private worlds that come into play in any classroom pedagogy.

If radical educators treat the histories, experiences, and languages of different cultural groups as particularized forms of production, it becomes less difficult to understand the diverse readings, responses, and behaviors that, for example, students exhibit in the analysis of a particular classroom text. In fact, a cultural politics necessitates that a pedagogy be developed that is attentive to the histories, dreams, and experiences that such students bring to schools. It is only by beginning with these subjective forms that critical educators can develop a language and set of practices that confirm and engage the contradictory forms of cultural capital that constitute how students produce meanings that legitimate particular forms of life.

Searching out and illuminating the elements of self production that characterize individuals who occupy and embody diverse forms of cultural capital is not merely a pedagogical technique for confirming the experiences of those students who are often silenced by the dominant culture of schooling; it is also part of an analysis that questions how power, dependence, and social inequality structure the ideologies and practices that enable and limit students around issues of class, race, and gender. Within this theoretical perspective, the discourse of lived cultures becomes valuable for educators because it can serve to illuminate how power and knowledge intersect not only to disconfirm the cultural capital of students from subordinate groups, but also how it can be translated into a language of possibility. That is, it can also be used to develop a radical pedagogy of the popular, one that engages the knowledge of lived experience through the dual method of confirmation and interrogation.

The knowledge of the 'other' is engaged in this instance not simply to celebrate its presence, but also because it must be interrogated critically with respect to the ideologies it contains, the means of representation it utilizes, and the underlying social practices it confirms. At stake here is the need to develop a link between knowledge and power, one that suggests realizable possibilities for students. In this sense, knowledge and power intersect in a pedagogy of cultural politics so as to give students the opportunity to not only understand more critically who they are as part of a wider social formation, but also to help them critically appropriate those forms of knowledge that traditionally have been denied to them.

The discourse of lived culture also points to the need for radical educators to view schools as cultural and political spheres actively engaged in the production and struggle for voice. In many cases, schools do not allow students from subordinate groups to authenticate their problems and lived experiences through their own individual and collective voices. As I have stressed previously, the dominant school culture generally represents and legitimates the privileged voices of the white middle and upper classes. It is important to stress that in order for radical educators to demystify and make the dominant culture an object of political analysis, they will need to learn and master what I loosely call the language of critical understanding.

In other words, if radical educators are to effectively understand and counter the dominant ideology at work in schools, they will have to interrogate and critically sustain those voices that emerge from three different ideological spheres and settings. These include: the school voice, the student voice, and the teacher voice. Each of these voices points to sets of practices that work on and with each other to produce specific pedagogical experiences within different configurations of power. The interests these different voices often represent have to be analyzed less as oppositional, in the sense that they work to counter and disable each other, than as an interplay of dominant and subordinate practices that shape each other in an ongoing struggle over power, meaning, and authorship. This type of analysis presupposes the necessity for analyzing schools in their historical and relational specificity, and it points to the possibility for intervening and shaping their outcomes. In order to under-stand and interrogate the multiple and varied meanings that constitute the discourses of student voice, radical educators need to affirm and critically engage the polyphonic languages their students bring to schools. That is, such educators need to learn 'the collection and communicative practices associated with particular uses of both written and spoken forms among specific social groups' (Sola and Bennett, 1985, p. 89). Moreover, any adequate under-standing of this language has to reach outside of school life into more encom-passing social and community relations that give it meaning and dignity.

Learning the discourse of school voice means that radical educators need to critically analyze the directives, imperatives, and rules that shape particular configurations of time, space, and curricula within the institutional and political settings of schools. The category of school voice, for example, helps to illuminate sets of practices and ideologies that structure how classrooms are arranged, what content is taught, what general social practices teachers have to follow (McLaren, 1986; Greene, 1984). Moreover, it is in the interplay between the dominant school culture and the polyphonic representations and layers of meaning that constitute varied student voices that a continuous interplay of dominant and oppositional ideologies are mediated so as to define and constrain each other.

Teacher voice represents the values, ideologies, and structuring principles that give meaning to the histories, culture, and subjectivities that define and mediate the day to day activities of educators. This is the voice of common and critical sense that teachers utilize to mediate between the discourses of production, texts and lived cultures as they are expressed within the asym-metrical relations of power that differently characterize public spheres such as schools. In effect, it is through the mediation and action of teacher voice that the very nature of the schooling process is often either sustained or challenged. That is, the power to shape schooling according to the logic of emancipatory interests is inextricably related, not only to a high degree of self understanding, but also to the possibility for radical educators to join together in a collective voice as part of a social movement dedicated to restructuring the ideological and material conditions that work both within and outside of schooling.

Thus, the category of teacher voice needs to be understood and interrogated critically, in terms of its own values and political project as well as in relation to the ways it functions, as part of the overall language of understanding, that is, the ways in which it shapes and mediates school and student voices.

In general terms, the language of critical understanding represents an acknowledgment not only of the political and pedagogical processes at work in the construction of forms of authorship and voice within different institutional and social spheres; it also represents an attack on the vertical ordering of reality inherent in the unjust practices that are actively at work in the wider society. Schools need to be viewed as democratic public spheres, as places where students learn the skills and knowledge to live in and fight for a democratic society. As such, they will have to be characterized by a pedagogy that demonstrates its commitment to engaging the views and problems that deeply concern students in their everyday lives. Equally important is the need for schools to cultivate a spirit of critique and a respect for human dignity that is capable of linking personal and social issues around the pedagogical project of helping students to become critical and active citizens.

## Summary

Each of the three major discourses I have briefly presented and analyzed as part of a radical pedagogy in this section involves a different view of cultural production, pedagogical analysis, and political action. Although each of these radical discourses involves a certain degree of autonomy in both form and content, it is important that a radical pedagogy be developed around the inner connections they share within the context of a cultural politics. For it is within these interconnections that a critical theory of both structure and agency can be developed that engenders an oppositional radical educational language in order to point to new questions, possibilities, and struggles. Worth repeating is the idea that essential to a viable form of radical pedagogy is the need for educators to redefine the political project that mediates and structures their teaching and educational research and to work and organize for the development of schools as democratic public spheres. In short, the central imperative behind a radical pedagogy, and the forms of inquiry it develops, have to be understood and embraced through an engagement in the world, by a commitment to praxis and the process of social transformation. The objective is nothing less than providing the conditions for educators and their students to become knowledgeable and committed actors in the world. To do so is to exhibit a voice that makes despair unconvincing, hope practical, and radical pedagogy possible.

## Acknowledgment

I am indebted to my colleague, Peter McLaren, for providing a critical reading of this article. Much of the material in the article has been drawn from my forthcoming book, *Schooling and the Struggle for Public Life*, to be published by the University of Minnesota Press.

## References

APPLE, M. (1977). *Ideology and Curriculum*. London: Routledge and Kegan Paul.
APPLE, M. (1982). *Education and Power*. London: Routledge and Kegan Paul.
ARONOWITZ, S. and GIROUX, H. A. (1985). *Education Under Siege*. South Hadley, MA: Bergin and Garvey.
BAKHTIN, M. (1981). *The Dialogic Imagination* (C. Emerson and M. Holquist, Trans.). Austin, TX: University of Texas Press.
BAKHTIN, M. (1984a). *Problems of Dostoevsky's Poetics* (C. Emerson, Trans.). Minneapolis, MN: University of Minnesota Press.
BAKHTIN, M. (1984b). *Rabelais and His World* (H. Iswolsky, Trans.). Bloomington, IN: Indiana University Press.
BELSEY, C. (1980). *Critical Practice*. New York: Methuen.
BERNSTEIN, B. (1977). *Class, Codes and Control* (Vol. III). London: Routledge and Kegan Paul.
BOURDIEU, P. and PASSERON, J. C. (1977). *Reproduction in Education, Society, and Culture*. Beverly Hills, CA: Sage.
BOWLES, S. and GINTIS, H. (1976). *Schooling in Capitalist America*. New York: Basic Books.
BREDO, E. and FEINBERG, W. (Eds). (1982). *Knowledge and Values in Social and Educational Research*. Philadelphia, PA: Temple University Press.
CARNOY, M. and LEVIN, H. (1985). *Schooling and Work in the Democratic State*. Stanford, CA: Stanford University Press.
CARR, W. (1985). 'Philosophy, values, and educational science'. *Journal of Curriculum Studies*, 17(2), 119–132.
DEWEY, J. (1916). *Democracy and Education*. New York: Macmillan.
DEWEY, J. (1984). *The Public and its Problems* [1927]. In J. A. Boydston (Ed.), *John Dewey, The Later Works, 1925–1953* (Vol. 2, 1925–1927). Carbondale, IL: Southern Illinois University Press.
DORFMAN, A. (1983). *The Empire's Old Clothes*. New York: Pantheon.
FEINBERG, W. (1983). *Understanding Education*. New York: Cambridge University Press.
FOUCAULT, M. (1981). *Power and Knowledge: Selected Interviews and Other Writings, 1972–1977* (C. Gordon, Ed.). New York: Pantheon.
FREIRE, P. (1970). *Pedagogy of the Oppressed*. New York: Seabury.
FREIRE, P. (1973). *Education for Critical Consciousness*. New York: Seabury.
FREIRE, P. (1985). *The Politics of Education*. South Hadley, MA: Bergin and Garvey.
GIROUX, H. (1981). *Ideology, Culture, and the Process of Schooling*. Philadelphia, PA: Temple University Press.
GIROUX, H. A. (1983). *Theory and Resistance in Education*. South Hadley, MA: Bergin and Garvey.

GIROUX, H. A., PENNA, A. N. and PINAR, W. F. (Eds). (1981). *Curriculum and Instruction*. Berkeley, CA: McCutchan.

GIROUX, H. and PURPEL, D. (1983). *The Hidden Curriculum and Moral Education*. Berkeley, CA: McCutchan.

GIROUX, H. A. and SIMON, R. (1984). 'Curriculum study and cultural politics'. *Journal of Education, 166* (Fall), 226–238.

GREENE, M. (1978). *Landscapes of Learning*. New York: Teachers College.

GREENE, M. (1984). 'Excellence, meanings, and multiplicity'. *Teachers College Record, 86*(2), 282–297.

JOHNSON, R. (1983). 'What is cultural studies anyway?' *Anglistica, 26* (1–2).

LIVINGSTON, D. (1983). *Class Ideologies and Educational Futures*. Philadelphia, PA: Falmer Press.

MACHEREY, P. (1978). *A Theory of Literary Production* (G. Wall, Trans.). London: Routledge and Kegan Paul.

McCLAREN, P. (1986). *Schooling as a Ritual Performance*. New York: Methuen.

MILLS, C. W. (1979). 'Mass society and liberal education'. In I. L. Horowitz (Ed.), *The Collected Essays of C. W. Mills*. New York: Oxford University Press.

OAKES, J. (185). *Keeping Track: How Schools Structure Inequality*. New Haven, CT: Yale University Press.

SHUKMAN, A. (Ed.). (1983). *Bakhtin's School Papers*. Oxford: RPT Publications.

SIMON, R. (1986). 'Work experience as the production of subjectivity'. In D. W. Livingstone (Ed.), *Critical Pedagogy and Cultural Power*. South Hadley, MA: Bergin and Garvey.

SOLA, M. and BENNETT, A. (1985). 'The struggle for voice: Narrative, literacy, and consciousness in an East Harlem school'. *Boston University Journal of Education, 167*(1).

SOLTIS, J. F. (1984). 'On the nature of educational research'. *Educational Researcher, 13* (December), 5–10.

TOURAINE, A. (1977). *The Self-Production of Society*. Chicago: University of Chicago Press.

VOLOSINOV, V. N. [Bakhtin, M. M.]. (1973). *Marxism and the Philosophy of Language*. New York: Seminar Press.

VOLOSINOV, V. N. [Bakhtin, M. M.]. (1976). *Freudianism: A Marxist Critique*. New York: Academic Press.

WEILER, K. (1988). *Gender and Schooling*. South Hadley, MA: Bergin and Garvey.

WELCH, S. D. (1985). *Communities of Resistance and Solidarity: A Feminist Theology of Liberation*. New York: Orbis.

WILLIAMSON, J. (1978). *Decoding Advertisements*. New York: Marion Boyars.

WISE, A. (1979). *Legislated Learning*. Berkeley, CA: University of California Press.

YOUNG, M. F. D. (Ed.). (1971). *Knowledge and Control*. London: Collier-Macmillan.

# Subject Index

# Index of Names